MEET THE
ANCIENTS
GATEWAY TO GREECE AND ROME

Robert Stephan
John Sutherland

ARGOS PUBLISHING, LLC

Meet the Ancients:
Gateway to Greece and Rome

Robert Stephan and John Sutherland

Published by:
Argos Publishing, LLC

ISBN-13: 9798385997930

Printed in the USA

For the Muses of
Fathom Drive

CONTENTS

INTRODUCTION

Meet the Ancients

Greetings, scholar of antiquity! Welcome to *Meet the Ancients: Gateway to Greece and Rome*. This book is meant to give you an introduction to the wonderful world of the ancient Mediterranean. It covers everything from the rise of civilization in the Bronze Age to the birth of democracy in ancient Greece to the formation and fall of the mighty Roman Empire. Along the way, you'll learn about some of history's most important events, most impactful inventions, and most colorful characters.

What makes this book different from the hordes of other textbooks out there? Well, the short answer to that is that it flips the proverbial script, making *you* the historian. Most books tell the story of the past through the eyes of the expert author; you get their vision of how history played out and why it went the way it did. This book, however, is focused on giving you actual ancient texts - from Bronze Age Egypt, from Classical Greece, from both the Roman Republic and Empire - so that you can create your own understanding of what happened in the past and why it matters.

These texts are meant to let you grapple with the messiness of ancient history. In order to figure out what's going on, for example, you'll have to unpack the biases and agendas and strategies of the authors who composed these ancient texts. Can you trust an Egyptian pharaoh when he says he crushed his enemy? Is Caesar's own personal account of his conquests reliable and factually correct? And if they don't portray a perfect reality, what, if anything, can we learn from these sources?

The following six chapters are meant to give you the experience of answering these questions for yourself. Each chapter begins with a relatively short overview of the period, just enough information to give you a bit of context. Then you'll get some background on one of the most important authors and texts that was created during that era. For example, you might learn about who the Greek poet Homer was and how the *Iliad* and *Odyssey* were composed. Finally, the bulk of each chapter will be an excerpt from an actual ancient text. Putting together what you know about the time period, the author, the genre, and the text itself, it will be up to you to figure out what it all means.

Each of the translations that form the core of this book have been specially constructed for you, the college student. Ancient Greek and Roman texts have, of course, been translated into English thousands of times over the course of hundreds of years. Many of these translations, however, are nearly as difficult to understand as the ancient Greek and Latin originals. Take for example the following example from Livy's *History of Rome*. In Daniel Spillan's 1854 translation, we get the following:

> *"Nor after that did the Aborigines yield to the Trojans in zeal and fidelity towards their king Æneas; relying therefore on this disposition of the two nations, who were now daily coalescing more and more, although Etruria was so powerful, that it filled with the fame of its prowess not only the land, but the sea also, through the whole length of Italy, from the Alps to the Sicilian Strait, though he might have repelled the war by means of fortifications, yet he led out his forces to the field."*

You almost need a PhD just to figure out what's being said there! The goal in these translations has been to sacrifice literalness to ease-of-reading. That is, we want you to actually be

10

able to understand what's going on, even if that means shifting the word order or turning poems into prose. You're still getting the exact story that the ancient authors told, just in a way that's actually comprehensible to someone without a PhD in Greco-Roman literature.

So that's the goal of this book. we don't just want you to learn about history; we want *you* to *do* history, to be a historian. There are often no "right" or "wrong" answers in terms of how to interpret these texts. Think about the context in which they were created, read the translations closely and carefully, and create your own conclusions about the exciting world of the ancient Greeks and Romans. Let's dive in!

Where to Begin

History's an interesting beast. In order to understand what happened at any given time, it's useful to know both the causes and effects. And if you buy that, then you need to have at least some understanding of what came before and what came after whatever event or period or person you're interested in. Seems straightforward enough, but taken to the extreme that means that we need to cover quite a lot to understand even a little.

Take this book, for example. The last chapter discusses the decline and fall of the Roman Empire. But to understand why the Roman Empire collapsed, you have to understand how the Roman Empire ran during the good times, the *Pax Romana* ("Roman Peace"), as the ancients themselves called it. To understand *that*, however, you need to have a sense for the Roman Republic, why it thrived and why it eventually descended into civil war for nearly 100 years. The Roman Republic doesn't make any sense, however, if you don't understand the rise and fall of the Roman kings during the city's earliest days. As it turns out, the last king of Rome - Tarquin the Proud - was such a bad ruler that (a) the senators kicked him out of power and (b) the guiding ideology of the Roman Republic for the next 500 years was centered on the principle that there should never be another king in Rome. The period of the Roman Monarchy corresponds with events going on in the Greek world, as well, so Rome can't be understood without looking east.

This same concept holds true in Greece. To understand the centuries of bickering between the Hellenistic kingdoms, you have to know about Alexander's march against the Persians and his construction of an empire that stretched all the way from Greece to India. But Alexander's conquest has its origins 150 years earlier with the Persian invasion of Greece. This led to one of the greatest military upsets in all of world history, with the measly Greek city-states somehow turning back the largest army the world had ever seen. In the years that followed, the Classical Period and the Golden Age of Athens led to some of the world's greatest achievements in literature, drama, philosophy, art, and architecture. But why was Persia attacking Greece in the first place? The answer to that question is inextricably bound with the birth of democracy and the Archaic Period of Greek history.

Complex civilization in Greece, however, stretches back a thousand years before democracy ever got off the ground. During the Bronze Age, mighty citadels and palaces sprouted up throughout mainland Greece and the islands. And the ruins of sites like Mycenae and Tiryns and Knossos became tourist attractions even in Classical antiquity. The Aegean Bronze Age was a relative latecomer to the game, and by the time the Mycenaeans were building their Cyclopean walls, the Bronze Age civilizations in the Nile River Valley and in Mesopotamia were already a millennium old, stretching all the back to around 3,000 BC. Not only that, these earliest of early civilizations gave us some of our most important cultural innovations - things like monumental architecture, economic specialization, and, perhaps most importantly, writing.

By now, you get the idea. Every period of interest is entangled with what came before it and what came after it. So, let's go ahead and start...in the beginning.

In the Beginning

"In the beginning, there was nothing." At least that's what there was according to the ancient Greek epic poet Hesiod, whose *Theogony* tells the story of the origin of the universe and the birth of the ancient Greek gods. The "nothing" Hesiod is referring to went by the name of "Chaos." But this isn't chaos like we're used to - frenzied madness or something like that. Rather, it refers to the "void" or the "chasm" or, as we've used here, "nothing."

It's doubtful that Hesiod, living almost 3,000 years ago, had a PhD in Astronomy. Despite this lack of training, Hesiod's assessment of what came first seems more or less right. As far as astronomers and cosmologists (i.e., people who study the origins of the universe) are concerned, we don't really have any sense for what came before the birth of our universe. For all we know, it could indeed have been nothing.

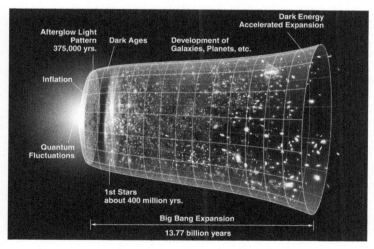

Fig. 1: The Big Bang and Universal Expansion

But then there was something. According to cosmologists, sometime around 13.8 billion years ago (that's 13,800,000,000 years ago, for those keeping track of the zeros), our universe burst into existence, an event we call the Big Bang today. To give you a better sense of how all these events relate to each other timewise, let's put all of universal history into a single calendar year. And we'll call the Big Bang January 1 at 12:00 AM on our cosmic calendar.

You can think of the Big Bang as the most extreme fireworks show you've ever seen, except everything was so hot and moving so fast that you wouldn't have been able to see anything at all. In that first fraction of a fraction of a fraction of a second, all the matter in our known universe burst forth, moving even faster than the speed of light. Things eventually slowed down, cooled off, and the laws of physics as we know them took hold. The soupy particles of the earliest flash started to come together, and eventually gravity started grouping matter into larger and larger chunks.

The way that scientists figured this out is actually pretty interesting. Back in the early 1900s, Edwin Hubble was looking at galaxies through his own telescope. He noticed that not just some, but *all*, of the galaxies in the universe were moving away from Earth. Not just that - they were all moving away from each other as well. And the further away the galaxy, the faster it was going. The logic from there is pretty simple: if things are moving away from each other now, then in the past they must have been closer together. Take that to the extreme, and, well, you get to a single point, a singularity, from which everything eventually arose.

In the middle of January on our cosmic calendar, about 13.4 billion years ago, we get the birth of the first stars. Stars and galaxies would be born, smash into each other, expire and then their matter would make new stars, in an ongoing cycle. When some of the biggest and brightest stars died, they'd release an enormous explosion - a supernova - that would send a diverse array of elements out into the universe. These elements would eventually form the building blocks for our sun, but the leftover junk - the dust and gas that didn't get eaten up by the sun - coagulated together to form our Earth, as well as the other planets and matter in our solar system.

We think this happened about 4.5 billion years ago, or

around September 2nd on our cosmic calendar. Although it might sound cool to have been hanging out on planet Earth at the beginning, watching everything take shape, it would have actually been a pretty miserable experience - and not just because they didn't have TikTok videos.

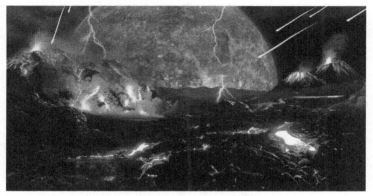

Fig. 2: An artist's rendering of "Hadean" Earth

It would have been insanely hot, with constant volcanic eruptions and noxious gasses throughout the atmosphere. Plus Earth was being bombarded with comets and asteroids, including one huge one that bounced off and created the Moon. It was so hellish, in fact, that the first 500 million years of the Earth's history are called the "Hadean" phase, after Hades, the Greek god of the underworld.

Let There Be Life

Somewhat amazingly, life began pretty quickly after the Earth's formation, at least in the scope of big picture universal history. Although it's still hotly debated, it is likely that the first organisms on Earth date back to around 3.7 billion years ago (or September 21st on our calendar). These are known as stromatolites, and they ride the line between living being and inanimate objects, partially bacterial microbes and partially stone.

It would actually take quite a while for things to get more interesting. Microorganisms ruled the world for billions of years until, about 500 million years ago, we get what's known as the Cambrian Explosion, where complex life expanded throughout the Earth's oceans. There were trilobites and fishes and squids and jellyfish, things that we'd consider actual living animals. Keep in mind, though, that in the big scheme of things, this is all really quite recent. This is all taking place near the end of the year - mid-December - on our cosmic calendar. To give you another sense, if you put this on a scale of 0 to 100, with 0 being the Big Bang and 100 being today, this explosion of life would have happened 96% of the way towards the present.

Fig. 3: A Trilobite fossil from the "Cambrian Explosion" around 500 million years ago

On our calendar, dinosaurs are booming on Christmas, and mammals don't get their start until after that. Primates have only evolved by December 30th, and Hominids - our human-like ancestors - in the afternoon (2:24 PM, to be exact) on New Year's Eve. Right before the New Year's Eve ball drops in Times Square, at 11:52 PM on December 31st of our cosmic calendar, we get the very first anatomically modern humans, about 200,000 to 300,000 years ago in absolute terms.

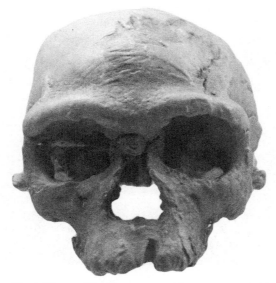

Fig. 4: The world's oldest preserved homo sapiens skull
(Jebel Irhoud, Morocco; ca. 300,000 years ago)

So we humans have only been around for a short 8 minutes (or a couple hundred thousand years) of cosmological history. In that amount of time, however, we have made some incredible strides. For the most part, however, the cultural developments aren't evenly spread out across the past 200,000 thousand years. In fact, for much of human history, life would have been pretty much the same no matter where or when you lived. The development of stone tools, for example, actually happens more than a million years *before* we are anatomically modern humans. Similarly, the domestication of fire goes back at least twice as far as the species *homo sapiens*.

With the help of these tools, humans went about doing the same thing for 95% of our species' existence: nomadically wandering the earth in search of food, shelter, and sex. Not a bad lifestyle if you can avoid being eaten by a saber-tooth tiger! That's not to say there were no developments at all. We get our earliest evidence for intentional burials - a possible sign of religious beliefs - about 100,000 years ago. And the earliest artistic creations - small figurines and cave paintings - arrived on the scene about 30,000 to 40,000 years ago.

Fig. 5: Replica of Upper Paleolithic cave paintings
(Chauvet, France; ca. 30,000 years ago)

These are clearly signs of "culture" in some sense, and certainly evidence for human creativity. But overall, most people in most places all over the world were looking for their next meal, trying to stay safe, and hoping to get laid once in a while.

The Neolithic Revolution

It was only with the end of the last Ice Age, around 10,000 BC (about 12,000 years ago) that we see a major shift. If you're keeping time, this is December 31st at 11:59 (and 32 seconds) PM on our cosmic calendar. As the climate warmed up, plants started growing a little better, and populations grew. This increase in population could lead to increased competition. Now, if you were pursuing your wooly mammoth from one region to the next, you might run into another group of people who decided that this particular wooly mammoth was now theirs. Then, not only do you have to find a way to bring down the beast, you've also got to fight off your neighbors.

The combination of better growing plants, increasing populations, and rising competition led some groups of people to try something entirely new. Instead of following the food - the herds of mammoths or bison or whatever was on the Menu du Jour - people decided to stay in one place and let their food come to them. They started adding a little extra water to the plants that were growing nearby, and breeding the tastiest grains and fruits and vegetables to get even bigger and better crops in succeeding generations. They did the same thing with animals, figuring out that if they built a fence around them, then they didn't have to chase them all over the globe. Selective breeding was also useful for animals, and they bred the strongest and most docile animals to eventually create fully domesticated species that they could use as a source of labor (and then eat afterwards as well).

Fig. 6: The positive feedback loop of the Neolithic Revolution

This whole process - of settling down in one place, of growing crops, and of domesticating animals - is known as the Neolithic Revolution. It got started around 10,000 BC and lasted until around 3000 BC, and while planting a few seeds might not sound very exciting, it had profound effects. For one, now that people had a permanent home, they could store extra food for long periods of time. Thus, when there was a drought or a cold spell, they had food saved up that could get them through the tough times. So the food surplus led to increased stability. This stability, in turn, allowed for the population to grow larger and larger. Then, the cyclical nature of farming, combined with the larger number of people, allowed a few of them to tinker with things other than just producing food. They could specialize in other sorts of activities - like experimenting with new crossbreeds of crops or designing new tools for farming. These steady, small technological advances would have led to even more food and greater surpluses . This relationship created a positive feedback loop that could create a perpetual cycle of growth. Surplus led to stability, stability led to population growth, population growth led to specialization, specialization led to technological advances, and technology led to food surplus, which then kept the cycle going.

So the Neolithic Revolution lays the seeds for complexity and growth that will set mankind on a trajectory of innovation for millenia to come. At the time, however, everyone was still pretty much the same. Sure, some people were nomadic hunter gatherers while others were farmers and breeders, but within each of those groups, there wasn't a lot of differentiation between families. Most people had similar houses, similar jobs, and led similar lives. Everything more or less looked the same.

Fig. 7: The Neolithic site of Çatalhöyük
(Çatalhöyük, Turkey; ca. 7500-5700 BC)

One place we can see this is at the site of Çatalhöyük, perhaps the most famous Neolithic site in the world. It's located in the middle of Anatolia (modern day Turkey), and it flourished from around 7500 to 5700 BC. It was a massive site for the time, with a steady population of around 5,000 to 10,000 people - vastly larger than the nomadic groups from millenia before. Despite the size of the site, however, there don't seem to be any public or monumental buildings. Everyone seems to have lived in somewhat similar houses, suggesting that there wasn't much stratification or hierarchy throughout the site. That doesn't mean that there was no complexity, however. These houses often revealed elaborate decorative wall paintings, numerous clay figurines, and animal skulls - especially bull skulls - mounted on house walls. These all suggest that there were religious and ritual practices taking place at Çatalhöyük.

Figs. 8 (left) and 9 (right): Reconstructions of the town of Çatalhöyük and a representative house

Overall, Çatalhöyük not only serves as a prime example of a Neolithic settlement, it also bridges the gap between the nomadic groups that predominated humankind for 190,000 years and the complex societies of the succeeding Bronze Age. The details of those Bronze Age societies, which bring us everything from the pyramids of Giza to the citadel of Mycenae, will be found in the pages to come.

CHAPTER I

Rise of Civilization

So far, we've seen that humans are a relatively late addition to the game, only arising about 200,000 to 300,000 years ago. Moreover, once *homo sapiens* finally comes on stage, things still progress at a caveman-like speed. For the first 190,000 years of our existence, most people in most places were all doing the same thing - wandering the world in search of food and shelter and a mate.

That all began to change about 10,000 BC. As the climate warmed and the Ice Age came to an end, populations increased and people began to settle down in one place. They built permanent houses, started farming, and domesticated plants and animals. These were major changes from what had gone on for the entire previous existence of humankind, and they put us on a trajectory that we're still feeling the impact of today. Essentially, it brought about a productive feedback loop - food surplus led to stability, stability led to population growth, growth led to labor specialization, specialization led to technological advances, and technology led to more food surplus, which kept the cycle going.

Populations began to rise, and people began living in towns

in much larger numbers than when they were nomadic. We have learned, for instance, about Çatalhöyük, the world's most famous Neolithic site located in modern day Turkey, a settlement that could house a population of thousands. But while they brought about impressive developments in architecture, art, and religion, everyone still seemed pretty much the same. There was no discernable social hierarchy, no public buildings, and no monumental structures.

Bronze Age Beginnings

That all began to change around 3000 BC (or December 31st at 11:59 and 48 seconds on our cosmic calendar). Around this time, culture became noticeably more complex in two different areas - Mesopotamia and Egypt. Mesopotamia, whose name comes from the Greek word for "the middle of the rivers," is located largely in modern day Iraq, between the Tigris and Euphrates Rivers. Egypt was, of course, centered on the Nile River Valley - the "Gift of the Nile" according to the Greek "Father of History," Herodotus. We call this period of growth, development, and complexity the Bronze Age, and it lasted from around 3000 to about 1200 BC.

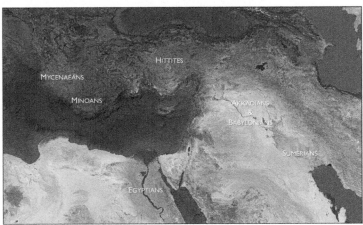

Fig. 10: Bronze Age Empires, ca. 3000-1200 BC
(Google, © 2023 TyerraMetrics)

While these areas are geographically distinct, they share an important trait: they are both centered on major river valleys. This is no coincidence, and scholars have suggested that it was large scale projects - like irrigation - that required centralized planning that led to differentiation and stratification within these societies. That is, someone had to do the planning, someone had to do the managing, and someone (well, most people) had to do the actual physical labor. We can see this emphasis on large scale projects and on the division of labor in artifacts like the Scorpion Macehead below. Over time, these different positions became entrenched, and we end up with a hereditary elite as the kings and priests of these Bronze Age empires.

Figs. 11 (left) and 12 (right): Macehead with King Scorpion wielding irrigation tool (Ashmolean Museum; ca. 3200-3000 BC)

This provides us some insight into how things began to change from a world where everyone was similar - that is, they lived in similar houses, worked similar agricultural jobs, and had similar levels of wealth - to a world where things became very, very different. All of a sudden, the house of a local leader was much larger than all the others, monumental tombs commemorated a ruling elite, and soaring temples were erected to glorify the gods. Cities arose that held ten times the number of people as Çatalhöyük, and they had differentiated spaces for public gatherings, private dwellings, and the political and religious elite. People became differentiated as well. Most were still involved in food production, cultivating crops or raising livestock, but some became full-time priests, or politicians, or military leaders. This also led to increased differentiation when it came to wealth, so some individuals had noticeably larger houses and richer burials than others.

Technological developments were both a cause and an effect of all this increased specialization and complexity, and during this period we see the invention of the wheel which aided transportation, bronze which helped in tool construction, and, perhaps most importantly, writing, which allowed for the transmission of knowledge across generations. At first, writing was primarily used to record economic transactions, but within a few hundred years - a drop in the proverbial cosmic bucket - we had everything from the world's first epic poem (Gilgamesh) to the earliest known magical spells (the Pyramid Texts).

Bronze Age Empires of the Near East

While these Bronze Age civilizations shared certain characteristics - full-fledged cities, socioeconomic hierarchies, political and religious elites - they each evolved in their own way. In Mesopotamia, for example, we have one culture regularly supplanting another. This began around 3000 BC with the rise of Sumerian city-states, places like Sumer, Ur, and Uruk. These could hold 50,000 people or more and had monumental political and religious buildings known as ziggurats, which resembled a flat-topped pyramid with a temple on top.

Figs. 13 (left) and 14 (right): Archaeological ruins and digital reconstruction of the Ziggurat of Ur (Ur, Iraq; ca. 2050 BC)

26

The Sumerians, and many of their successors, operated according to a theocracy, where the political leaders derived their power from the gods themselves. It makes it tough to argue with authority when they're backed by supreme deities, after all.

Towards the end of the 3rd millennium (the 2000s BC), the independent city-states of the Sumerians fell under the centralized leadership of a single city-state known as Akkad. These people, the Akkadians, are sometimes known as the world's first empire, uniting diverse peoples and lands under the rule of a single political leader. Their founding and most famous leader was known as Sargon the Great. He became legendary for his conquests, and more than a millennium after his reign, he was still remembered in the Near East for his skill at battle.

Fig. 15: The so-called "Mask of Sargon." Scholars now think, however, it likely belonged to his grandson, Naram-Sin. (Iraq Museum; ca. 2300 BC)

The Akkadians held control of the region for only about 200 years, however, and by the early 2nd millennium BC, the Babylonians had become the dominant ruling force in the area. Scholars today call this the Old Babylonian Empire, and it too only lasted a couple hundred years from around 1800 to around 1600 BC. Their most famous leader was a man named Hammurabi, famous for being the first to establish a written, codified set of laws. Today we often refer to his method of justice as "an eye for an eye," meaning that if you do something criminal, the offended person can do the same thing to you. A closer examination, however, shows that was only true *within*

27

a social class. If a rich person harmed a poor person, then equal justice wasn't quite on the table. Nonetheless, the fact that these laws were written down meant that the elites couldn't keep changing them to fit their needs at any given moment, at least everyone had to play by the same rules.

Fig. 16: Basalt stela featuring Hammurabi's Code
(Louvre Museum; ca. 1800-1750 BC)

By the middle of the 1000s BC, the Hittite Empire had grown powerful in Anatolia, an ancient name for modern day Turkey. The Hittites were known as incredibly prolific warriors, and they were almost always at war with someone. They were the first to make effective use of iron - a valuable discovery for improving weapons - and they were the first to invent the war chariot as well. As we will see in the ancient texts below, these war-loving Hittites came to blows with the Egyptians at the Battle of Kadesh towards the end of the Bronze Age.

Bronze Age Egypt

Speaking of the Egyptians, they had their own thing going on while power in the Near East was constantly changing hands. Egypt was more geographically isolated than Mesopotamia, with desert to the east and west of the Nile, cataracts (i.e., steep rapids) to the south, and the Mediterranean to the north of the Egyptian Delta. In the earliest days, Egyptian cultures developed separately in the south, known as Upper Egypt because it was upstream, and the north, known as Lower Egypt because it was downstream.

About 3000 BC, the disparate regions of Upper and Lower Egypt became united under a single ruler. How that actually happened is still a matter of debate, but archaeological evidence provides some clues. The Narmer Palette, a decorative, ceremonial instrument used for grinding minerals into makeup, depicts King Narmer wearing the White Crown of Upper Egypt on one side. He stands tall, ready to smite his enemy, supposedly a captive from Lower Egypt. Above and to the right a depiction of Horus, the falcon god of kingship, holds another captive, this time with reeds growing out of his back, which is thought to symbolize the reeds of the Nile Delta of Lower Egypt. The back of the palette then shows Narmer wearing the Red Crown of Lower Egypt, suggesting that he has now become the lord of the two lands. Two mythical beasts with extended necks are intertwined, thought to symbolize the coming together of Upper and Lower Egypt. And captives from Lower Egypt are shown in the upper register, with mutilated phalluses sitting on top of their decapitated heads. Thus we think that the unification of Egypt was a rather bloody affair, with Upper Egypt eventually subduing and incorporating Lower Egypt.

Fig. 17: The Narmer Palette (British Museum; ca. 3000 BC)

In the years that followed, known as the Early Dynastic Period (Dynasties 1-2, ca. 3100-2700 BC), Egyptian rulers associated themselves with the gods and experimented with different ways to proclaim their divinity. They buried themselves in mastaba tombs, which were like pyramids that were chopped off just above the ground. These were meant to represent the primordial mound from which all life arose. In the earliest days, some scholars think that the kings practiced human sacrifice, forcing all their servants to be executed when they themselves died so that they could continue to serve the king in the afterlife. Thankfully for future generations of servants, this practice soon ended, and the burial of executed servants was replaced with the burial of ushabtis, or small figurines that could then help serve the king in the afterlife.

The Old Kingdom (Dynasties 3-6, ca. 2700-2200 BC) saw the creation of Egypt's most famous monuments - the pyramids. These began with the Djoser, the first king of the Old Kingdom, when he built the step pyramid of Saqqara (ca. 2650 BC). He created the pyramid by taking the mastaba tombs of the Early Dynastic period and layering them one on top of the other, with successive layers being slightly smaller in area, thus creating the stepped look. By the Fourth Dynasty, Egyptian kings were experimenting with true pyramids. The pharaoh Sneferu built no fewer than three pyramids trying to get it right. He had one pyramid collapse upon itself and another had to be adjusted half way through before he finally got it right.

For most, however, it is the pyramids of Giza which stand as the pinnacle of Egyptian architecture. The three major pyramids at Giza were built by the kings of the Fourth Dynasty, Khufu, Khafre, and Menkaure. Khufu's pyramid, what we call the Great Pyramid today, is the largest of the three, covering a whopping 13 acres of ground and rising 481 feet into the air. Inside, the pyramid is mostly solid stone. But there are a series of corbeled passages that one can traverse, and these end in the burial chambers for both the king and queen. These help us conclude, of course, that the pyramids themselves were not just monuments of power, they were funerary structures, meant to house the royal family for all of eternity.

Fig. 18: The Pyramids of Giza (Giza, Egypt; ca. 2600-2500 BC)

After a century or so of relative instability, power was reconsolidated during the Middle Kingdom (ca. 2050-1650 BC). Individual pharaohs or kings once again ruled the entire country, but the way they portrayed themselves had evolved. Rather than the eternally strong, youthful depictions of the Old Kingdom, pharaohs in the Middle Kingdom portrayed themselves as the shepherds of their people. They would intentionally exaggerate certain features to show how much they cared - large

31

ears to show they were listening, severe faces to show how hard they were working, and wrinkled brows to show the toll it took upon them.

The Middle Kingdom also saw the peak of literary culture in Egypt. We get texts that go beyond simple royal decrees and instead discuss the life, concerns, and struggles of everyday people. Texts such as the "Tale of Sinuhe," "The Dispute between a Man and His Ba," and "The Tale of the Eloquent Peasant," show Egyptian authors engaging with the difficulties and complexities of what it meant to be human.

Fig. 19: The Papyrus of Hunefer showing a scene from the Egyptian "Book of the Dead" (British Museum; ca. 1275 BC)

In the middle of the 17th century BC, there was a large invasion from the Levant. A group known as the Hyksos swooped in, riding on a brand new technology - the war chariot - and brought the Middle Kingdom to a close. A century later, Egyptians had reconsolidated power and the New Kingdom (ca. 1550-1050 BC) had begun. They adopted the Hyksos' war chariot as well as several other technologies they brought with them, like the horse and the composite bow. And using these new tools, the pharaohs set out to expand their empire. More than ever before, Egypt started looking beyond the Nile River Valley to incorporate new lands: Nubia to the south, Libya to the west, and the Levant to the north and east. This brought them into conflict with the major empires of the Near East - like the Hittites - and the translated texts below give you a first-person perspective of how the 19th dynasty pharaoh Ramesses the Great went to battle against this rival empire.

The New Kingdom also saw a shift in resource allocation. Back in the Old Kingdom, the pyramids were, without a doubt, the biggest expenditures of the Egyptian pharaohs. As cool as they looked, however, it turns out that building giant, conspicuous tombs was like putting up a sign that read "valuable objects buried here," and all the pyramids were broken into and looted in antiquity. During the New Kingdom, the pharaohs began to bury themselves in the Valley of the Kings, a region in the western desert near the capital of Thebes. Here they dug their tombs underground in an attempt to conceal them from looters. For the most part this didn't work, and the vast majority of them were indeed still robbed thousands of years ago. One, however, the tomb of Tutankhamun, lay undisturbed until the Egyptologist Howard Carter unearthed it in 1922. Tutankhamun was not a particularly spectacular or famous pharaoh, and his burial was likely no richer than most others, yet the sarcophagus and mask of Tutankhamun stand today as a testament to the wealth of the mighty pharaohs because it survived.

Fig. 20: The burial mask of King Tutankhamun
(Egyptian Museum in Cairo; 1332-1323 BC)

Despite the riches of King Tut's tomb, New Kingdom pharaohs were actually spending less money on their own tombs and more money on their temples. It was the New Kingdom that saw religious sanctuaries like Karnak and Luxor rise to prominence. And sites like Hatshepsut's temple at Deir el-Bahri or Ramesses II's temple near Thebes show us that individual pharaohs spent more on their funerary temples than they did on the tombs that accompanied them.

Fig. 21: The Temple of Karnak, dedicated to the Theban Triad of Amun, Mut, and Khonsu, flourished during the New Kingdom (Karnak, Egypt; 1550-1069 BC)

Bronze Age Collapse

Waging war, as we see with the Battle of Kadesh, was naturally a part of imperial expansion. But it was actually outside invasion that brought the New Kingdom - and the Egyptian Bronze Age - to close. In the early 11th century BC, a diverse group of naval marauders, who the Egyptians call the "Sea Peoples," launched a series of attacks. Royal texts claim the pharaoh and his people forcefully repulsed these naval assaults, but the collapse of the New Kingdom and the rise of fragmentation and instability during the Third Intermediate Period suggests that they had more of an impact than the Egyptians were willing to admit.

*Fig. 22: Relief showing Ramesses III "defeating" the Sea Peoples
(Medinet Habu, Egypt; ca. 1200 BC)*

Taking a broader view, we actually see that places far beyond Egypt were also destroyed right around this time, during the 12th and 11th centuries BC. The Hittite capital of Hattusa was burned to the ground. Mighty Troy, located in western Turkey, was destroyed twice. The Aegean palace of Knossos collapsed, as did the citadel of Mycenae on mainland Greece. And many of the sites in Cyprus and the Levant (including Kadesh itself) suffered the same fate.

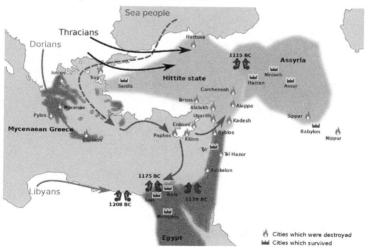

*Fig. 23: Destruction and migration during the Bronze Age Collapse
(ca. 12th century BC)*

For a long time, scholars suggest that the same "Sea Peoples" that invaded Egypt were responsible for this widespread destruction. And even today most people acknowledge that the external invasion was part of the cause. Now, however, we see this widespread downfall - what we call the Bronze Age Collapse - as being more multifaceted in nature, a combination of external invasion, climatic issues like natural disasters and drought, internal rebellions, and economic network fragmentation. This collapse has a lasting impact. Gone are the palaces, the citadels, and the monumental tombs and temples. For centuries the region, especially the Aegean (i.e., the sea between Greece and Turkey) experienced a reduction in wealth and complexity, before things rose again at the dawn of the Iron Age.

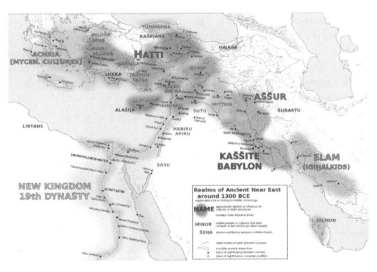

Fig. 24: Map of Egypt and Hatti just prior to the Battle of Kadesh (ca. 1300 BC)

The Battle of Kadesh

The New Kingdom (1550 - 1069 BC) in Egypt was a time of empire and expansion. By this point, the pyramids of Giza were already 1,000 years old, and the Egyptian pharaohs had started burying themselves underground in the Valley of the Kings. The largest royal building projects shifted from monumental tombs, like those at Giza and Saqqara, to massive temples, like those at Karnak and Luxor. Egypt had also already been through several periods of boom (the Old and Middle Kingdoms) and bust (the First and Second Intermediate Periods). The New Kingdom was the first time, however, that Egypt made a concerted effort to expand outside the Nile River Valley. They pushed south into Nubia (modern Sudan), west into Libya, and north and east into the Levant. It was there, near the border of modern-day Syria and Lebanon, that the burgeoning Egyptian Empire came into contact with the Hittite Empire of central Anatolia (modern Turkey).

The Hittites, for their part, had been growing in power for most of the 2nd millennium BC. The Near East, at this point, had a long history of one empire supplanting another - the Sumerians were overtaken by the Akkadians who were in turn overtaken by the Babylonians. Now the Hittites had become the strongest power in the region. They were known as particularly fierce warriors, and as expert archers and charioteers. During the second half of the 2nd millennium BC, their expansion outside of central Anatolia brought them into contact with the Egyptians. We know from Hittite cuneiform texts found at Amarna - the new Egyptian capital of the heretic king Akhenaten - that the Hittites had been in correspondence with Egypt decades before the Battle of Kadesh broke out, but our general sense is that these letters were largely ignored by the Egyptian pharaoh.

By the 13th century BC, however, the Hittites had moved further south, while Egypt had moved further north. This area, right around Kadesh, served as a lucrative crossroads for trade between Egypt, Anatolia, and the Near East, and thus held strategic value for all parties involved.

Ramesses II (ruled 1279-1213 BC), also known as Ramesses the Great, sat on the Egyptian throne. By the time the Battle of Kadesh broke out, he had already made a name for himself by defeating the Sherden sea pirates and by founding a

Fig. 25: Monumental statue of Ramesses II from the Ramesseum in Thebes (British Museum; 13th century BC)

new capital, Pi-Ramesse, in the Nile Delta. Now he confidently marched north with approximately 20,000 infantry and perhaps 2,000 chariots, broken into four divisions. The Pharaoh himself commanded the Amun division and led the way, far in front of his other troops. The remaining divisions - the Ra, the Ptah, and the Set - were spread out southwards along the road to Kadesh. We know from the texts that are translated below that the battle took place in the 5th year of Ramesses II's reign, that is, in 1274 BC.

Meanwhile, Muwatalli II (ruled 1295-1272 BC) was the King of the Hittites. Like Ramesses, he had established a new capital, moving it from the traditional site of Hattusa to the new town of Tarhuntassa. Towards the end of his reign, in

1274 BC, he marched his army south towards Kadesh. While exact numbers are hard to come by, most scholars estimate that the Hittites had about twice as many troops as the Egyptians, perhaps 40,000 infantry and 3,000 chariots. Rather than march straight out to face the Egyptians, however, Muwatalli had his troops hide behind the old city of Kadesh, and he sent out spies to convince the Egyptians his army was still over 100 miles away.

Fig. 26: Relief depicting a Hittite chariot from Carchemish (Museum of Anatolian Civilization; 9th to 8th centuries BC)

In terms of big picture historical impact, the Battle of Kadesh was just one of many battles that took place during the Bronze Age. It didn't launch one empire into world dominance while bringing another to its knees. In fact, as you'll see from the ancient sources, it can be difficult to tell who won the battle at all.

The Battle of Kadesh is extremely important for historians, however, because of the records that have been left behind. It is the earliest battle for which we can reconstruct, at least to some extent, the play-by-play events of the fighting itself.

Although pinpointing what actually happened, and separating it from the copious amounts of propaganda layered in these texts, can be quite the challenge. The Battle of Kadesh is also unique for its time in that we have evidence from both sides of the battle - the Ramesses II placed accounts of the battle on the walls of his temples, while Muwatalli and his successors referenced it in their letters and future treaties. The Egyptian sources are more robust and detailed, but that doesn't make them any more "true" or reliable in a historical sense. Finally, the Battle of Kadesh is the earliest conflict for which we have the peace treaty. Not only that, we have textual evidence for it in both places, both in Egypt and the Hittite homeland.

Thus, in some ways, we have a dream scenario for historians. Play-by-play accounts of the battle; descriptions of what happened from both empires involved in the conflict, and a treaty that set the terms of peace for both sides. As with all texts, and especially royal texts from the ancient world, these sources are a mix of historical reality, royal propaganda, and genre-specific constructions. Each source will be introduced in more depth below, so keep in mind these contexts as you try to piece together what happened at Kadesh for yourself.

The Egyptian Sources

Ramesses the Great had his accomplishments at Kadesh recorded in several different texts – the *Bulletin*, the *Poem of Pentaur*, and the *Peace Treaty of Kadesh*. The *Bulletin* was inscribed on the walls and pylons of numerous Egyptian temples, including those at Karnak, Luxor, Abydos, and Abu Simbel, using hieroglyphs to tell the tale and full scale relief carvings to illustrate several of the most important scenes. The *Bulletin* is useful on many accounts. It gives us the date of the battle (the 5th year or Ramesses II's reign), and it also delivers a play-by-play account of the Battle of Kadesh. The events of the battle, however, are entangled with some not-so-subtle propaganda glorifying the Egyptian Pharaoh, which can make it tricky to determine what actually happened.

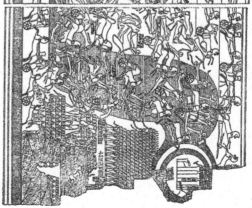

Fig. 27: *Drawing of a sculptural relief depicting the Battle of Kadesh from the Ramesseum (Thebes, Egypt; 13th century BC)*

The *Poem of Pentaur* is the other major account of the Battle of Kadesh. It differs from the *Bulletin* in that it mixes together a prose account of the battle with a poetic account of Ramesses II's courageous deeds. Like the *Bulletin*, it was published on a variety of temples, including those at Luxor, Abydos, Abu Simbel, Karnak, and the Ramesseum. As you might expect from such locations, it was meant to be seen far and wide. To give you a sense of scale, one of the panels spans 50 feet in width and stands 40 high, with thousands of individual figures.

Fig. 28: The Poem of Pentaur *from the north side of the first pylon at the Temple of Luxor (13th century BC)*

It was also written down on papyrus. One of the most complete forms, known as the *Papyrus Sallier III*, even records the person who put the proverbial pen to paper – a man by the name of Pentaur. That name provides the title to the work as a whole. No one really knows whether he was the author of the poem or just the scribe, but either way his name has stood the test of time.

Most scholars believe it is indeed a mix of prose and verse, although there is still debate about whether or not it is truly a poem. Either way, Ramesses II certainly plays the role of the hero. He laments being left all alone – abandoned by his troops and by Amun himself – and then he extols his bravery, strength, and prowess in single-handedly defeating the enemy. The possibly-poetic nature of the text, combined with his heroic deeds, have led some to call this the "Epic of Pentaur" or the "Egyptian Iliad" as a precursor to the Greek war-based epic that would arise half a millennium later.

Fig. 29: Papyrus Sallier III with the final lines of the Poem of Pentaur *and the name of the scribe (British Museum, 13th century BC)*

The texts below are adapted from Miriam Lichtheim's translation from her book *Ancient Egyptian Literature: The New Kingdom.*[1] This translation attempts to prioritize readability and comprehension at the expense of literalness or exact word or phrase order. The poetic verse is especially difficult to capture in English, since we can't produce the same meter and it didn't have a rhyme scheme. In an attempt to capture the "poetic" nature of those parts of the text, we have included Rawnsley's 1894 translation,[2] which uses a basic rhyme scheme

1   Lichtheim, Miriam. *Ancient Egyptian Literature. Volume 2, The New Kingdom.* 2nd ed. Berkeley, CA: U of California, 2006, pgs. 57-72.

2   Rawnsley,H. D. *Idylls and Lyrics Of the Nile.* London: David Nutt, 1894, pgs. 109-121.

to make it read more like a poem. We've also made slight updates to modernize the language. We hope it helps you piece together the puzzle that is the Battle of Kadesh.

Words of the Ancients
Bulletin of the Battle of Kadesh

It was late May in the 5th year of the reign of the immortal Ramesses II - the King of Upper and Lower Egypt, the glory of Ra-Horakhty,[3] the mighty Bull of Truth, the son of Ra himself, and the one Amun[4] loves most.

At this time, the Pharaoh made his way into southern Canaan, looking for his second victory. All was good in the tent of the King - everyone healthy and wealthy - as they sat in the hills south of Kadesh. Then, in the morning, the Pharaoh made an appearance, looking like Ra himself, dressed in the armor of his father Montu.[5] And the Pharaoh took his army north, reaching the southern outskirts of the town of Shabtuna.[6]

SPIES DECEIVE THE PHARAOH

Soon, two messengers from the local bedouin[7] people brought the king a message. They said, "Our brothers are the leaders of some local tribes allied with your enemy, the Hittites. [10] But they sent us here to let you know that we'll abandon them and serve you, great Pharaoh!." The Pharaoh responded

---

3   Ra-Horakhty is a mix between Ra, the god of the sun, and Horus, the god of kingship.

4   Amun was the patron god of the city of Thebes, in Upper Egypt. He rose to prominence in Egyptian religion during the New Kingdom, and was sometimes fused with Ra, the sun god, as Amun-Ra.

5   Montu was a god of war, particularly popular in Upper Egypt. Thus, he's a metaphorical, not literal, father of the Pharaoh.

6   Shabtuna was a town just south of Kadesh. It was of strategic importance because it offered a place to cross the Orontes River.

7   The Egyptian term used is *Shosu* which refers to a local bedouin group, and the term "bedouin" is an Arabic term for "desert dwellers," referring to the fact that these people were nomadic.

to the two messengers, "Where exactly are your brothers who sent you to deliver this message?" And the heralds said to the Pharaoh, "They're with the King of the Hittites. Your enemy from Hatti[8] is far away, currently near Aleppo, just north of Tunip.[9] He was too scared of you, Pharaoh, to travel south once he heard you were marching north."

Now the two nomads were lying to the Pharaoh, since it was actually the King of the Hittites who had sent them to deliver this message, to discover the whereabouts of the Egyptians [20] and to prevent them from preparing for war with the Hittites. In reality, the enemy from Hatti had indeed traveled south, bringing with them all their infantry and chariots and leaders from every group under Hittite control. And they stood ready for battle, hiding behind the Old City of Kadesh so that the Pharaoh didn't realize they were there.

Once the two bedouin messengers were let go, the Pharaoh led his army north, reaching a place northwest of Kadesh. [30] There, on the west side of the Orontes River just north of Kadesh, they set up the royal camp, with the Pharaoh taking his seat on a beautiful golden throne.

Then an Egyptian scout brought in two scouts from the Hittite enemy. They were led before the Pharaoh, and he said to them, "Who are you?" They replied, "We're servants of the King of the Hittites. He sent us to find out where you were." And the Pharaoh responded, "Where is the King of the Hittites and his army? I've heard he's up near Aleppo, just north of Tunip."

The Hittite Attack

[40] The captured scouts told the Pharaoh, "That's what you think? The evil King of the Hittites has come down here! Not only has he brought all the people under his control, he's brought many allies as well. There are the Trojans, the Mi-

---

8   Hatti is the name for the kingdom of the Hittites.

9   The Egyptian text calls the location "the land of Khaleb." This corresponds to modern Aleppo, about 120 miles north of Kadesh.

tanni, the Kaskians, the Mysians, the Pitassa, the Carians, the Lycians, the Carchemish, the Arzawa, the Ugarit, the Irun, the Inesa, the Phrygians, the Kadesh, the Aleppans, and all people from Kedy. They have a strong infantry, many chariots, and plenty of weapons for battle. [50] There are more of them than sands on the seashore. Take a look; they're armed and ready for battle, right behind the Old City of Kadesh."

Then the Pharaoh brought in his senior officials so that they could hear what the scouts from the enemy Hittites had just said. The Pharaoh said to them, "Listen to what's going on with our Egyptian officials and our foreign allies. Everyday these people tell me, 'The evil King of the Hittites is up near Aleppo, just north of Tunip. He ran away when he heard you were coming, Pharaoh.' [60] But just now I heard from these two captured scouts that the Hittite enemy has come down here with all his people and his allies, that they're more numerous than sands on the seashore. Check it out for yourself; they're hiding their army right behind the Old City of Kadesh, and my foreign allies and Egyptian administrators couldn't tell me they were there."

Ramesses' senior officials responded to the divine Pharaoh, "It is truly criminal that your foreign allies and Egyptian leaders [70] couldn't find the enemy Hittites wherever they were and report their location to you each day." Then the vizier[10] was ordered to speed up the Egyptian army as it approached the southern part of the town of Shabtuna, marching it double time to bring it up to where the royal camp was pitched.[11]

But while the Pharaoh was speaking with his senior officials, the enemy Hittites launched an attack with their infantry and chariots and all their allies as well. After fording the river to the south of Kadesh, the Hittite army charged at the Pharaoh's troops, who were caught completely off guard. The

---

10 In ancient Egypt, the *vizier* was the highest-ranking official under the Pharaoh.

11 We can see here that the Egyptian army was divided into multiple divisions. As we learn in the *Poem of Pentaur*, Ramesses was out in front with the Amun division, while the Ra, Ptah, and Set divisions trailed behind.

Egyptian infantry and chariots were dealt a major blow while they marched north to the Pharaoh's royal camp. Then the enemy Hittites surrounded the Pharaoh's royal camp itself.

Fig. 30: The Bulletin of the Battle of Kadesh *depicting Ramesses attacking from his chariot (Abu Simbel, Egypt; 13th century BC)*

TRIUMPH OF RAMESSES II

When the Pharaoh saw what was happening he jumped up, raging with the spirit of his father Montu. He snatched his weapons and put on his armor, appearing like the god Set[12] in his prime. He jumped on his mighty horse "Victory-in-Thebes" and swiftly headed out by himself, all alone. [90] The Pharaoh was so powerful, so courageous, that no one could stand in his way. The ground before him was engulfed in flames, and he scorched the enemy hordes with fireballs. His fierce eyes flickered as he stared them down, his strength blazing like fire against his enemy. He treated the hordes of foreign foes as if they were nothing, considering them no more than chaff.[13]

The Pharaoh charged into battle against the enemy Hittites and their many allies. He was like Set with his power and

---

12 Set was the Egyptian god of violence and chaos. As such, he was particularly known for his strength in battle. According to Egyptian mythology, Set killed his brother Osirirs and battled Osiris' son Horus for control of Egypt. After losing that battle, he became god of the desert, of violence, and of chaos. He is often depicted as a jackal.

13 Chaff refers to the covering of the seed on a stalk of grain, along with any other debris that is meant to be discarded.

47

Sekhmet[14] with his rage. The Pharaoh killed all the troops of the enemy Hittites, slaughtering their leaders and generals, and he slew all their allies that had come to fight as well. [100] Their infantry and chariots were annihilated, ending up face down in the dirt. The Pharaoh cut them down right where they stood, and they littered the ground in front of his horses. And all this time the Pharaoh was alone, not another person with him.

Fig. 31: The Bulletin of the Battle of Kadesh *depicting Ramesses smiting his enemies (Abu Simbel, Egypt; 13th century BC)*

---

14 Sekhmet is an Egyptian goddess of war and healing and is depicted as a lioness. She is the daughter of the sun god Ra and often embodies his vengeful spirit. According to Egyptian mythology, Sekhmet was sent to cleanse the world of humans who were conspiring against Ra. After killing them, however, she continued to rage, killing almost all mankind. To stop her, Ra poured out beer that was dyed red, so that it looked like blood. Sekhmet drank the beer thinking it was indeed blood, and in doing so, she became so drunk that she stopped killing the mortals. Hence her association with rage in the text above.

I, the Pharaoh,[15] destroyed the enemy Hittites, and they fell on their faces, one on top of another, just like crocodiles fall into the Orontes River. I flew at them like a griffin,[16] attacking every nation that stood against me. I alone did this, for my infantry and chariots had abandoned me, never even looking back. With my infantry and chariots as my witnesses, I swear on my life, on Ra who shines upon me, and on my father Atum[17] who blesses me, [110] that everything I, the Pharaoh, have said is true.

Words of the Ancients

The Poem of Pentaur

[1] Listen to the glorious victory of Ramesses: King of Upper and Lower Egypt, Usermaatre-Setepenre, Son of Ra, Beloved of Amun, and Recipient of Eternal Life![18] He won this victory over the nations of Hatti, of Mitanni, of Arzawa, of Pitassa, of Troy, of Mysia, of Caria, of Lycia, of Carchemish, of Kedy, of Kadesh, or Ugarit, and of Phrygia.[19]

The Pharaoh was just a young king,

---

15 The switch from Third Person ("The Pharaoh") to First Person ("I, the Pharaoh") is in the original Egyptian text. It's a common element in royal New Kingdom inscriptions.

16 A griffin has the head and wings of an eagle (or, perhaps, a falcon in ancient Egypt) and the body of a lion.

17 Atum is the primordial god in Egyptian mythology, the god from which all others arose. Since the Pharaoh is considered divine, Atum would be an ancestor (if not the direct father) of Ramesses.

18 Egyptian Pharaohs had five names: their personal name, their throne name, their Horus name, their Golden Horus name, and their Nebty name. Ramesses was the personal name of the pharaoh who fought the Battle of Kadesh, while Usermaatre Setepenre was his throne name. It translates as something like "Chosen by Ra whose Justice is Powerful." The Greeks called Ramesses II "Ozymandias," which was their transliteration of the first part of his throne name, Usermaatre, and which Percy Shelley used to title his famous sonnet.

19 According to Lichtheim (2006: 57-72), the *Poem of Pentaur* includes both prose and verse components. Here we see the first shift to verse. Because Egyptian verse doesn't translate well to English, we've used a basic rhyme scheme to convey its poetic nature.

So mighty no one could compare;
His arms were strong and his heart did sing,
The power of Montu was in his air.

Like Atum he was ideal of form,
Praised for his beauty wherever he went;
[10] All lands he won, a perfect storm,
Always attacking until they're spent.

For his soldiers he stood a bastion of defense,
Their shield when the battle began;
His skill with a bow was truly immense,
And he conquered many a man.

Into enemy hordes he'd headlong charge,
Never doubting his pure skill;
In battle his courage loomed ever large,
Like a flame that looked to kill.

His heart was stout like a raging bull,
Fearless against enemies combined;
A thousand men he'd surely pull,
A hundred thousand more would be maligned.

The Duke of Doom and Ruler of Renown,,
He was beloved through all the land;
Awesome to behold, the glorious crown,
Like Set on a mountain he'd stand.

Fear he struck in his enemies' hearts,
A ferocious lion among a herd of goats;
[20] And triumphs arose from valorous starts,
But always humble were his quotes.

Steadfast in both action and thought,
His first move was always right;
A savior when battle was brought,
His charioteers he helped in the fight.

His people he brings home alive,
Always saving all his men;
His heart of steel lets them thrive,
And like a mountain they rise again.

His name is Usermaatre-Setepenre,
The King of Upper and Lower Lands;
Beloved of Amun and Son of Re,
Ramesses' life eternally stands.

THE MARCH TO KADESH

Then the Pharaoh prepared his infantry and chariots, and he assembled the Sherden[20] hostages he had captured in his previous victories. He armed his troops and gave them orders, and then started his strong march northward, bringing both his infantry and chariots with him, in May of the 5th year of this reign. [30] As he made his way out of Egypt, he passed by the fortress of Sile,[21] as though he were Montu himself with all his strength. And as he went, all the foreign nations of the land trembled in fear, and their leaders brought him gifts while their people bowed before the strength of the Pharaoh. He was truly traversing these small paths as though they were the broad avenues of Egypt itself.

After passing through this area, the Pharaoh made his way to Ramesse Meramun, a town located within the Cedars of Lebanon, and kept pushing north. When he reached the hills surrounding Kadesh, he crossed the Orontes River with the first part of his army, the "Amun" division. [40] And there he pitched his camp next to the town of Kadesh.

Meanwhile, the Hittite enemy had come down and brought with them allies of every nation, from sea to shining sea. They,

---

20 The Sherden are a foreign group that are best known for being one of the "Sea Peoples," the diverse coalition of naval marauders that lay siege to Egypt and the rest of the eastern Mediterranean at the end of the Bronze Age. Scholars don't really know who these people are, and hypotheses range from Sardinians to Akkadians.

21 Sile was a fortress along the "Way of Horus," a road that led out of Egypt into Canaan.

of course, brought everyone from their homeland of Hatti, but also people from Mitanni, Arzawa, Troy, Kaskia, Mysia, Pitassa, Irun, Caria, Lycia, Cilicia, Carchemish, Urgarit, Kedy, Syria, Mushanet, and Kadesh itself. The King of the Hittites, brought them all, not leaving a single nation behind, and all those groups brought their kings and generals and infantry and chariots, [50] the largest army ever to be assembled. The enemy hordes were like locusts, covering the lofty mountains and the low plains. There wasn't an ounce of silver left in Hatti, for it had all been used to hire these foreign mercenaries for the upcoming battle. And the evil King of the Hittites and his allied hordes hid themselves behind the old town of Kadesh, northeast of the city.

The Pharaoh, on the other hand, was alone with his attendants and only the Amun division of his army. The Ra division of the army was still attempting to cross the ford near the southern town of Shabtuna, [60] about 6 miles away from the Pharaoh. The Ptah division was further south still, near the town of Ironama. And the Set division was still marching along the road at this time. So the Pharaoh assembled the troops from the leading Amun division, the best his army had to offer, and placed them on the shores of Amor.[22]

The evil King of the Hittites stood in the center of his army, not daring to come out and fight for fear of the Pharaoh. However he was good at marshaling his troops, for he had gathered hordes of soldiers and chariots, more numerous than grains of sand on the seashore. They were able to place three men in each chariot, armed with every imaginable weapon of war. [70] And there the army stood hiding behind the old town of Kadesh.

THE HITTITE ATTACK

Then the Hittite army came rushing out around the south side of Kadesh, launching an assault and attacking the very center of the Ra division of the army, which was totally sur-

---

22 Amor was previously the home of the Amorites, a Semitic speaking group that once controlled the region. The "shores of Amor" refer to the Mediterranean Sea.

prised and unprepared for battle. The Egyptian infantry and chariots were dealt a major blow, while the Pharaoh was still camped north of Kadesh on the west side of the Orontes River.

When his messengers told him what happened, the Pharaoh jumped up like his father Montu. He grabbed his weapons and donned his armor, looking at this moment like Ba'al[23] himself. He mounted his royal horse, named "Victory-in-Thebes" from the stables of the Pharaoh, who is most loved by Amun. [80] Then the Pharaoh rode towards the enemy, charging the Hittite troops all by himself, not another man by his side. As he made his way into the fray, the Pharaoh saw 2,500 enemy chariots starting to surround him. They were the swiftest of the Hittite troops along with the foreign allies from Arzawa, Mysia, Pitassa, Kaskia, Irun Cilicia, Aleppo, Ugarit, Kadesh, and Lycia - each chariot with three men acting as one team.[24]

Fig. 32: Archival photo of the Poem of Pentaur *inscription and reliefs from the Temple of Karnak (13th century BC)*

---

23 Ba'al was a Canaanite god that caught on in Egypt during the Middle Kingdom. He was original a sky and weather god, but soon became the head of the pantheon. He's often equated with the Egyptian god Set, and hence his reference as Ramesses II prepares for battle.

24 Following this section, Lichtheim (2006: 65) notes the *Poem of Pentaur* transitions back into verse. To give a sense of the poetic nature of this section of the text, we have included Rawnsley's translation (1894: 109-121), with slight updates to modernize the language.

RAMESSES' HEROIC DEFENSE

And not one of my princes, none of my people most great,
Was with me, not a captain, not a knight;
[90] For my warriors and chariots had left me to my fate,
Not one was there to take his part in the fight.

Then spoke the Pharaoh: "Father Amun, where are you?
Should a father forget his son?
Is there anything without your knowledge I have done?
Haven't I given you credit for everything I have won?
Have I ever gone against your word?
Disobeyed, or broken a vow?
Is it right that Egypt's lord,
Should be forced in front of foreigners to take a bow,
Or own their rod?
Whatever may be the plan of this Hittite horde.
Surely Amun should be above those who know no god?

Father Amun, is it nought
That to you I dedicated many monuments, and filled
Your temples with the prisoners of war?
[100] That for you, long-standing temples I dared to build?
That for you grand palaces I have brought,
That tribute to you from afar
A whole land comes to pay,
That to you 10,000 oxen for sacrifice I fell,
And burn upon your altars the sweetest woods that smell;
I did all your heart required; did my hand ever sway?

I have built for you wondrous works beside the Nile,
I have raised you mast on mast,[25]
For eternity to last,
All the way from Elephantine's isle[26]

---

25 These would be the flagstaffs that traditionally stood outside Egyptian temples.

26 Elephantine was an island in the middle of the Nile in the far south of Egypt. Thus it would have been a big deal for Ramesses to bring obelisks from there all the way to Amun's temple at Thebes

The obelisks for you I have conveyed,
It is I who brought alone
The everlasting stone.

It is I who sent for thee,
The ships upon the sea,
To pour into your coffers the wealth of trade;
Is it told that such a thing
By any other king,
At any other time, was done at all?

Let the wretch be put to shame
Who refuses your commands.
But bring honor to his name
Who praises Amun with his hands.
To the full of my endeavor,
With a willing heart forever,
I have acted like this for you.

[110] And to you, great god, I call;
Look at me Amun, look at it all,
I am in the midst of many peoples, all unknown,
As plentiful as grains of sand,
Here I stand,
All alone;
There is no one at my side,
My warriors and chariots are scared,
They have deserted me, none have dared
Listen, when for help I cried.

But I find that Amun's grace
Is far better to me
Than a million fighting troops and chariots could ever be.
Yes, better than 10,000, even if they were a brother or son,
When with hearts that beat like one.
Together to help me they are gathered in one place.
The might of men is nothing, it is Amun who is lord,
[120] What has happened here to me is by your word,
And I will not disobey your command;

But alone, as here I stand,
To you my cry I send,
Unto earth's farthest end.
Saying, 'Help me, father Amun, against the Hittite horde.'"

Then my voice found an echo in Hermonthis' temple-hall,[27]
Amun heard it, and he listened to my call;
And for joy I gave a shout.
From behind, his voice cried out,
"I have come to you, Ramesses the Great,
Behold! I stand with you,
Behold! You know it is true,
I am your father, the great god Ra,[28] destined by fate.

Behold! My hand is with you and shall fight,
And my arm is strong above
The hundreds of ten thousands, who against you unite,
Of victory am I lord, and a brave heart I do love,
I have found in you a spirit that is right.
And my soul it rejoices in your valor and your might."

Then all this came to pass, I was changed in my heart
Like Montu, god of war, was I made,
[130] With my left hand hurled the dart.
With my right I swung the blade.
Fierce as Ba'al in his time, before their sight.
Two thousand and five hundred pairs of horses were around.
And I flew into the middle of their ring,
By my horse's hooves they were dashed to pieces on the
ground.

None raised his hand in fight.
For the courage in their hearts had sunken quite;

---

27 Hermonthis was the location of the Temple of Montu (also spelled Mont or Monthu). Montu was the embodiment of the power of the pharaoh.

28 During the New Kingdom, Amun, the patron god of Thebes, was sometimes merged with Ra, god of the sun, and was frequently worshiped as the combined Amun-Ra.

And their limbs were struck with fear,
And they could not hurl the dart,
And they had not any heart
To use the spear;
And I cast them to the water,
Just as crocodiles fall in from the bank,
So they sank.

And they tumbled on their faces, one by one,
[140] At my pleasure I made slaughter.
So that none
Ever had time to look behind, none turned and fled;
Where he fell, did each one lay
On that day,
From the dust none ever lifted up his head.

Then the wretched King of the Hittites, he stood still,
With his warriors and his chariots all about him in a ring,
Just to gaze upon the valor of me, the mighty king
In the fray.
And I, the king, was all alone,
Of my men and chariots none
To help me; but the Hittite of his gazing soon had fill,
For he turned his face in flight, and sped away.

Then his princes were sent.
To battle with me, the lord.
Well equipped with bow and sword
And all goodly armament,
[150] Chiefs of Luka, Masa, Kings of Malunna, Arathu,
Carchemish, of the Dardani, of Keshkesh, Khihbu.
And the brothers of the king were all gathered in one place.
Two thousand and five hundred pairs of horse —
And they came right on in force.
The fury of their faces to the flaming of my face.

Then, like Montu in his might,
I rushed on them apace.
And I let them taste my hand

57

In a twinkling moment's space.
Then cried one to his mate,
"This is no man, this is he.
This is Set, god of hate,
With Ba'al in his blood;
[160] Let us get out of here, let us flee,
Let us save our souls from death,
Let us try to save our lungs and breath."

And before the king's attack.
Hands fell, and limbs were slack.
They could neither aim the bow, nor thrust the spear,
But just looked at him who came
Charging on them, like a flame.
And the King was as a griffin in the rear.
(Behold thus speaks the Pharaoh, let all know),
"I struck them down, and there escaped none.
Then I lifted up my voice, and I spoke,
Ho! my warriors, charioteers.
Away with craven fears.
Halt, stand, and courage awoke,
[170] Behold I am alone.
Yet Amun is my helper, and his hand is with me now."[29]

-----

[203] When my Menna, charioteer, beheld in his dismay.
How the horses swarmed around us, his courage fled away.
And terror and affright
Took possession of him quite;
And straightway he cried out to me, and said,
"Gracious lord and bravest king, savior-guard
Of Egypt in the battle, be our ward;
[210] Behold we stand alone, in the hostile Hittite ring,
Save for us the breath of life,
Give deliverance from the strife.
Oh! protect us, Ramesses Miamun! Oh! save us, mighty
King!"

---

29 Lines 172-202 of Lichtheim's translation (2006: 57-72) are omitted in
Rawnsley's verse translation (1894: 109-121). They have been left out
here as well to preserve the continuity of the poem.

Then the King said, "Stop! take courage, charioteer,
As a sparrow-hawk swoops down upon his prey,
So I swoop upon the foe, and I will slay,
I will hew them into pieces, I will dash them into dust;
Have no fear,
Cast such evil thought away.
These godless men are wretches that in Amun put no trust."

[220] Then the king, toward the Hittite host he flew,
"For the sixth time that I charged them," and listen well,
"Like Ba'al in his strength, on their rear guard I fell.
And none escaped, and I slew, and slew, and slew."[30]

HITTITES BEG FOR MERCY

Then the evil King of the Hittites wrote to me, worshiping me as though I were Ra himself. He said, "You truly are Set, Ba'al in human form. And fear of you spreads like wildfire in the land of Hatti." [300] So the Hittite king sent a messenger with a letter addressed to the Pharaoh, saluting the Egyptian King.

Fig. 33: Archival photo of the Poem of Pentaur *inscription and reliefs from the Temple of Karnak (13th century BC)*

---

30 According to Lichtheim (2006: 71), the prose text resumes here.

"Ramesses the Great: Ra-Horakhty, mighty Bull of Truth, protector of the army, most powerful in all the realm, shield for his soldiers in times of war, King of Upper and Lower Egypt. Usermaatre-Setepenre, son of Ra, strongest of the strong, most loved by Amun, and receiver of eternal life. I am now your servant, and I must say that you are truly the son of Ra himself. He has delivered all the world to you. The land of Egypt and the land of Hatti both serve you, kneeling at your feet. [310] Ra, your divine father, has given these to you. Please, do not destroy us. You are indeed the all-powerful, way too strong for the land of the Hittites. We now bow to you, so please don't kill us, your servants. There's no need to continue raging against us mercilessly. Yesterday you killed a hundred thousand of us, and today you returned to ensure not a single one of our kings had an heir still living. Please don't continue this rampage, victorious Pharaoh! [320] Make peace, not war. Let us breathe!"

Then the Pharaoh softened his soul, like Montu after the battle was over. The Pharaoh ordered all of his senior officials and generals - commanders of the infantry and of the chariots - to gather together to listen to what had transpired. And he let them hear what the King of the Hittites had written to him. The officials and generals responded as one, "Making peace is a wonderful idea, Your Majesty! There's no shame in making peace when someone else begs for it. [330] Not a single nation could stop you if you chose to attack."

The Pharaoh listened to the words of his senior officials and generals, made peace with the Hittites, and started his journey southward. He returned to Egypt peacefully, with his infantry and chariots in tow. All the gods and goddesses protected him, granting him life, prosperity, and health. He had crushed the enemy and struck fear in their hearts, while at the same time protecting his own army. Now all nations praise his name.

He peacefully arrived back in Egypt, coming to Pi-Ramesses.[31] There, he relaxed in his palace, full of life and power. Like Ra on the horizon, all the gods of Egypt praised him,

---

31 Pi-Ramesses was a new capital built in the Nile Delta area of Egypt by Ramesses II.

"Welcome, dear son! King Usermaatre-Setepenre, the son of Ra, most loved by Amun, receiver of eternal life, Ramesses the Great!" And they gave him millions of jubilee festivals[32] so that he would forever sit upon the throne of Ra, with the lands of every nation - low and high - bowing at his feet for the rest of time.

Supplement by the Ancient Author

This was written in the during the summer of the 9th year of the reign of Ramesses the Great: the King of Upper and Lower Egypt, Usermaatre-Setepenre, the son of Ra, the most loved by Amun, the receiver of eternal life (just like his father Ra).

This text was commissioned by the Chief Officer of the Archives, the Royal Treasury, the Scribe Amenemone of the Royal Treasure, and the scribe Amenemwia of the Royal Treasury.

This text was created by the scribe Pentaur.[33]

The Hittite Sources

One of the most interesting aspects of the Battle of Kadesh is that we have accounts – or at least references – to the battle from both sides, the Egyptians and the Hittites. The Hittite sources for the battle of Kadesh are far less extensive than those of the Egyptians. They are not monumental texts that give us a play-by-play of the battle from the Hittite side of things. None-

---

32 A "jubilee" festival is one that commemorates a certain anniversary or length of rule. In Egypt, the most famous of these was the Sed (or Heb-Sed) Festival, which was celebrated after the king ruled for 30 years and then again every 4 years after that. In general, these were festivals of celebration but also regeneration, giving the king the power to continue to rule effectively.

33 Parts of the *Poem of Pentaur* are found on temple walls throughout Egypt, with sites like Karnak, Luxor, and Abydos being some of the most famous. It was also, however, recorded on papyrus. The final part of this translation is found on what's known as the *Papyrus Sallier III*. This particular papyrus, one of several well-preserved accounts, bears the name of its scribe, Pentaur. Modern scholars have used that scribe's name to refer to the entire text.

theless the fragments we do have are incredibly valuable for clarifying how things actually turned out.

The first source below is a fragment of a letter, written by Hattusili III to his brother Muwatalli II. At the time of the battle, Muwatalli was the Hittite king and Hattusili was a regional governor. After Muwatalli II's death years after Kadesh, Hattusili would take over as king. The second Hittite source is found in a later treaty between the Hatti, homeland of the Hittites, and Amurru, the region near modern day Syria and Lebanon. Amurru was also the region that contained Kadesh, hence the reference to it in the preamble to this later treaty. The translations for both texts are found in Trevor Bryce's *The Kingdom of the Hittites*.[34]

Fig. 34: Hittite treaties were posted on bronze tablets. This image depicts a treaty between the Hittite King Tudhaliya IV and Kurunta of Tarhuntassa. (Museum of Anatolian Civilizations; ca. 1235 BC)

34 Bryce, Trevor. *The Kingdom of the Hittites*. Oxford: Oxford University Press, 2005, pgs. 239-40.

Words of the Ancients
Letter from the Hittite Governor to the King

Because my brother Muwatalli campaigned against the king of Egypt and the king of Amurru, when he defeated the kings of Egypt and Amurru, he went back to Aba. When Muwatalli, my brother, defeated Aba, he...went back to Hatti, but he left me in Aba.[35]

Words of the Ancients
Treaty between the Hittites and Amurru

When Muwatalli, the brother of the father of My Sun, became king, the people of Amurru broke faith with him, and had this to say to him: 'From free individuals we have become vassals. But now we are your vassals no longer!' And they entered into the following of the king of Egypt. Thereupon Muwatalli, the brother of the father of My Sun, and the king of Egypt did battle with each other over the people of Amurru. Muwatalli defeated the king of Egypt and destroyed the Land of Amurru with his weapons and subjugated it.[36]

The Peace Treaty of Kadesh

Not only do we have Egyptian and Hittite accounts of the Battle of Kadesh, we also have the peace treaty between the two groups that ended the conflict. This is the world's earliest extant peace treaty.

The treaty itself was composed 16 years after the actual battle of Kadesh, in the 21st year of the reign of Ramesses II. By this time, Muwatalli II had died, and his brother, Hattusili

---

35 Translation from Bryce (2005: 240). Text originally published in *Keilschrifturkunden aus Boghazköi* XXI, 17 and *Catalogue des textes hittites* 86, I, 14-21. Translated into English by Beal, R. *The Organisation of the Hittite Military*. Heidelberg, 1992, pg. 307.

36 Translation from Bryce (2005: 240). Originally from the *Catalogue des textes hittites* 105, I, 28-38.

III had taken over as king of the Hittites, thus the treaty was between him and Ramesses II.

Incredibly, we actually have copies of the peace treaty from both the Egyptian and Hittite side of the conflict. The way this would have worked is a little convoluted. The kings, or diplomats on behalf of the kings, would have first agreed to the terms of the treaty. Then each side wrote up the treaty using the traditional naming conventions of their own king. So for the Egyptians, that would mean something like "Ramesses II, most loved by Amun, King of Upper and Lower Egypt, son of Ra, receiver of eternal life." Then they sent their copy to the other side's capital. The Egyptian composition, for example, was inscribed on a silver plate, then sent to Hattusa, the Hittite capital. There, it would have been translated into the Hittite language and inscribed on cuneiform tablets. Likewise, the Hittites would have sent their own copy to Egypt, where it was translated into the Egyptian language and then inscribed on the walls of temples.

Fig. 35: The cuneiform version of the Peace Treaty of Kadesh *from the Hittite capital of Hattusa (Istanbul Archaeological Museum; 13th century BC)*

The text below is derived from the cuneiform tablets found at the Hittite capital of Hattusa. It is an adaptation of Gary Beckman's translation in *Hittite Diplomatic Texts*.[37] In creating this adaptation, we have sacrificed some literalness and omitted some of the royal titles to make it easier to understand.

Fig. 36: The hieroglyphic version of the Peace Treaty of Kadesh *from the Temple of Karnak in Egypt (13th century BC)*

37 Beckman, Gary M. *Hittite Diplomatic Texts*. Atlanta: Society for Biblical Literature, 1996, pgs. 90-95.

Words of the Ancients
Peace Treaty of Kadesh

PREAMBLE

[1] This is the treaty that Ramesses II, most loved by Amun and Great King of Egypt, signed on a silver tablet with Hattusili III, the Great King of the Hittites, to bring about eternal peace and brotherhood between the two nations.

THE PARTIES

[2] The Great King Ramesses II, the son of Seti I, grandson of Ramesses I, King of Egypt, Most loved by Amun, and Hero of all the Lands.

[3] The Great King Hattusili III, son of Mursili II, grandson of Suppiluliuma I, King of the Hittites, and Hero of all the Lands.

[4] The Great King Ramesses II writes the following to the Great King Hattusili III.

PURPOSE OF TREATY, PREVIOUS RELATIONS

[5] We - the Great Kings Ramesses II and Hattusili III - have established eternal peace and brotherhood. Similarly, our nations - Egypt and Hatti - also establish eternal peace and brotherhood.

[6] As far as we are concerned, the gods have never allowed war between these two nations, going all the way back to the beginning of time. We are doing this in order to re-establish the peaceful relationship that our gods - the Sun God and the Storm God[38] - intended for Egypt and Hatti since the dawn of time, so there is never any conflict between them.

---

38 The "Sun God" refers to the Egyptian god Ra, and the "Storm God" refers to the chief deity of the Hittites.

FUTURE RELATIONS

[7] This is the treaty that Ramesses II, Great King of Egypt,[39] signed on a silver tablet with Hattusili III, the Great King of Hatti, to bring about eternal peace and brotherhood between the two nations. He is my brother, and I am his. And together, we will create a brotherhood of peace, one that is even better than the earlier peace between Egypt and Hatti.

[8] Ramesses, the Great King of Egypt, is on good, peaceful terms with the Great King Hattusili, the Great King of Hatti. And the sons of Ramesses will forever be at peace with the sons of Hattusili for all the rest of time. Just like us, our sons will maintain this peaceful relationship, so that Egypt and Hatti will be like brothers for all of eternity.

NON-AGGRESSION

[9] The Great King Ramesses II will never start a conflict against the Hittites nor take anything from them. And the Great King Hattusili III will never start a conflict against the Egyptians nor take anything from them. The Sun God and the Storm God have created this eternal pact of peace and brotherhood for Egypt and Hatti so that there will never be any conflict between them. Ramesses, the King of Egypt, will abide by this pact to create eternal peace. Egypt will live in peace and brotherhood with Hatti forevermore.

DEFENSIVE ALLIANCE

[10] If an enemy ever attacks the Hittites and their Great King Hattusili III, he will send a message to Ramesses II saying, "Come help me against my enemy." And the Great King Ramesses II must send both his infantry and chariots to defeat this enemy and take vengeance for Hatti.

---

39 The actual text continually refers to both Ramesses II and Hattusili III with a long string of titles. For Ramesses, it is usually, "Ramesses, beloved of Amun, Great King, King of Egypt." We have shortened this to "Great King of Egypt" or simply "the Great King Ramesses II" to make the text read a little more smoothly.

[11] If Hattusili III, Great King of the Hittites, ever has his own people turn against him, he will send to Ramesses II, Great King of Egypt. And the Great King Ramesses II will send both his infantry and chariots to destroy whoever has angered the Great King.

[12] If an enemy ever attacks the Egyptians and their Great King Ramesses II, he will send a message to Hattusili III saying, "Come help me against my enemy." And the Great King Hattusili III must send both his infantry and cavalry to defeat this enemy and take vengeance for Egypt.

[13] If Ramesses II, Great King of Egypt, ever has his own people turn against him, he will send to Hattusili III, Great King of Hatti. And the Great King Hattusili III will send both his infantry and chariots to destroy whoever has angered the Great King.

SUCCESSION

[14] After the long reign of the Great King Hattusili III, his son shall take the throne and become King of Hatti. And if the people of Hatti rebel against him, the Great King Ramesses II must send both his infantry and cavalry to punish them.

FUGITIVES

[15] If an important noble ever flees Hatti, or if a group of people under Hittite control ever leaves its territory, the Great King Ramesses II must take them into custody and send them back to the Great King Hattusili III.

[16] If even one or two regular men come to Ramesses II to join up with him, then the Great King Ramesses II must take them into custody and send them back to the Great King Hattusili III.

[17] If an important noble ever flees Egypt, or if a group of people under Egyptian control ever leaves its territory, the Great King Hattusili III must take them into custody and send them back to the Great King Ramesses II.

[18] If even one or two regular men come to Hattusili III to join up with him, then the Great King Hattusili III must take them into custody and send them back to the Great King Ramesses II.

[19] If an official or two ever flee Hatti and come to Egypt so that they don't have to serve the Great King Hattusili III anymore, then the Great King Ramesses II must take them into custody and send them back to his brother [Hattusili III].

[20] If an official or two ever flee Egypt and come to Hatti so that they don't have to serve the Great King Ramesses II anymore, then the Great King Hattusili III must take them into custody and send them back to his brother [Ramesses II].

[21] If this does happen, and a person or two flee from Hatti and come to Ramesses II, then Ramesses II must take them into custody and send them back to Hattusili III, for they are brothers. However, he should not punish these fugitives for their crimes. He shouldn't tear out their tongues or their eyes or cut off their ears or their feet. And he shouldn't destroy their family - their wives and children - either.

[22] If this does happen, and a person or two flee from Egypt and come to Hatti, then Hattusili III must take them into custody and send them back to Ramesses II, for they are brothers. However, he should not punish these fugitives for their crimes. He shouldn't tear out their tongues or their eyes or cut off their ears or their feet. And he shouldn't destroy their family - their wives and children - either.

The Rest of the Story

The treaty continues from here, but the remainder of the text is lost. Fragmentary remains, however, suggest that it goes on to discuss the issue of fugitives in more detail. The treaty then appears to conclude with blessings for the two parties - the Great Kings Ramesses II and Hattusili III - and curses if the treaty should ever be broken. The text also suggests that the original treaty - the one that would have been signed on a silver table (which no longer exists) - contained two Egyptian seals, one of Ramesses II and one of the Sun god Ra.

What we do know, however, is that the Battle of Kadesh was one of the last major conflicts during the peak of both the Egyptian and Hittite Empires. A century later, the Mediterranean was thrown into turmoil as powerful cities and civilizations throughout the region were burned to the ground. Known as the Bronze Age Collapse, this period, starting around 1200 BC, saw the downfall of the Hittite Empire and the destruction of its former capital of Hattusa.

Even the Egyptians, who had been going strong for nearly 2,000 years at this point, were thrown into chaos. They record the "People of the Nine Bows" and the "Sea Peoples" as a diverse group of naval marauders who laid siege to Egypt during the 12th and 11th centuries BC. Just like Ramesses II did for the Battle of Kadesh, Egyptian Pharaohs at the time erected monuments depicting their total domination of these invaders. In reality, however, we see the collapse of the New Kingdom and the rise of the Third Intermediate Period – a time of invasion, destabilization, and decentralization – in the aftermath of these attacks. The days of mighty Bronze Age empires had finally come to a close.

CHAPTER II

Becoming Greek

𝕴t's important to remember that the political landscape is very, very different today than it was 3,000 years ago. Not just that different people govern different places today, but rather the whole concept is fundamentally different. Today, we have countries or nation-states. That means that we can draw hard, clear-cut lines on a map to determine what area is owned by which country. And each country, in turn, has its own capital city which is the seat of government for the country as a whole. In antiquity, however, there were a wide variety of political entities. In some places like Egypt, a central king ruled something akin to a country. In the Near East, a king might rule a diverse group of people and places, something closer to an empire. And in the Aegean - mainland Greece, the islands, and the western coast of Turkey - you frequently have independent city-states. They share a culture and a religion and a language, but they are all separate, independent political entities.

The independent city-states of the Greek world go back to the Bronze Age, a thousand years before Athens invented democracy around 500 BC. We saw that in Egypt and the Near East, Bronze Age civilizations arose around 3000 BC, but those of the Aegean world - that is, the area in and around the Aegean Sea, which lies between modern day Greece and Turkey - were relatively late starters. It wasn't until the 2nd millennium BC (the 1000s BC), that this region started to develop the same level of wealth and complexity as their Near Eastern counterparts. Once things did get off the ground, two different cultures arose in the area, Minoan culture centered on Crete and the islands, and Mycenaean culture centered on mainland Greece.

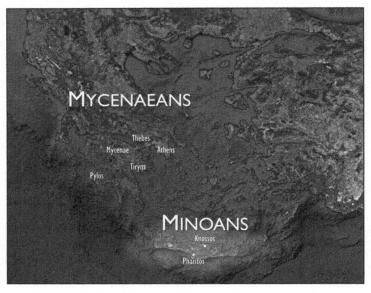

Fig. 37: Map of Mycenaean and Minoan cultures during the Aegean Bronze Age (Google, © 2023 TerraMetrics)

Minoan culture is named after the legendary King Minos, the first King of Crete, and the ruler who established the labyrinth that held the hideous half-man, half-bull minotaur. According to Greek mythology, the minotaur would annually devour seven boys and seven girls from Athens, at least until the hero Theseus put an end to his subterranean meals. The actual Minoans, however, were far more peaceful. At numerous sites throughout Crete, we have archaeological evidence for Minoan palaces. These were large, complex structures that serve polit-

*Fig. 38: Ruins of the Palace of Minos at Knossos
(Knossos, Greece; ca. 1900 - 1200 BC)*

ical, religious, and economic functions, and the complexity of the grandest of these, at the site of Knossos, makes it look like it is indeed a labyrinth. Strangely, however, none of these palaces have any defensive fortification walls, which is normally the first thing you build if you're a major Bronze Age site. On top of that, the decoration is profoundly peaceful: depictions of dolphins swimming, amphoras with tentacled octopi, and frescoes with acrobats leaping over the top of bulls are all found at sites like Knossos. You can think of this group as the hippies of the Bronze Age.

*Fig. 39: Restored dolphin fresco from the Palace of Minos
(Knossos, Greece; ca. 1500 BC)*

The Mycenaeans - the mainland Greek counterpart to the Minoans - were the exact opposite. If you look at their palaces, at sites like Mycenae and Tiryns, they are surrounded by incredibly massive fortification walls, making them true citadels. The stones of these walls are so big, in fact, that early scholars called them "Cyclopean" walls, since only a mighty Cyclops could move stones so large. Artifacts found in the graves of Mycenae further suggest their militaristic nature. We have daggers inlaid with hunting scenes, bronze armor and boar's tusk helmets, and golden burial masks just to name a few of the highlights. Mycenaean palaces centered on what's known as the megaron, a large room with a fire burning in the middle, and it was from here that the local king would conduct his business.

Fig. 40: Cyclopean walls and the so-called "Lion Gate" at the Bronze Age citadel of Mycenae (ca. 1550 - 1150 BC)

Texts written on clay tablets using a script known as Linear B gives us even greater insight into these early Greek cultures. The script was only deciphered in the middle of the 20th century, and it was shown to be a very early form of the Greek language. Once translated, these tablets have revealed important clues to how Mycenaean society functioned. In large part, these are accounting documents, and they record the diversity of goods that were shipped to the central citadels, and also the goods that then got shipped back out to the surrounding

Fig. 41: Linear B Tablet from the Bronze Age site of Pylos recording how animal hides were distributed to leather workers
(National Archaeological Museum of Athens; ca. 1450 BC)

countryside . This makes us think that these palaces stood at
the center of a partially redistributive economy, where goods
would flow into the center, which would then redistribute them
as needed to the rest of the population. This would have allowed for a greater level of agricultural specialization, meaning
that if your land was best for olives, you could grow only olives, send some to the citadel, and then receive other types of
goods from the center.

The Greek Dark Ages

Even the colossal Cyclopean walls couldn't prevent these
Bronze Age Aegean cultures from collapsing in the 12th century
BC. At the same time sites were being destroyed in Egypt and in
the Levant, these palaces and citadels were burnt to the ground
on mainland Greece and in the islands as well. The legend of
sites like Mycenae would live on. They became the inspiration-
al setting for the Homeric epics, the *Iliad* and the *Odyssey*, and
they even became tourist attractions in later Greek and Roman
antiquity. But the Bronze Age palaces had come to an end, and
as a result the Aegean plunged into what is commonly known
as the Greek Dark Ages (ca. 1200 - 800 BC).

Why are they called the Greek Dark Ages? Well, scholars
know less about them, because our evidence is scanty compared
to other periods. The massive citadels of the Bronze Age com-

75

pletely disappear, and the sites we do have are much smaller in scale than those of the preceding period. This suggests a fundamental change in social, political, and economic organization, with large state governments and redistributive economies falling out of use, eventually replaced with smaller social units and greater self-sufficiency. Not only that, we also just have fewer sites to begin with, so they are smaller and less numerous. When we look at the funerary realm, burials are far less rich than they used to be. And the grave goods that do exist are significantly less sophisticated than those of the Bronze Age. You can see, for example, what a Bronze Age octopus amphora looks like and compare that to the protogeometic amphora of the Greek Dark Ages.

Fig. 42 (left): Bronze Age "Marine" style amphora depicting an octopus (Heraklion Archaeological Museum; ca. 1500 BC)

Fig. 43(right): Dark Age "Protogeometric" style amphora with concentric circles (British Museum; ca. 975-950 BC)

Analysis of pottery and artifacts from the Dark Ages also shows us that the frequency of imported goods dramatically declines, suggesting that the long distance trade networks of the Bronze Age have largely disintegrated. Perhaps most surprisingly, all the major Bronze Age Linear B writing completely disappears. That's right, people forget how to write for nearly half a millennium!

The 8th Century Renaissance

Sometime around 800 BC, however, the pendulum started to swing back. The following hundred years - the 8th century BC - was an exciting time in the Greek world as it started to spread its culture across the Mediterranean and create some of the institutions that we think of as fundamentally Greek. During the 700s BC, increasing population pressure caused some of the Greek city-states to send out settlers to found new colonies. They sailed far and wide across the Mediterranean, establishing colonies on the French Riviera like Massilia (modern Marseille) and even on the east coast of Spain. Southern Italy and Sicily eventually became so dense with Greek colonies that the region was called Magna Graecia, or Greater Greece. Still other settlers found their way into the Black Sea, founding cities which would serve as important sources for food and grain for centuries to come.

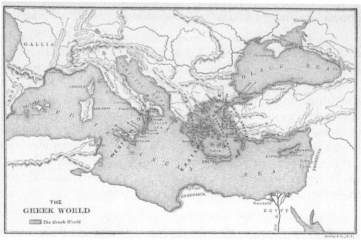

Fig. 44: Greek colonization during the Archaic Period stretched across the Mediterranean, from the Black Sea to Spain.

Some of Greece's most important institutions and cultural developments also had their origins in the 8th century BC. The ancient Olympics, for example, date all the way back to 776 BC, and they played an important socio-political role. Remember, the Greek city-states were all politically independent, and they often fought with each other as much as with any outside group. The Olympics, then, allowed people from these diverse, independent city-states to come together peacefully, and encouraged athletic competition as a way to build common social and cultural bonds. The Olympics weren't just a flash in the pan either; they were held every four years for more than a millennium, before early Christian emperors put an end to the practice because of its pagan religious connotations.

Although it had never really disappeared, religion also became far more visible in the archaeological record in the 8th century BC. We get the first recognizable Greek temples dating back to this period. And while most of them were built over many times in antiquity, small models like the one of the Temple of Hera at Argos   show that the earliest Greek temples looked much like houses, literally a house for the god. The style of Greek temples changed, of course, over time, but that function of housing the god or goddess would remain for centuries.

Art was part of the 8th century renaissance as well. We saw that during the Greek Dark Ages, the level of sophistication and complexity of vase decoration dramatically declined, ending up in a series of straight lines and concentric circles (Fig. 41). In the 8th century, the inclination towards geometric design remains, but we see an increase in its detail as well as the return of pictorial iconography. The *krater* above (Fig. 42), originally found near the Dipylon Gate of the Kerameikos cemetery in Athens, shows just how detailed these vases could be. It depicts the funerary preparations and procession of the deceased, and the vase itself would have served as the grave marker.

Perhaps most importantly, the 8th century BC saw the resurgence of writing. After 400 years of silence (or darkness, if you will), writing was back, and this time it was better than ever. Remember that the Linear B tablets of the Bronze Age primarily focused on accounting, goods flowing to and from the palaces. Now, however, writing returned in alphabetic form. The alphabet itself was borrowed from the Phoenicians, and these 24 simple letters could be recombined in an almost infinite number of ways to write down almost any sound a per-

Fig. 45: Archaic Period "Geometric" style amphora from Athens
(Metrpolitan Museum of Art; ca. 750-735 BC)

son could make. As a result, the earliest texts we have aren't economic in nature; rather, they're literary and poetic. The very first Greek alphabetic inscription, for example, is on a small cup and references a scene from the *Iliad*. In fact, it makes a joke that says whoever drinks from this cup will make Aphrodite, goddess of love, fall in love with him.

*Fig. 46: "Nestor's Cup" contains the earliest Greek alphabetic
inscription and references the Homeric epics
(Archaeological Museum of Pithecusae ca. 725 BC)*

Our earliest longer texts are also far different than the
Bronze Age tablets. They are, of course, the epic poems composed by Homer: the *Iliad* and the *Odyssey*. We'll cover more
about both the author and the texts as we introduce the translations below, but for now it's important to know that this was
a major break from what came before it. People weren't using writing to only record their economic transactions, they
were using it to entertain, to tell stories, and convey values that
would govern Greek life for centuries.

Archaic Greece

The "8th Century Renaissance" is essentially the first part
of the time period we call Archaic Greece, which lasted from
around 800 BC to 479 BC, when the Greeks surprisingly defeated the Persians who had invaded their homeland. Although
we call this the Archaic Period, almost everything that we consider quintessentially Greek gets its start during this time. We've
already seen that the Olympics, temples, intricate vase painting,
and literary writing all got their start in the first hundred years
of the Archaic Period. But that was just the beginning.

Politically and socially, the Archaic Period in Greece saw
the move towards equality, which eventually culminated in the

birth of democracy. During the Bronze Age, powerful kings known as *wanakes* in early Greek ruled from their citadels. In the Greek Dark Ages, leaders were known as *basileis*, which were less powerful monarchs. By the archaic period, however, many city-states had adopted oligarchies, which meant that a small group of people, usually aristocrats, ruled the city-states. Occasionally, a single person would try to overthrow the group and take power all for themselves, and we (and the ancient Greeks) call these people tyrants.

By the end of the Archaic Period, however, at least some of the Athenians had become discontent with the tyrannical rule of the city. Two of the citizens, guys by the name of Harmodius and Aristogeiton, actually tried to assassinate the last two tyrant leaders of the city. They were only partially successful, but in the chaos that ensued, democracy was born.

Fig. 47: The "Tyrannicides" (Harmodius and Aristogeiton) who attempted to assassinate the last tyrants of Athens (National Archaeological Museum of Naples; Roman copy of a 5th century Greek original)

81

An Athenian named Cleisthenes decided that all citizens should have a say in how the city-state operated, and thus we get one of the world's earliest participatory governments. It's important to remember here that "citizens" meant free men who were from the city-state, so women, children, slaves, and foreigners were all left out. Nevertheless, this was a major step towards equality during a time when other cultures, like the Persians, were consolidating more and more power in the single person of the king.

The Archaic Period also saw the development of architecture that we tend to associate with Greece. We saw that temples emerged during the 8th century BC but over the next few centuries, these small house-like structures were replaced with large stone buildings. These became peripteral in style, meaning they were surrounded on all sides with columns, and they became monumental in size. The earliest were known as *hecatompeda*, or hundred-footers, due to their length. It was during this time that the standard elements and layout of Greek temples was set. They were usually composed of three rooms: the *pronaos* or entry vestibule, the *naos* or sanctuary where the cult statue would have stood, and the *opisthodomos* or treasury where gifts for the gods would have been kept. Many city-states, especially those in southern Italy and Sicily, poured immense amounts of wealth into building numerous temples as a way to compete with one another for regional prestige.

Fig. 48: Archaic Period Temple of Apollo at Corinth (ca. 560 BC)

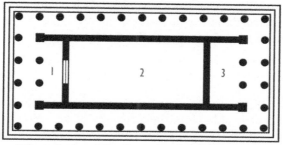

Stylobate=platform on which columns stand   Peristyle=exterior colonnade

1=Pronaos (Entry)   2=Naos (Sanctuary)   3=Opisthodomos (Treasury)

Fig. 49: Plan of a typical Greek temple

Vase painting also developed into what we think of as "Greek" during the Archaic Period. We learned above that the 8th century BC saw the re-emergence of iconography on vases, and this continued to develop over the Archaic Period. By 700 BC, Protocorinthian vases merged this geometric approach with Near Eastern motifs. And a century later, full-fledged Corithian-style pottery drew heavily on Near Eastern animal imagery. Around 600 BC, Athenian potters and painters invented the first "Black Figure" pottery, which is exactly what it sounds like, with the background in reddish orange and the figures on the vase portrayed in black.

Fig. 50: Attic black-figure Panathenaic prize amphora
(Metropolitan Museum of Art; ca. 530 BC)

These tend to be what we think of when we imagine "Greek" pottery. The vase above (Fig. 47) is a Panathenaic amphora, awarded to the winners of sprint race at the Panathenaic games during the 6th century BC.

Greek sculpture also emerged during the Archaic Period. When the Greeks set up their first colony in Egypt in the 7th century BC, they were enamored with the style of Egyptian sculpture that dated back at least 2000 years earlier. They adopted this general look for their own sculptures, showing a person standing upright and rigid, arms at their side, and one foot striding forward. This type of statue is known as a *kouros* if it's of a man and a *kore* if it's of a woman and they proliferated throughout Greece during the 6th century BC.

Fig. 51: Old Kingdom statue of striding figure from El Kab, Egypt (Metropolitan Museum of Art; ca. 2500 BC)

Fig. 52: The Kroisos Kouros from Anavyssos, Greece (National Archaeological Museum of Athens; ca. 530 BC)

Finally we have the emergence of Greek philosophy during the Archaic Period. This wasn't quite the time of Socrates, Plato, and Aristotle, but we do get people starting to ask deep questions about the way the world worked. Many of these philosophers came from the city of Miletus in the region of Ionia, which corresponds to the western coast of Turkey, and thus we call this the Milesian school of philosophy and the period the Ionian enlightenment. Some of the most famous philosophers were Anaximander, Anaxagoras, Anaximenes, and Thales, and this group started questioning how the world worked if the gods weren't actually controlling everything. They were looking for explanations that could cut across different natural phenomena, and many of their explanations focused on elements. Thales, for example, thought that everything was composed of water's different forms - gaseous steam, solid ice, and liquid water. He wasn't exactly right, of course, but he was on the right track in thinking that everything is made up of small parts that combine in different ways.

Thus, the Archaic Period is a bit of a misnomer. Sure, it's older (or more "archaic") than Classical Greece, but just about everything we associate with ancient Greece gets its start during the Archaic Period. Around 500 BC, however, right in the middle of this meteoric rise, Greece became embroiled in a conflict with the mighty Persian Empire. The existence of their very culture was at stake. To find out how that played out, however, you'll have to read the next chapter.

Homer's *Iliad*

The *Iliad* is one of the oldest and most influential works in all of Greek, and indeed world, literature. Along with the *Odyssey*, it was one of two ancient Greek epic poems attributed to the blind poet Homer, who most scholars imagine writing or composing some time in the 8th century BC. Generally considered the earlier of the two poems, the *Iliad* stands as the oldest surviving work of ancient Greek literature, and it was as famous in Greek antiquity as it is today - for while the tale is set during the epic Trojan War, the story actually focuses on individual experiences and emotions: the desire for glory, the role of fate, and the concept of heroism. Because of this, its themes connected - and still connect - with its audience on a personal and meaningful level.

It is the Greek hero Achilles that stands at the center of *Iliad*, and honestly he seems a little strange when compared to our modern group of superheroes. Achilles isn't out fighting crime or trying to save the world or on a quest for some mythical object. Instead, he spends much of the *Iliad* sitting in his tent on the beach, moping about and pouting about how his fellow Greek leader - King Agamemnon of Argos and Mycenae - has taken away the prize of honor he was awarded when the Greeks sacked a small town near Troy. Achilles, in fact, does this for more than half the book, only entering the fray about ⅔ of the way through.

Fig. 53: Attic black-figure vase depicting Ajax and Achilles playing a game during a break in the Trojan War (Vatican Museums; ca. 550-530 BC)

Once he does start fighting, his strength and speed and skill in battle are unparalleled; he truly is an extraordinary warrior. But his deeds off the battlefield are questionable at best and by no means exemplary. It is his rage at the dishonor he has been subjected to that serve as the centerpiece of this story, and while not everyone might be able to associate with the feeling of heroic warfare, all of Homer's readers or listeners could certainly empathize with these very human emotions of anger and indignation at the perceived slight of another individual.

Fig. 54: Bronze Age boar's tusk helmet from Mycenae
(National Archaeological Museum of Athens; 14th century BC)

We say Homer's readers or listeners because the origins of the *Iliad* are somewhat shrouded in mystery. Scholars believe the story was created sometime in the 8th century BC, the dawn of the Archaic Period in Greece. The narrative itself, however, is meant to be set about half a millennium earlier, sometime around 1,200 BC in the Late Bronze Age, a time of massive citadels and palaces, only the ruins of which remained by Homer's own time. Evidence for this discrepancy can be found in the material and cultural references of the text. For example, some soldiers in the *Iliad* wear "boar's tusk helmets" (which are exactly what they sound like, protective helmets made from boar's tusks), which existed only in the Bronze Age of the 2nd millennium BC.

However, the deceased in the *Iliad* are often cremated on funeral pyres rather than interred in the ground, a practice which only arose much later in the Archaic Period. It's almost as though Homer was trying to place the setting in the Bronze Age but just didn't get all the details right, and some of the practices from his own time slipped into the text. Images from the story start showing up in art, like ancient Greek vase paintings, in the 600s BC, so we can feel confident it predated those creations.

One of the ways in which these small mistakes may have arisen is through the oral transmission of the story by a series of bards, or oral poets, across a long period of time. Almost like a game of telephone 500 years long, you can't help but have a few things change along the way. This is how most scholars view Homer - as a person (or a group of people) who helped standardize the story of the *Iliad* and performed it orally for aristocratic families in the early days of Archaic Greece.

Fig. 55: Statue of Homer singing and playing the lyre
(Louvre Museum; 1812)

The poem is composed in dactylic hexameter (giving each line six feet, and each foot a single long and two short syllables), and this meter would have been conducive to the oral performance of a long poem. Other clues to this early oral performance include the heavy use of epithets and formulae. Epithets are nicknames of various syllables that the singer could insert into any line to ensure that every line would precisely fit the meter, and formulae are standardized scenes that get repeated, like the steps in hosting a feast or preparing for war. You can think of it like a set of Lego blocks of various sizes, rather than composed entirely of 1 x 1's, the *Iliad* and *Odyssey* were created using standardized blocks of various sizes.

As you will see, the story of the *Iliad* begins right in the middle of the Trojan War. The backstory for why the Greeks have come to Troy is only briefly referenced in the *Iliad*. In fact, the *Iliad* and *Odyssey* were just two poems of what scholars call the Epic Cycle, a series of eight epic poems that tell the entire story of the Trojan War. These include the Judgment of Paris (*Cypria*), the story of Achilles (*Iliad*), the arrival of the Trojan allies (*Aethiopis*), the Trojan Horse and sack of Troy (*Iliou Persis*), the return of the Greeks (*Nostoi*), the homeward journey of Odysseus (the *Odyssey*), and Odysseus' final adventure and death (*Telegony*). The *Iliad* and *Odyssey* are the only stories that we still have in full and were the most famous in Greek antiquity. These are also thought to be the earliest of the eight, but clearly audiences would have been expected to know the rough outline of the entire Epic Cycle even in its earliest days.

The prequel to the *Iliad*, known as the *Cypria*, tells the story of the Judgment of Paris and the abduction of Helen. First, a little background on Helen: she was the daughter of Zeus and Leda, and was renowned for her beauty long before the Trojan War. She was so beautiful, in fact, that the Greeks envisioned this causing problems. So when she became of marriageable age, all of her suitors swore an oath to support whomever Helen chose as her husband. If anyone were to attack Helen's husband in an attempt to steal her away, they would all join forces against the traitor. So when Helen married King Menelaus of

Sparta, all the other Greeks swore to support him if anyone were to steal her away.

The other half of the story begins with another wedding, this time of Achilles' parents - the mortal man Peleus and the divine sea-nymph Thetis. Zeus hosted the celebration, and all the gods were invited; all, that is, except for Eris, the goddess of discord and strife. Eris, however, sent along a present, a golden apple inscribed with the Greek word *kallisti* ("for the fairest"), which was to be awarded to the most beautiful goddess. Zeus, not wanting to upset Hera again, forced the Trojan prince Paris to make the decision. Hera offered to make him lord of Europe and Asia; Athena offered him skill in war and wisdom; and Aphrodite offered him the most beautiful woman in all the land (which, of course, was Helen). Paris, of course, chose Aphrodite, and on a subsequent trip to Sparta, Paris abducted Helen, the wife of King Menelaus, and returned with her to Troy.

Fig. 56: The Judgement of Paris by François-Xavier Fabre
(Virginia Museum of Fine Arts; 1808)

As a result of the oath that the Helen's suitors had sworn to Menelaus, the diverse group of Greek tribes gathered together to sail to Troy to win her back. The mighty walls of Troy, however, prevented an easy victory, and the *Iliad* picks up in the 9th year of the siege. While Troy remains impenetrable, the Greeks have had success sacking and pillaging surrounding towns. As was customary in the ancient Greek world, they collectively decided how to divide the spoils of war from these successful raids among the soldiers. And thus Homer's story begins.

Words of the Ancients

Homer's *Iliad*

Book 1

Sing to me, goddess, about the rage of Achilles (son of Peleus),[1] which brought endless woes to the Greeks (Achaeans).[2] For it was this rage that sent many brave souls rushing down to the realm of Hades, and it was this wrath that turned so many glorious heroes into food for the vultures. Tell me of that fateful day on which the prophecies of Zeus came true, when kingly Agamemnon (son of Atreus)[3] and mighty Achilles first

---

1 Peleus, a mortal man, was married to Thetis, an immortal sea-nymph, and their child was the hero Achilles. All the gods attended the wedding of Peleus and Thetis, except for Eris, the Goddess of Strife, who sent along the golden apple of discord as a present. This was retrieved by the Trojan prince Paris, who gave the apple to the goddess he deemed to be the fairest: Aphrodite. In return, Aphrodite promised Paris the most beautiful woman in the world, Helen, the wife of King Menelaus of Sparta. Paris' abduction of Helen leads to the Trojan War (and thus to Homer's *Iliad*, which starts in Year 9 of a 10-year long siege of the city of Troy).

2 Here we have translated the word "Achaeans" as "Greeks." Homer sets the *Iliad* within the context of Bronze Age Greece. During that time, city-states were politically independent of one another. They all would have thought of themselves as Greeks (even the Trojans), but they also all would have had their own identity in addition. So Agamemnon is king of the Achaeans; Achilles is king of the Myrmidons; and Priam is king of the Trojans.

3 In the original Greek, Homer simply says "the son of Atreus" instead of referring to Agamemnon directly. His readers or listeners would have known the mythological background well enough to understand who this referred to. In this translation, we will begin by referring to the characters directly while also stating their parentage. In subsequent mentions, we will try to balance faithfulness to the original Greek with ease of understanding for the reader.

began to quarrel.

Which god made these two start to argue? It was Apollo (son of Zeus and Leto), who was so upset that the son of Atreus (Agamemnon) dishonored his priest Chryses, [10] that he sent these evils to plague the Greek people. For Chryses had come down to the Greek ships in order to free his daughter by paying a hefty ransom. And as he entered the camp, he held in his hand the scepter of Apollo, complete with a wreath indicating he was coming in peace. Once there, he sought out Agamemnon and Menelaus (the two sons of Atreus).

A PRIEST'S PLEA DENIED

"Sons of Atreus and all you other Greeks," Chryses pleaded. "May the Olympian gods bless you and allow you to destroy the city of Priam (Troy)! And after your victory, may you return to your homes safely. [20] But please, accept the gifts that I have brought as ransom in exchange for my daughter, for they are sacred to Apollo, the son of Zeus."

Fig. 57: Detail from an Apulian red-figure volute crater depicting Chryses begging Agamemnon for the return of his daughter (Louvre Museum; ca. 360-350 BC)

The Greeks listened intently to Chryses, for they all had a great respect for him. And they were unanimous in their opinion – accept the proposal and take the ransom in exchange for his daughter. But Agamemnon alone was unmoved by the priest's plea. He angrily shouted at Chryses and sent him away. "Listen up old man. I better not find you hanging out near our ships or in our camp. Your fancy scepter and wreath won't get you any special treatment here. There's no way I'm freeing your daughter. She's mine, and she will grow old in my house in Argos,[4] [30] spending her days at my loom and her nights in my bed. So get the hell out of here or things will get even worse for you!"

The old man was scared, and he obeyed the words of Agamemnon. He said nothing on the way out of the Greek camp, silently making his way to the seashore. There he prayed to mighty Apollo, the son of Leto. "Hear my prayer, god of the silver bow (Apollo), protector of Chryse and holy Cilla, and ruler of Tenedos.[5] I beg you, hear my prayer, Mouse God (Sminthe).[6] [40] If I have ever honored you – decorating your temple with flowers and sacrificing the fattest bulls in your name – please hear my prayer. Avenge my tears, and let loose your arrows upon these impious Greeks (Danaans)!"

And Apollo indeed heard his prayer. He was furious as he descended the craggy peaks of Mount Olympus. His bow and quiver was slung over his shoulder, and his arrows clanged together as he shook with rage. Cloaked in darkness, he sat far away from the ships, and his silver bow resounded as it sent an

---

4   Agamemnon is the legendary king of Mycenae and/or Argos. While these are different sites in later periods, it is thought they were different names for roughly the same region during the Bronze Age.

5   The names get a little tricky here. Chryse is the town near Troy with a Temple to Apollo, Chryses is the priest of Apollo, and Chryseis is the daughter of Chryses. Cilla is a nearby town south of Troy, while Tenedos is an island near Troy, just off the coast of modern day Turkey.

6   Smintheus or "mouse" is one of the epithets of Apollo. In the ancient Greek world, mice were thought to be inspired by the vapors of the earth, thus serving as a symbol of oracles and prophecy. As an oracular god, Apollo is logically connected to such an animal. According to the ancient Greco-Roman geographer Strabo, the Temple of Apollo at Chryse (where Chryses was a priest), contained a cult statue of Apollo with a mouse under his foot.

arrow of death into the middle of the Greek camp. The first to perish were the pack animals and hunting dogs. [50] But then he set his aim upon the people themselves. And for the entire day, the camp burned as the funeral pyres were stacked high with Greek soldiers.

Fig. 58: Ivory statue of Apollo reaching into his quiver for an arrow (Stoa of Attalus Museum; 3rd century BC)

This went on for nine straight days, with Apollo's arrows bringing death and destruction to the Greeks. Then, on the tenth day, Achilles called them all together. For he had been inspired by Hera, who saw that the Greeks were on their last legs, and she took pity on them. Once the Greeks had gathered together, Achilles stood and addressed the crowd.

"Son of Atreus (Agamemnon)! We need to get out of here now if we're going to escape with our lives, [60] for our men are perishing from war and disease all at once. Let's get a priest or prophet or an interpreter of dreams in here quickly – some one who can tell us why Phoebus Apollo is so furious.[7] Is it an oath we have broken? Or a sacrifice we have failed to make? We must figure out whether an offering of our finest lambs will be enough for Apollo to take this plague away from us."

Achilles then sat down, and Calchas, the son of Thestor

---

7   Apollo's epithet Phoebus means something like "bright" or "pure" and
     emphasizes his connection to the sun (*Helios*).

and the wisest of all the prophets (for he knew everything that was, is, and will be), stood up to speak. [70] It was Calchas who had guided the Greek fleet to the shores of Ilium (Troy), [8]and he spoke to them honestly and as best he could.

"Most blessed Achilles, you want me to tell you about the fury of divine Apollo, and I will certainly do so. But first, I need you to promise that you will be on my side, both in words and actions, since what I am about to say will undoubtedly enrage the king of the Argives[9] who leads all the Greeks (Agamemnon). You know a regular person like me can't stand against a king. [80] For even if he acts like everything is okay now, his rage will burn within until he can exact his revenge. So think about whether you really want to protect me before I speak my piece."

And Achilles answered the seer, "Don't worry! Tell it like it is, just as you have received it from the heavens. Let us know, Calchas, what Apollo – the god to whom you pray – has revealed to you.[10] I promise that not one of the Greeks here down by the ships will touch a hair on your head while I am still alive. [90] Not even Agamemnon shall touch you, even though he is the most powerful of all the Greeks."

And so Calchas the prophet spoke courageously, "Apollo is not angry about a broken oath nor a missed sacrifice. Rather, he rages because of the mistreatment of his priest, whom Agamemnon dishonored. For Agamemnon would not release the daughter of the priest of Apollo, even though he had brought him plenty of gifts to ransom her. So now Apollo will not stop destroying the Greeks until Agamemnon returns the priest's daughter, this time without any ransom at all. And on top of that, he must send a hundred oxen to Chryse as well. If we do all that, we might just have a shot at appeasing Apollo."

---

8 *Ilium* is another name for the city of Troy, and the city that gives the story its title of *Iliad*.

9 People from the city of Argos.

10 Apollo is an oracular god, one who had knowledge of the future and could be consulted to reveal such knowledge. Thus it makes sense that Apollo is "the god to whom Calchas prays.

FEUD OF AGAMEMNON AND ACHILLES

[100] Then the prophet sat down, and Agamemnon furiously erupted out of his chair. His black heart pounded with anger, and fiery flames danced in his eyes. He glared at Calchas and spewed, "Prophet of doom! You never once have foreseen anything good coming my way. Your words never, ever bring me any solace. And you come into the Greek camp rambling about how Apollo has plagued us because I wouldn't take a ransom and return the daughter of the priest Chryses. [110] You don't understand how deeply I care for her; I love her even more than my own wife Clytemnestra! For she is every bit as beautiful and loving and smart and impressive as her. But I'll return her if I must, for I'd rather see my people live than die. Only on one condition, though – you need to get me a new prize[11] to replace her. Otherwise, I'll be the only person here without one, and that's just not a good look for the leader of the Greeks."

[120] Achilles responded to Agamemnon, "Most honored son of Atreus, why are you acting so jealous? How in the world are we supposed to find another prize for you? It's not like we have some storage room full of gold and silver and women to distribute whenever we'd like. The spoils of war we took from the cities have already been doled out, and we can't take away what has already been awarded. Give this girl back to Apollo and his priest, and if Zeus allows us to sack Troy, then you'll be paid back tenfold."

[130] But Agamemnon answered him, saying "Achilles, you might be brave, but you're all brawn and no brain. You forget your place in the pecking order; there's no way you're going to convince me to give her up. Think about it; you'd be sitting there with your own prize, but I'd look like a fool, having given mine up – and done so at your order to boot! So let the Greeks find me another prize worthy of my stature, or else

---

11 The taking of "prizes" was something that was done after being victorious in combat. You can think of it like the "spoils of war." In this period, after sacking a city, the victorious group would have come together to collectively decide who got what part of the booty.

I'm coming for yours – or Ajax's or Odysseus' – and whomever I come for, well, that person is going to be sorry. But for now, let's follow the prophet's advice. [140] Get a ship ready, find a crew, and load it up with Chryseis and the hundred oxen. And make sure that one of our best men serves as captain – Ajax or Idomeneus – or even you, mighty Achilles (son of Peleus). That gives us our best chance of offering an appropriate sacrifice and appeasing Apollo."

Achilles glared at him and responded, "You greedy bastard! [150] How are you going to get any of the Greeks to fight for you if you keep acting like this? I didn't sail all the way here to fight the Trojans because they had wronged me – I have no beef with them. They didn't show up in my fertile fields of Phthia and steal my cattle or my horses or my crops. I live halfway across the world from them, and the mountains and the sea keep us far apart. We came here to follow you, King Asshole![12] We're here for your glory, not our own, so that you and Menelaus[13] can take vengeance on the Trojans. [160] You seem to forget all this, while you sit here threatening to take away my prize, which the Greeks have rightly bestowed upon me. Yet when we Greeks sack any of the wealthy Trojan towns, my spoils of war never compare to yours, even though I'm the one doing all the fighting! You swoop in, take the lion's share of the booty, and I'm left down by the ships to thankfully scrape together whatever I can get now that the fighting is done. Honestly, it's probably best if I just take my ships and go back to my homeland of Phthia,[14] [170] since I have no interest in staying here to be insulted while I drum up golden treasures for you.

Then Agamemnon retorted, "Good, get the hell out of here if that's what you want! I'm not going to beg you to stay. I've got plenty of others here who actually respect me. And most

---

12 The original Greek is *o meg' anaides*, which translates literally as something like "O great shameless one."

13 Menelaus is the king of Sparta, the brother of Agamemnon, and the husband of Helen. The Trojan prince Paris abducted Helen and brought her back to Troy, which is what started the war in the first place.

14 This is the hometown of Achilles and his group of Myrmidons. It is thought to be located in the region of Thessaly in northeastern Greeks.

of all, I have Zeus, the Lord of Olympus, in my corner. None of the other kings here hate me the way you do; you're always such an angry jackass. Oh, and you say you're brave? Wasn't it the gods who made you that way? Go on home with your ships and your soldiers and lord your bravery over your Myrmidons. I don't care. [180] But I'm going to do this: since Apollo is taking Chryseis from me, I'm going to send her along with my boat and my crew. But in exchange, I'm coming to your tent and taking your war prize, Briseis, just so you know how much stronger I am than you. Let that be a lesson to everyone else as well."

Fig. 59: Ancient Roman mosaic of Achilles arguing with Agamemnon from the House of Apollo at Pompeii
(National Archaeological Museum of Naples; 1st century AD)

Achilles, the son of Peleus, was outraged, and his heart pounded in his chest as he tried to decide between drawing his sword, pushing the crowd aside, [190] and slaying Agamemnon on the spot, or checking his anger and calming down. While he was deciding between these options, and preparing to draw his deadly sword from its sheath, Athena swooped down from Olympus – Hera had sent her since she loved both Achilles and Agamemnon – and she grabbed the son of Peleus (Achilles) by his golden hair. This, of course, was visible to Achilles alone, and none of the others could see what was happening. He swung around, and from the fiery flames in her eyes, he knew immediately that this was the goddess Athena. [200] "What are you doing here, daughter of Zeus the aegis-bearer?" he asked. "Did you come to check out how arrogant Agamemnon, the son of Atreus, has become? Let me tell you, this guy is going to pay for his hubris with his life."

Then Athena spoke to Achilles. "Look, I just came all the way from Olympus; listen to me and calm your anger. Hera sent me down here, since she likes both of you. So please, put away your sword and stop this fighting. [210] Yell all you want at him, and honestly, that will be more useful. You'll get three times the benefit from jabbing him with words than you will stabbing him with your sword. So calm down, and listen to me."

ACHILLES' VOW TO WITHDRAW

And Achilles responded to Athena. "Divine goddess, it doesn't matter how furious I am. If you and Hera command me to do something, I am at your service. This will work out better for me anyway, since the gods always listen to the prayers of those who obey their commands."

So Achilles loosened his grip on the silver hilt of his sword, and he jammed it back into its sheath, just as the goddess had requested. [220] Athena, then, returned to Olympus to live among the gods in the house of Zeus, the aegis-bearer.

But the son of Peleus (Achilles), was still furious, and he kept up the verbal assaults on the son of Atreus (Agamemnon). "You filthy drunk! You've got the face of a bitch and heart of an ass. Never ever do you dare to go out with our troops onto the battlefield, nor do you lie in wait with our men to ambush the enemy. You avoid these things like you do death itself. Instead of doing anything useful, you spend your days stealing things from anyone who dares to contradict you. [230] Because this is how you treat your people, they have all become weak; you are the King of Cowards, otherwise you wouldn't be able to insult anyone."

And Achilles continued, "I swear by the gods themselves

– by this sacred scepter which shall never sprout another leaf since the very day it was plucked high up in the mountains, the sacred rod which the Greeks carry as a symbol of the judgment of men and the laws of the heavens, by these things I swear - [240] that when the Greeks desperately look for Achilles on the battlefield, they shall not find him. In your darkest days, when your men are dying at the hands of Hector,[15] you're going to have no clue how to help them. And your black heart will eat you from the inside out, as you rue the day that you insulted the bravest of the Greeks."

Achilles, the son of Peleus, then threw his golden scepter to the ground and sat back down, while Agamemnon, the son of Atreus, angrily leapt out of his seat on the other side of the room. Just then, however, the smooth-talking Nestor stood up, the most-persuasive king of Pylos, whose words were sweeter than honey. [250] He was wise with age, and already had out-lived two generations of men under his rule. And he addressed the crowd earnestly, as best he could.

"Honestly, a darkness has fallen upon the Greeks. If Priam[16] could see this, he and all the Trojans would be overflow-ing with joy to hear you two – who are such great fighters and such wise leaders – argue like this. I'm older than both of you though, so listen to my sage advice. For men greater than either of you have heeded my guidance. [260] I'll never see the likes of those men again – of Pirithous or Dryas, of Caeneus or Exadius, of godlike Polyphemus or Aegeus' son Theseus, every bit as im-pressive as the immortal gods.[17] These were the greatest fighters ever to grace the face of the earth. And whenever they went up against one of the barbarian tribes, they would utterly destroy them. I came from Pylos, in the farthest reaches of Greece, but

---

15 The greatest warrior of all the Trojan princes, and the one who will be-come the primary foe of Achilles later in the *Iliad*.

16 Priam was the king of the Trojans during the war.

17 This whole group constitutes a previous generation of heroes - ones that lived long before the Trojan war. Pirithous, Dryas, Caeneus, and Exadi-us were all heroes from the region of Thessaly in northeastern Greece, whereas Theseus became a distinctly Athenian hero after his labors and slaying of the Minotaur.

when I met up with them, I fought the best that I could.[18] [270]
Not a single living person could stand against these heroes. But
guess what? When I talked, they listened and were persuaded
by what I had to say. Let it be the same for you, for I'll give you
a much better way forward. Agamemnon, we know you're the
foremost among the Greeks, but don't take Achilles' girl away
from him, for the Greeks have already awarded her to him.
And Achilles, quit raging at Agamemnon, for no other person
who carries such a scepter is as honored as he is. Let's be realis-
tic; you are strong, and your mother is indeed a goddess, [280]
but Agamemnon is stronger than you, since he has more troops
under his command. Son of Atreus (Agamemnon), I beg of you,
calm your anger, and end this argument with Achilles. For in
the heat of battle, he is a beacon of strength for the Greeks."

*Fig. 60: Ancient Roman mosaic of King Nestor of Pylos overseeing
the removal of Briseis (Getty Villa; 2nd century AD)*

And Agamemnon replied, "Wise Nestor, everything you've
said is true. But this fool Achilles acts like he wants to be master of the universe, the king of kings, the lord of everyone and
everything. And this simply won't happen. I'm happy to admit
he's a great fighter, but what gives him the right to speak with

---

18 Pylos is located in the southwestern corner of the Peloponnese, which
itself is in the southwestern corner of mainland Greece. Thus, Pylos would
have been about as far away from Thessaly (and the heroes Nestor just
mentioned) as you can get.

such animosity and disrespect?"

[290] Then Achilles butted in, "I would be a coward if I went around obeying every little thing you said. From now on you can boss other people around because I'm not going to listen anymore. And furthermore – and take this to heart – I'm not going to argue any more about this girl. For the people taking her away are also the ones who gave her to me. But that's it – you're not getting anything else from my ship. [300] Give it a shot and see what happens: my spear will drip with your blood."

And so the hostilities finally ended, and the Greek troops dispersed. The son of Peleus (Achilles), went back to ships with the son of Menoetius (Patroclus)[19] and his crew. Meanwhile, Agamemnon dragged one of his ships into the water and selected a crew of twenty rowers. He then brought Chryseis on board along with a hundred oxen as gifts for the god, [310] and he appointed Odysseus as captain.

So these men boarded the ship and sailed across the sea. Then the son of Atreus (Agamemnon), ordered the people still around to purify themselves by bathing in the sea. Afterwards, they offered sacrifices of a hundred bulls and perfect goats right there on the beach. And the savory scent of the burning meat wafted up into the heavens.

While the men made their sacrifices, Agamemnon thought about his threat to Achilles, and he called in his faithful messengers Talthybius and Eurybates. [320] He said to them, "Go over to Achilles' tent, grab Briseis, and bring her back here. If he's not going to give her to me willingly, then I'll just have to get you guys to take her away. That'll show him who's boss."

So he gave them their orders and sent them away, and the two of them trudged sadly along the beach until they came to the ships and tents of the Myrmidons.[20] They found Achilles sitting there next to the ships and tents, and he was already pissed

---

19 Menoetius was the father of Patroclus, Achilles' best friend and probable lover.

20 Again, the Myrmidons are the specific group of Greeks from the region of Thessaly that Achilles led.

off when he saw them coming. [330] They stood there trying to be respectful and so frozen with fear that they couldn't get a word out. But Achilles knew why they had come, and said, "Come on over, messengers of gods and men. Don't worry, my fight's not with you; it's with Agamemnon who sent you over here to take away Briseis. Patroclus, go get her and hand her over to these two. But I do want you to listen to what I have to say – by the divine gods and mortal men, and by the unquenchable rage of Agamemnon. [340] If the Greeks ever need me to save everyone from death and destruction, they can call, but I won't answer. Agamemnon has truly gone mad, and that short-sighted fool has put all the Greeks in danger."

THETIS HELPS HER SON

So Patroclus did as his friend asked, and he retrieved Briseis from the tent and gave her over to the messengers. And they took her to the ship even though she clearly didn't want to go. Then Achilles wandered down the edge of the dull gray water, and he cried as he stared at the endless barren sea. [350] He threw his hands in the air and called out a prayer to his divine mother. "Mother," he blubbered, "when you gave birth to me, you knew I was in for a short life. The least Zeus, who thunders upon Olympus, could do is fill it with a little bit of glory. But there's none of that. Agamemnon, the son of Atreus, has completely dishonored me, taking away my prize by sheer force."

He cried while he spoke, and in the depths of the sea his mother listened as she sat next to her father, the Old Man of the Sea.[21] Immediately she shot up to the surface, spraying a gray mist as she crested the waves. [360] After coming ashore, she sat by Achilles, holding his hand and asking him, "Son, why are you crying? What's bothering you? Don't keep it bottled up; let me know so we can deal with this together."

Achilles took a deep breath and responded, "You already

---

21 This is a nickname for Nereus, the son of Pontus (the Sea) and Gaia (the Earth). He was a sea god, inhabiting the Aegean, and was known for giving birth to 50 daughters, known as the Nereids, including Thetis, Achilles' mother.

know, mother. Why bother explaining it again? It started when we sacked the city of Thebe, the stronghold of Eetion,[22] and brought home all the spoils of war. We Greeks split up the booty just like we're accustomed to doing, and Agamemnon was given the beautiful maiden Chryseis. As it turns out, her father, Chryses, was a priest of Apollo. [370] He came to us with a huge amount of gifts to ransom his daughter's freedom. And not only that, he brought the scepter of Apollo, wrapped in the wreath of treaty, begging all the Greeks for help, but especially Agamemnon and Menelaus, the two sons of Atreus.

"And the response from the Greeks was unanimous – take the gifts he offered and return the girl! But Agamemnon wouldn't listen, and he yelled at the poor guy and sent him packing. So Chryses angrily stomped off and prayed to Apollo for vengeance, [380] and the god heard him loud and clear. Apollo sent a deadly curse upon the Greeks, and their corpses piled high as deadly arrows flew through our entire camp. Finally, one of our seers used his gift of prophecy to determine that it was Apollo who was causing this destruction, and I was the first one to say we should do whatever it takes to make Apollo happy again. But the son of Atreus (Agamemnon), got angry and started making threats, which he is now following through on. Right now, the Greeks are sending a ship to Chryse with his daughter on board as well as a bunch of gifts to sacrifice to Apollo. [390] But at the same time, Agamemnon's messengers have come to take away Briseis, who the Greeks awarded me as my share of the spoils of war.

"So help out your heroic son, if you can. Head up to Olympus, and if you've ever done anything nice for Zeus, start calling in his favors. I've often heard you bragging about how, out of all the immortal gods, you were the only one to save the son of Cronus (Zeus) when all the others would have had him thrown in chains. [400] You said you called up the hundred-handed beast that gods call Briareus and men call Aegeaon because

---

22 The city referenced here, Thebe, is located in Cilicia (a region in modern day western Turkey near the site of Troy). Its king was Eetion, who was also the father of Andromache, the wife of the Trojan prince Hector.

Fig. 61: Fresco of Thetis consoling her son Achilles by Giovanni Batista Tiepolo (Villa Valmarana ai Nani; 1757)

he's so strong.[23] And when that absolute monstrosity sat next to Zeus, none of the other gods dared to bind him in chains. So

---

23 Briareus was one of the three Hecatoncheires, beastly sons of Uranus (Sky) and Gaia (Earth), who had 100 hands and 50 heads. Briareus was associated with powerful deadly sea storms, hence the name the mortals gave him of Aegeaon (of the Aegean Sea). The Hecatoncheires were originally chained up in Tartarus, but fought on the side of Zeus and the Olympians, helping them defeat the previous generation of gods known as the Titans.

go remind Zeus who's responsible for making him the Lord of Olympus. Get on your knees and beg him to give strength to the Trojans, so that the Greeks are surrounded, pushed back to their ships, and die on the beaches. Then we'll see how they like their king, [410] and maybe then Agamemnon will regret being a blind fool and insulting the greatest of the Greeks.

Thetis cried as she listened, and she responded, "Son, poor me for ever having bore you! I wish that you could live a long life free from all this sadness. It is really terrible to have both such a short life and one filled with more sorrow than all your comrades. So curse the hour I gave birth to you! But I will help you if I can, and I'll head straight to the snowy peaks of Mount Olympus and beg Zeus to listen to your prayer. [420] You just stay here with your ships, fan the flames of your rage, and stay out of this fight while I'm gone. Yesterday, Zeus and all the other Olympians went all the way to Oceanus to feast with the Ethiopians.[24] They won't be back for twelve days, so I'll wait until then to go to his bronze palace and plead with him. I think I should be able to convince him to help."

RETURN OF CHRYSEIS

So Thetis left, still upset that Briseis had been taken from her son. [430] In the meantime, Odysseus had reached Chryse with the oxen for sacrifice. As they rowed into harbor, they brought down the sails and stored them in the hold, loosened the ropes tying the jib to the mast, and finally lowered the mast itself. Then they rowed over to the appropriate spot, dropped the anchors, and fastened the ropes to the dock. The hundred oxen were led off the ship, and Odysseus led Chryseis to the altar of Apollo to give her back to her father. [440] There he said, "Chryses, King Agamemnon sent me to return your daughter and bring you a hundred oxen as a gift for Apollo, which will hopefully appease him, so that he might put an end to the destruction of the Greeks."

24 Not to be mistaken with the population of the modern country, the Ethiopians mentioned by Homer are a vague group of people living at the farthest eastern and western edges of the world.

*Fig. 62: Sculpture from the Parthenon frieze showing cattle led to
sacrifice (British Museum; 5th century BC)*

After his speech, he gave the girl back to her father, who
was overwhelmed with joy. They then arranged the hundred
oxen around the altar of Apollo, washed their hands, and sprinkled the sacrificial animals with barley. Chryses then raised his
hands to the sky and prayed, [450] "Hear me, god of the silver
bow, and protector of Chryse and Cilla, ruler of Tenedos with
ultimate power. Just as you listened to my previous prayers,
and brought death and destruction to the Greeks, now please
listen again, and end this curse upon their people."

Once again, Apollo indeed listened to his prayer. And when
the words had been spoken and the barley had been sprinkled,
they pulled back the heads of the sacrificial oxen, sliced their
throats, and butchered them. [460] Then, they removed the
thigh bones and wrapped them in fat, putting a few pieces of
the meat on top. And Chryses placed these in the wood-burn-
ing fire and poured some wine over the sacrifice. All around,
the men stood holding five-pronged skewers, and after they
burned the thigh bones and tasted the entrails, they butchered
the rest of the cattle, cutting them into small meaty chunks,

107

putting them on the skewers, and barbecuing them until they were nicely seared. Once the meat was cooked, they all feasted, with each man getting a full share of the beef, and everyone feeling perfectly happy. [470] Then the mixing-bowl was filled with wine and water, and passed around from man to man, with enough wine that each could drink their fill and still pour one out for the god Apollo as well.

So the men spent the whole day celebrating the god with their sacrifices and songs, chanting the holy hymns as Apollo looked down cheerfully from Olympus. As the sun set, the men slept right on the beach next to their ships. And the next day, as rose-fingered Dawn emerged once again, they made their return to the Greek camp. Since Apollo was pleased by their sacrifices, he sent them a helpful wind, and the men raised the mast and hoisted the sails. [480] The white sails billowed in the wind, and the ships knifed swiftly through the blue water as a foam sprayed constantly against the bows. When they arrived at the Greek camp, they brought their ships up onto the dry beach, propping them up to keep them in place. And then the troops dispersed, heading back to their own ships and tents.

All the while, Achilles sat near his own ships, fanning the flames of his rage. He didn't attend the meetings of the Greek leaders, nor would he enter the fight. [490] He just sat there, sinking deeper into his fury and frustration as he longed to enter the battle.

Zeus Agrees to Aid the Trojans

After the twelve days passed, the immortal gods returned to Olympus with Zeus at the head of the pack. Thetis did not forget her son's plea, so she rose to the surface from the depths of the sea, and accompanied the Dawn (Eos) up to Olympus, where the son of Cronus (Zeus), sat alone on his lofty throne. [500] Thetis knelt before him, grabbing his knee with her left hand and his chin with her right, and she pleaded for her son, "Zeus, if I've ever done anything to help you, please hear my prayer and restore honor to my son who is doomed to die so young. Agamemnon has disrespected him by stealing away his prize and keeping her for himself. Most wise lord of Olympus, please help restore his honor by helping the Trojans win the war until the Greeks pay my son back for everything they took from him."[25]

Fig. 63: Thetis asking Zeus to restore honor to Achilles by Jean Auguste Dominique Ingres (Granet Museum; 1811)

[510] For a while Zeus just sat there silently. But Thetis continued to grasp his knee, begging him a second time, "Please nod your head and promise me you'll help, or at least just say no so I can get a sense for how little you care. No need to worry about how I'll respond."

After hearing this Zeus got worried, "I'm going to be in real trouble if you get me arguing with Hera. She's always trying to drag me into a fight with her sassy taunting. Already

---

25 Grasping the knee and chin is a pose one would take when begging for something.

she's ripping into me in front of all the other gods, just for giving the Trojans as little bit of help. [520] You should probably get out of here before she finds out what you're asking for. I'll think about it. No, you know what? I'll do it, just as you wish. And I'll even give you the nod of approval so you know that I'm serious. This is the most serious promise I can make. For I never break a promise, or fail to deliver, once I give my nod of approval."

And as these words came out of his mouth, Zeus bowed his head. His golden locks of hair swayed upon his mighty brow and all of Olympus shook with thunder.

[530] After making their plans, the two went their separate ways - Zeus to his palace, and Thetis leaving magnificent Mount Olympus and plunging back to the bottom of the sea. All the gods stood as the king of Olympus strode through its halls, not a single one daring to remain seated. But the second Hera saw him, she knew that he'd been plotting with silver-footed Thetis, the Old Man of the Sea's daughter, and she immediately ripped into him, "You deceitful jerk! Which goddess are you keeping secrets with now? [540] You're always running around behind my back, and you haven't spilled a single word to me about your plans."

And the father of gods and men replied, "Hera, I can't keep you in the loop about every single one of my meetings. Sure, you're my wife, but you'd find these affairs awfully difficult to understand. When you need to know something, there's no one on heaven or earth that will be told sooner. But when I choose to keep something to myself, don't go prying and asking endless questions."

[550] "Mighty Zeus, son of Cronus," Hera responded, "what are you talking about? Prying and asking questions? Me? Never! I always let you do whatever you want. But still, I have this uneasy feeling that the Old Man's daughter, Thetis, has been working you over. I saw her grasping your knees and begging you just earlier this morning. I'm guessing that you promised her that you'd bring glory to Achilles and kill hordes of Greeks down by their ships."

[560] "Dearest wife," said Zeus, "I could be sitting alone doing nothing and you'd still think I was plotting against you. If you keep this up, I'll only get angrier with you, and you'll be the worse off for it. But yeah, you're right this one time. I do intend to do this. So sit down, and shut up. For if I have to raise my hand to you, all of Olympus could be on your side and it still wouldn't help."

This scared Hera, so she calmed her temper and sat down silently. Indeed, all the Olympian gods throughout the palace of Zeus were unnerved, that is, [570] until Hephaestus tried to soothe his mother Hera. He pleaded, "Mother, it will be unbearable if the two of you start fighting and send all of Olympus into disarray just because of a few mortals. If these stupid plans actually come about, there will be no peace in the palace or fun at our feasts. Let me give you my two cents, mother, and you know I'm right: quit being bull-headed and patch things up with my dear father Zeus, if only to keep him from berating you again and ruining our feast. [580] If the God of Thunder wants to cast us down from our Olympian seats, he certainly could do so; there's no double he's the strongest. So say something sweet to him, and he'll be back in a good mood in no time."

As he was telling her this, Hephaestus took an extra large cup of nectar and gave it to his mother. "Don't be sad, mother, keep your chin up. You know how much I love you, and I'd hate to see Father take a swing at you. No matter how much I might want to help, there's nothing I could do; there's just no standing up to Zeus. Remember the last time I was trying to help you, [590] he grabbed me by the ankle and flung me entirely out of Olympus. I fell for an entire day - from morning until evening - and only at sunset did I come crashing down on the island of Lemnos. And I just laid there, barely alive, until the Sintians came to help me out."[26]

This made Hera smile, and with a grin she took the cup

---

26 This is one version of the origin story for Hephaestus' disabled leg and limp. The Sintians originally inhabited the region of Sintice and the island of Lemnos in the far northern part of the Aegean, near Thrace. Later in Greek history they became known as marauding pirates.

Fig. 64: Ancient Roman sculptural relief showing Hephaestus thrown from Olympus (Museum of Ostia; 2nd century AD)

of nectar from her son's hands. Then Hephaestus filled a few more cups of nectar from the mixing-bowl and passed them around to the rest of the gods, going around the circle from left to right. And at this sight, the divine gods burst out in laughter and applause as the God of the Forge played waiter in the palace of Olympus.

[600] And so they feasted for the entire day, from sunup to sundown. Each got a full share, and all were satisfied. Apollo plucked away at his lyre, while the Muses sang with the sweetest of voices, one starting the song and then passing it along to the others. And as the sun went down, the gods went to bed back in their own homes, which limping Hephaestus had constructed for them with his exceptional craftsmanship. [610] In this way, Zeus, the Olympian God of Thunder, also went to sleep in his own bed, with his wife Hera, who sits upon the golden throne, laying by his side.

The Rest of the Story

Like the *Odyssey*, the *Iliad* is composed of 24 books, and we have seen how Book 1 sets the scene with the argument between Achilles and Agamemenon, resulting in Achilles sitting out the war. From there, the *Iliad* almost ends before it even gets going. Shortly after Book 1, Paris agrees to a one-on-one battle with Menelaus. It is a winner-take-all fight for Helen, which would bring the war to an end one way or the other (Books 2-4). Menelaus, a mighty warrior, of course agrees, and while he bests Paris on in the contest, Aphrodite whisks away both Paris and Helen to the Trojan citadel before Menelaus can deliver the death blow.

This launches a series of duels between the heroes of Greece and Troy (Books 5-7). Diomedes, one of the legendary Greek heroes, takes on the Trojan Aeneas, the ancestor of Romulus, Remus, and all the Roman people. Diomedes looks to have the upper hand until Aphrodite, mother of Aeneas, intervenes to save her son (but not before Diomedes slices the wrist of Aphrodite herself). Now the other gods start getting involved: Apollo warns Diomedes about fighting the immortals, but Athena - defender of the Greeks - boosts Diomedes' courage and strength to the point that he is able to wound Ares, the god of war. Zeus eventually has had enough, and he prevents the gods from getting further involved in the war.

Despite Diomedes' impressive feats, the tide soon turns, and the Trojans take control of the war (Books 8-15). Under the leadership of Prince Hector, greatest of the Trojan warriors, they push the Greeks all the way back to their wall, soon breaking through and pinning them against their own ships. It is at this point that Patroclus - Achilles' best friend and lover - can take it no longer. He begs Achilles to rejoin the fight, yet his plea is ignored (Books 16-18). Achilles does, however, allow Patroclus to wear his own armor into battle, and Patroclus fights with such ferocity and skill that the Trojans think Achilles has indeed re-entered the combat, even killing Sarpedon, the son of almighty Zeus. Patroclus continues to push back the Trojans until he is confronted - and ultimately slain - by Hector, who takes the armor, which is actually that of Achilles.

Now we see Achilles rage once again, no longer focused on his fellow Greek Agamemnon, but rather on the Trojan prince Hector (Books 19-22). Achilles re-enters the battle, and the gods, too, rejoin the fray, with Apollo trying to divert Achilles away from the action. All the Trojans make it back inside their walls except for Hector, who, after a brief attempt to escape, faces Achilles head-on. The duel is swift and ends with Achilles stabbing Hector through the neck, then desecrating his body as he drags it behind his chariot around the walls of Troy. Achilles has taken revenge on Hector for the death of Patroclus, and Agamemnon has even returned Achilles' war prize Briseis, but these actions seem to bring little solace to the tragic hero.

Fig. 65: Achilles drags the body of Hector around the walls of Troy (Achilleion; 1892)

The last two books of the *Iliad* are about coming to peace with the events that have occurred (Books 23-24). Patroclus' ghost visits Achilles and asks him to hold the proper funerary rites, and Achilles responds with a set of funeral games before Patroclus' eventual cremation. And then Priam, the king of Troy, sneaks into Achilles' tent to beg for the return of Hector's body. After an initial refusal, Achilles finally breaks down in tears, lamenting the losses and pain that both of them have suffered as a result of the war. Achilles returns Hector's body to King Priam, who carries it back to Troy for burial. The story ends with death, burial, and mourning - both for the Greeks and the Trojans.

Homer's *Odyssey*

The *Odyssey* is an epic poem that recounts the tale of the Greek hero Odysseus as he attempts to make it back home after fighting in the Trojan War. The work, like the *Iliad*, is attributed to Homer. The *Odyssey* is one of the most widely read pieces of literature to come out of the ancient world, one of the oldest, and one of the most influential, impacting authors like Dante, James Joyce and others. Odysseus is a different kind of hero than Achilles or Agamemnon who we met in the *Iliad*, however. Instead of strength alone, or power, Odysseus is associated with wit, cunning, and tricks. He is the one who devises the stratagem that ends the Trojan War favorably for the Greeks: build a giant wooden horse, hide soldiers in it, hope that the Trojans bring the horse inside the city walls, and then sack the city from the inside.

Odysseus is a fully-fleshed out, multidimensional character who feels very familiar to modern audiences. Although he has great brawn, he relies on his brains. Although he expects to be treated well as a guest, he doesn't hesitate to sack cities and kill. Although he is on an arduous journey home to his loyal wife, he is unfaithful to her. He has a sense of humor and he is a great story-teller, but is he reliable? The moral ambiguity of his character is not unlike modern superheroes and other popular characters such as Batman, Anthony Soprano, Severus Snape, or Frankenstein's monster.

The poem, like the *Iliad*, is divided into 24 books. The *Odyssey* is a "sequel" to the *Iliad* in the sense that most of the events recounted take place after the events of the *Iliad*. In fact, there is no overlap between events described in each work. Both works are attributed to Homer as the "author," a fact not doubted by ancient audiences, but modern scholars feel that the works were ultimately written down by different people based on stylistic differences. Yet both came from the same story-telling tradition of oral poetry in the region and were a part of the Epic Cycle, as mentioned in the preceding introduction to the *Iliad*. Just as with the *Iliad*, we see frequent use of epithets and formulas to assist the bard to either memorize sections or compose them on the spot.

Whereas the entirety of the *Iliad* takes place in one location, the *Odyssey* has a much wider geographic scope. Recall that the poem was likely composed in the 8th or 7th centuries BC and is set in an earlier period around the 12th century

BC during the Bronze Age. Discussions of historical context are thus difficult, but this is about the time of the formation of cities (*poleis*) and trading posts (*emporia*) across the Greek world corresponding to the Archaic period. This is a time when the Greeks spread throughout the Mediterranean and into the Black Sea, establishing colonies. The Greek alphabet was being developed, and there were cultural and political developments taking place that would set the scene for Classical Greece. There were active trade networks between cities. The movement, geographic awareness, and sense of danger/adventure that we see in the *Odyssey* finds its context in what was becoming a more connected Mediterranean region.

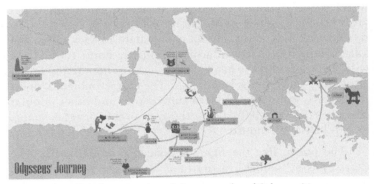

Fig. 66: One interpretation of the geography of Odysseus' journey

The *Odyssey* has a rather complicated structure. The first four books, rather than picking up Odysseus' narrative after the sack of Troy, tell the story of Odysseus' son, Telemachus. The boy, about 20 years old, is on Ithaca, Odysseus' home island, with his mother (Odysseus' wife), Penelope. Not only does he lack news about his father after the end of the war, he is also dealing with his mother's 108 suitors who presume Odysseus is dead and are living at Odysseus palace and waiting for Penelope to choose a new husband. Penelope is delaying this decision through a weaving ruse - she is as crafty as her husband, after all - saying she will marry when she has finished a death shroud for Odysseus' father, but she unravels it each night. The goddess Athena comes down to Ithaca in disguise and helps Telemachus get to the mainland to try to find news about his father. He visits Nestor and later Menelaus and Helen and learns that his father may be the captive of the nymph Calypso. The suitors, meanwhile, devise a plan to attack Telemachus' ship as he returns.

In Books 5-8 we first find Odysseus who is indeed a captive of Calypso. As Odysseus will recount at the start of Book 9, Calypso has fallen for Odysseus who won't marry her (thus turning down an offer of immortality). Poseidon is angry with Odysseus for reasons we will learn in Book 9, so while Poseidon is away from Olympus, Athena convinces Zeus to send Hermes to Calypso to order her to release Odysseus, who then builds a raft and sets sail. But Poseidon catches wind of Odysseus' journey and wrecks his raft. Odysseus swims to the shore of an island and wakes up to a young girl, Nausicaä, who has been convinced by Athena in a dream to explore the shore. She assures Odysseus that he is in good hands and indeed her father Alcinous takes Odysseus in and offers him a ship to return home, before he even knows who Odysseus is.

At the very end of Book 7, Odysseus heads to the king's feast but hasn't yet given away who he is. There, Odysseus gives a blind poet a piece of his meat so that he will sing about the Trojan Horse, even referencing Odysseus' own role in the deception. The bard sings the song and Odysseus cries. Alcinous sees this and asks the bard to stop singing since the song has made his guest sad. Alcinous is curious about his guest's true identity and asks him where he has been, who he has met, and why he is so sad about the story of the fall of Troy. Book 8 picks up immediately from there and Books 9-12 consist of Odysseus' story of how he left Troy and eventually lost all his men and ships. As you read the story, consider the sophistication of this ancient work: even though it is one of our oldest written works, it contains a story within a story, one told by a hero known for his guile and trickery. Can this narrator be trusted? Let us find out.

Words of the Ancients

Homer's *Odyssey*

Book 9

And so Odysseus replied:

"King Alcinous, it is such a pleasure to be here at this banquet and hear your gifted musician sing like a god. Is there a greater joy in life than to spend a summer's evening listening to a harpist in the great hall, eating at tables filled with bread and meat, with the servers topping off your wine, keeping your cup always full? [10] I think not! But, you've asked why I am sad and I will tell you, even though I think it'll make me cry even more. Where do I start and what should I save for the end? It's a long story because the gods have given me a lot of trouble .

*Fig. 67: Head of Odysseus, part of set of statues capturing the moment he blinds Polyphemus
(National Archaeological Museum of Sperlonga, 1st century AD)*

I suppose first I should tell you my name so that even if I die early and never make it home, our shared guest-friendship[27]

---

27 The relevant Greek term is *xenia*, which was an institution of generosity between hosts and guests. The rules and customs around xenia were commonly held through the Greek world and we can see them at play in many scenes within the *Odyssey*. Here Odysseus is treated properly with a meal and entertainment before he is even asked to identify himself. Alcinous goes above and beyond by offering the stranger a ship. The Greeks held these customs in such esteem that Zeus himself was the protector of this moral obligation toward guests. *Xenia* was meant to be reciprocal, which

118

can be extended to you and you can be hosted in my home if you ever visit. I'm Odysseus, son of Laertes. [20] As I think you've heard, I'm famous worldwide for my skill both at war and during peacetime.

My home is Ithaca, an island with a mountain you can see from far out at sea called Mount Neritum, which is covered in trees. Nearby, a bit further from the mainland are three other islands, Doulicium, Same and tree-lined Zakynthos. Ithaca is rocky and rugged but a good place to raise resilient children, and I miss it dearly.

For a long time, I was held captive by Calypso, a very beautiful goddess, [30] who kept me in a cave saying she wanted to marry me.[28] I was then held captive by Circe,[29] a cunning woman, who was also trying to get me to marry her. Even though I did stay with them for a while, it didn't mean anything. Plus, there is no place like home! But let me tell you about my homecoming from Troy,[30] which Zeus made extremely challenging and dangerous.[31]

---

is why Odysseus explicitly mentions that Alcinous can be hosted on Ithaca now that he knows who his guest is.

28 Odysseus spent about 7 years with Calypso on Ogygia, an island sometimes identified with modern day Malta, but no one really knows. Odysseus had been gone from his home nearly 20 years by the time he reached Scheria, the town of the Phaeacians: the war for Troy lasted ten years and Odysseus' homecoming took another ten years. This is the last leg of his journey but first we get to hear part of his journey from Odysseus' own perspective.

29 He spent about one year on the island of Aeaea (a very consonant-averse island!) with Circe.

30 Scholars do not know exactly where Scheria, home of the Phaeacians, is located and aren't even sure about the location of Ithaca, in fact. That said, in 1871, following the directions mentioned in the ancient texts, Heinrich Schliemann and Frank Calvert excavated a mound located in western Turkey just where the Mediterranean meets the Sea of Marmara. There they found layers and layers of settlements going back to the early Bronze Age that certainly could be "Troy," though the connection between this site and the legends is hazy at best.

31 Later in Book 9, we'll see why Poseidon becomes angry with Odysseus but here he cites difficulties from Zeus. These stem from Odysseus' journey to the underworld in which his men take and eat some of the cattle of

Fig. 68: Circe and Odysseus
(Academy of Fine Arts of Vienna; 1785)

FLIGHT FROM TROY

I set sail from Troy and the wind took me to Ismaros where the Cicones live.[32] [40] I sacked and plundered the town, killing the men and taking the women,[33] and I divided our winnings evenly amongst the crew. I urged the men to leave the

---

Helios, who demanded that Zeus punish Odysseus (despite the fact that he was asleep when his men did this).

32 The Cicones were allies to the Trojans and their city Ismaros was located in ancient Thrace, which roughly correlated to modern northeast Greece, Bulgaria and northwest Turkey, at the northernmost part of the Aegean Sea. The area was reputed to have very good wine which becomes relevant to the story later on.

33 There is no further mention of these women who, if taken aboard the ships, must not have survived the ordeal.

city quickly, but the fools wouldn't obey because they were barbecuing on the beach, and they'd had a bit too much wine to drink. Meanwhile, some prisoners got away and ran inland to seek help from their neighbors, who showed up in force. The enemy appeared in the morning like blooming leaves or flowers and these guys could really put up a fight - [50] both on foot and from chariots. It didn't look good, like the gods themselves were against us. My men made a strong stand, spear on spear with their backs against their ships, and they held their own in the morning, but by late afternoon (around when you'd normally let the oxen stop working), we started to take on heavier losses, [60] six people per ship, and so we retreated to our ships and sailed off. We were glad that we got away but sad about our fallen brothers, and as we fled, we poured one out three times for each of those who'd been killed by the Cicones.

Then Zeus raised a big storm with heavy winds and clouds so thick it was as dark as night. [70] At first we let the ships get carried by the wind but it started ripping the sails to tatters, so we pulled those down and rowed as hard as we could for land. Exhausted and still grieving over our mates, we spent two days and nights recovering offshore. On the third day, we got our act together, raised masts and sails, and let the wind and rudderman bring us home. And I probably would have made it home pretty soon after that except, [80] as we came around Melea, there was more weather and a strong current and we got pulled off course again, past Kythera.[34]

For nine days, we drifted around, getting pushed by winds, but on the tenth day we made it to the land of the Lotus-Eaters, who do in fact eat lotus flowers.[35] We disembarked to refresh our water stores and have some lunch. After we had eaten and drunk our fill, [90] I sent two of my men, who brought a

---

34 To this point, we can roughly sketch Odysseus' journey through the geography of the ancient world. After this, though some scholars have made efforts to locate Odysseus' wanderings, he seems to pass into more of a fantasy land.

35 We don't know for sure what the lotus is. Some suggestions have included a date (a jujube perhaps), a poppy-pod, marijuana, or persimmon. In modern parlance, a lotus-eater is someone who lazes about in luxury rather than tending to business.

third with them, to learn about the local peoples. They found the Lotus-Eaters who didn't have bad intentions but fed the men the sweet lotus flower which was so delicious that the men forgot why they were there, didn't want to report back, and even failed to remember that we were trying to get back home. When I found them, they wanted to stay forever and keep eating the fruit, but I dragged them, kicking and screaming, back to the ships and had to tie them under the benches. [100] I got the rest of the men on board and warned them not to eat any lotus fruit because of the effects, and so they sat down and beat the waves with the oars, back to work.

Fig. 69: Engraving of Odysseus on the island of the Lotus-Eaters (Rijksmuseum; 1633)

LAND OF THE CYCLOPES

Constantly distressed by the conditions at sea, we came to the land of the utterly lawless Cyclopes.[36] They don't plant or plow their fields, trusting to the heavens instead, [110] yet wheat and barley grow naturally and the grape vines grow

---

36 "Cyclopes" is pronounced sy-KLOH-peez and is the plural of "Cyclops," which literally means "round-eyes." There is no explicit mention in Homer that they only have one eye, but it is probably imagined that the audience assumed this.

wild. The Cyclopes don't have government or formal laws; instead they each live in their own mountain caves, masters of their own domains and families, and pay little notice to their neighbors.

Not too far away from the shore (but not too close, either) there is an island full of wild goats whose populations aren't kept in check with hunting. [120] Hunters normally climb mountains and work their way through heavy forests for their prey, but none set foot here. And again, the fields are not planted or plowed, it's just the goats. That's because the Cyclopes don't have good ships like ours and no shipbuilders, [130] so they are unable to travel between cities along the coast, let alone travel across open water. If they did have good enough ships, they would definitely have settled the island. The fields on the island go all the way to the shore, get good rain, have good soil and are lush with green. It's the perfect terroir for wine grapes, too. Plus, there's a great harbor where you wouldn't need to anchor or tie your ships down, just glide gently into the beach and wait for fair winds before setting off again. [140] There's even a fresh water spring at the harbor, flowing down from a cave, and a poplar grove surrounds the spring.

We approached the island at this harbor in the pitch black, with the moon hidden. We must have been guided safely by a god because the lookout couldn't even see that there was an island there until suddenly our ships glided to a stop on a beach. So we put away the sails, [150] disembarked and slept on the beach for the rest of the night.

When Dawn arrived, with her rose-colored fingers,[37] we woke up in awe of the land and started exploring it, and the nymphs, Zeus' daughters, drove some goats toward us for an easy meal. We grabbed our spears and bows from our ships and in three groups hunted the goats and were blessed with easy pickings. [160] We killed nine goats for each of the twelve

---

37 This is one of the formulae mentioned in the introduction, an often repeated phrase or line that we'll see a few times in Book 9. Dawn was the goddess Eos, sister to Helios (Sun) and Selene (Moon). Dawn is thus both representative of the morning sunrise and an anthropomorphic deity, as so often occurs in Hesiod's *Theogony*.

ships, with my ship getting ten. With this bounty we were able to feast all day, eating the meat and drinking our fill of wine, which didn't run out because we had stolen plenty of jars from the Cicones on Ismaros. Meanwhile, we wondered at the Cyclopean mainland, seeing smoke from their fires and maybe the faint sounds of voices and bleating goats. The sun set, and we slept again on the beach. [170] The next morning, I summoned my men to a meeting and told them, "Brave men, all of you wait here while I take my own ship, cross to the mainland, and find out whether this race is without law and order or whether they are respectful of the gods and welcoming to guests."

I hopped on board my ship with my men, whom I ordered to release the mooring cables, [180] take their seats, and begin striking the gray seas with their oars.[38]

We rowed across the bay, and before long, as we were approaching the mainland, we saw a cave opening from the face of the cliffs, fronted by laurel bushes. There were many sheep and goats grazing there inside of a field that was enclosed by sections of stone wall built between pine and oak trees. This was the home of a monster of a man who at that time was out with his flocks. [190] He lived a solitary life away from the other Cyclopes, even more lawless than the others. And he looked not like us bread-eating men, but rather like an old mountain, sticking out from the rest of the mountain chain.[39]

We beached the ship, and I took my twelve best men with me, ordering the rest to stay behind and guard the ship. I took with me a goatskin full of rich, dark wine, a gift of Euthanthes' son, Maron, who was a priest of Apollo back on Ismaros. During our sack of the city, we had protected[40] Maron, his wife and his child, who lived within the wooded grove of Apollo's temple, [200] out of respect. His gifts were seven perfectly shaped talents of gold, a silver bowl, and twelve jars of

---

38 Odysseus likely has 12 ships total at this point.

39 Despite the description, Odysseus hasn't yet seen the Cyclops.

40 Protected is a generous word here. Odysseus and his men spared Maron and his family from all the murdering and pillage they were performing.

Fig. 70: Polyphemus mosaic from Villa Romana del Casale in Sicily. Notice here that Polyphemus has an extra eye, not just one. (Piazza Armerina; early 4th century AD)

sweet, unmixed wine, a heavenly beverage. The wine was a secret known only to Maron, his wife, and a servant and even though when he drank it, he mixed it with twenty parts water to one part wine, [210] the scent from the mixing bowl was so sweet that you couldn't prevent yourself from drinking it. I took a large skin and filled it with this wine and took a pack of provisions, all because I had a foreboding thought that some-day soon I might meet a beastly man who wouldn't properly respect customs or laws.[41]

In the Cave of Polyphemus

We quickly entered the cave - he was out with his flocks of sheep - and marveled at the bounty inside. He had bins brimming with cheeses and pens [220] packed full of lambs. The pens were well-ordered with the newborns in one pen, the

---

41 If it is true that Odysseus had this premonition, perhaps he could have avoided his subsequent troubles?

slightly older in another pen, and the adolescents in a third pen. His milk vessels, bowls and pails were all filled with whey. My shipmates requested that we burgle some of the cheeses, deliver them to the ships and then come back and shepherd some of the lambs down to the ship as well and then take off. I myself wanted to meet the owner in hopes of receiving a gift as a guest,[42] so I didn't listen to my men although I should have. [230] It turned out that the man was not an easy one to deal with.

So we waited for the Cyclops, lit a fire and ate some cheeses, making sacrifices to the gods as well. He arrived carrying a big load of seasoned firewood which he threw down with such a crash that it scared us into hiding in the back of his cave. He divided his flock, driving into the cave the female goats and sheep for milking and keeping the rams and billy goats in the outside pen. [240] Then he blocked the cave entrance with a giant stone slab, large enough that twenty-two strong, four-wheeled wagons wouldn't be able to budge it. He sat down and milked the ewes and goats each in their turn, and then allowed their young to nurse.[43] He curdled half of the milk and put it into wicker baskets to strain[44] and set the other half aside to drink with his dinner. [250] After he had performed all his chores, he lit a fire and finally noticed us, saying, "Strangers, who are you? Where have you sailed from? Did you come here on trading business or do you wander the seas, ravaging other people's lands?"[45]

We were horribly frightened by his voice and his shape, but I was able to answer him, saying, "We are Achaeans (Greeks)[46]

---

42 Odysseus expects the treatment of *xenia* or guest-friendship.

43 This is another formula. The Cyclops will do this a few times as part of his chores.

44 This is the start of the cheese-making process.

45 It does not bode well that the Cyclops is already ignoring the customary host obligation to take care of the comforts of guests before asking them questions. Then again, his cave has been invaded and his stocks eaten, so he has cause for suspicion

46 Achaeans is one way that the Greeks refer to themselves, along with Danaans, Argives, and Hellenes. We generally use the term "Greeks" in our

trying to reach home on our way back from Troy, but have been tossed about [260] by winds and thrown off our course by Zeus' hand. We are men of Agamemnon, the son of Atreus, who has won world-wide fame by sacking such an illustrious city as Troy and killing such multitudes. We humbly ask for your hospitality and the gifts which are our right as guests. Oh Mighty One, be reverent to the gods: we are your guests, and [270] Zeus himself is the avenger of the mistreated visitor."

He answered without any compassion in his voice, saying, "You are a fool or a stranger to these lands if you are going to stand there asking me to fear and respect the anger of the gods. The Cyclopes aren't afraid of *aegis*-bearing Zeus,[47] or any of the other blessed gods, because we are stronger than them. I wouldn't spare you or your friends just because I thought Zeus might be driven to anger; I would only do so if I felt like it. Tell me, though, where is your ship right now? [280] Did you moor it close by or down the coast?"

He had asked me this in hopes I might reveal our location, but I was too smart for that, so I lied and said "Poseidon pushed my ship from open water toward the shore on the other side of your country and then dashed it on the rocks. My friends here and I made it out alive."

The wicked beast didn't even answer but quickly put his hands on two of my men and started smashing them against the ground like puppies. [290] Their bashed brains were everywhere and the blood soaked the ground. He ripped them apart, limb by limb, and ate the pieces. He feasted like a wild lion, eating every piece: skin, organs, and bones. The rest of us cried and threw our arms up to the heavens in complete shock, what else could we do? Once the Cyclops had packed his esophagus with human meat and washed it down with some milk, he laid down on the floor among his sheep and went straight to sleep. I thought [300] to grab my sword in this moment and thrust it

---

translations but here used the other term to add some spice to the text. The term "Greek" is a Latin one, first used by Roman authors.

47 The *aegis* is associated with Athena and Zeus and was a shield (sometimes a breastplate) offering protection.

right into his chest, but fortunately I realized that if I did this, we'd be done for, because we'd never be able to move the giant rock that the monster had used to block the entrance to the cave. So we whimpered and cried right where we were until morning.

When rose-fingered Dawn appeared, the Cyclops made a fire, milked the ewes and goats each in their turn, and then allowed their young to nurse. [310] Immediately after that, he grabbed two more of my men and started eating them for breakfast. Once he was finished, he moved the stone door aside to let out his herd, but shut the door again right away. He did this as easily as one might close the lid on a quiver of arrows. He yelled to drive his flock away toward the mountains. I would have to devise a crafty way to get revenge and win glory at the same time.

ODYSSEUS' DECEPTION

The following plan seemed like it would be the best one. The Cyclops had placed a massive club near one of the pens; [320] it was unseasoned olive wood, perfect for a staff when dried. It was the size of a mast of a twenty-oared trading ship, one big enough to handle open water. I cut a six foot section and had my men smooth it out and I worked on creating a point at one end, hardening it in the fire. I then hid the stake in a pile of dung, [330] which was all over the cave. I asked my men to choose four among them at random who would help me lift it up and thrust it into the monster's eye as he slept. As luck would have it, the four men picked randomly were the same ones I would have chosen.[48]

At day's end, the Cyclops came back from pasturing his flocks and drove them into the cave. Not one was left outside in the courtyard, through either his own initiative or through divine will. [340] He pushed the great stone door back into place, milked the ewes and goats each in their turn, and then allowed their young to nurse. When he was done with his tasks,

---

48 Odysseus' men would have drawn lots, perhaps by placing small tokens for each man in a helmet and drawing or shaking them out.

Fig. 71: Archaic or late geometric period krater depicting Odysseus and a friend stabbing the Cyclops Polyphemus in his only eye (Archaeological Museum of Argos; ca. 670 BC)

he snatched two more of my men and ate them for dinner, as if it was nothing. I then approached him holding out an ivy-wood bowl of dark wine[49] and said, "Cyclops, now that you've eaten all that human meat, take this wine and drink it.[50] It's from my ship and I was bringing it to you as a gift in hopes you would [350] take pity on us and help us get home, but instead you've raged at us way beyond reason. Do you really think anyone will visit you if this is how you treat your guests, with such lawlessness?"

He took the cup and drank it and seemed really impressed with the quality of the wine so he asked me for another cup full. "Kindly give me more wine!" he said, "and tell me what your name is so that I can give you a present that you'll be pleased

---

49 This is the wine Odysseus was talking about having received as a "gift" from Maron on Ismaros. Remember that this wine was normally diluted with 20 parts water to one part wine (the standard was 4 parts water) so this is an extremely strong wine that the Cyclops is drinking.

50 Odysseus' words in Greek make it sound like an offering to a god.

with. The Earth here grows beautiful sun-ripened grapes that we make into wine, but this drink is godly nectar and ambrosia."

[360] I gave him three more cups full of wine, one at a time, and he chugged them easily. When I saw he was a little buzzed, I put on my best act and spoke to him, saying, "Cyclops, you asked for my name so I will tell you, and then you can give me my gift as promised. My name is Norman and that's what my mother, father and comrades all call me."[51] The monster replied, "Norman! Your present is that I will eat all of your friends first [370] and then eat No'man last." As he finished speaking, he plopped backwards falling on the ground and fell into a deep sleep. Because of his drunkenness, he then turned his head and threw up the wine and the human meat he'd been binge eating.

I immediately snatched up the post of wood, reheated the tip in the embers of the fire, and roused the courage of my men so they wouldn't wimp out. When the post, even unseasoned as it was, started to glow in the fire, [380] I took it out and my men bravely gathered around me. We jammed the sharp end of the post hard into the Cyclops' eye; I put all my weight into it and twisted it back and forth as if I were drilling a hole in a piece of timber for a ship, the way two men could do continuously by holding both ends of a belt. Just like that, we stabbed the hot post into his eyeball until blood poured out as we twisted, and the steam singed his eyelids and eyebrows, [390] and the roots of his eyes burst in the heat. It was like when a blacksmith quenches a hot ax in cold water to make it stronger and it sizzles and steams - that's exactly what the Cyclops' eye was like around the olive post, and he screamed out a horrible shriek that echoed throughout the cave.

Afraid, we scurried away. He pulled out the post, which was covered in eye juices and blood, and threw it aside in his

---

51 Odysseus tells the Cyclops that his name is *outis* which translates literally as "no one" or "no man." We feel the translation "Norman / No'man" is a fun one, since it is a real name in our language and could maybe create the confusion we will see later on in the story. The name "NoOne" or "NoMan" is common in other translations.

Fig. 72: Detail of the neck of a funerary proto-Attic amphora depicting Odysseus and his men blinding the Cyclops Polyphemus (Archaeological Museum of Eleusis; ca. 660 BC)

anger and agony. As he did this, he shouted to the other Cyclopes living [400] near him along the coast and they approached his cave from all around in response to his screaming, and they asked what was happening.

"What's the matter, Polyphemus? Why are you screaming in the quiet of the middle of the night, waking us up? There is no man stealing your sheep, right? And there is no man trying to murder you through deceit or strength?"

Polyphemus[52] yelled back to them from inside his cave, "Norman is killing me through deceit! No'man is killing me through strength!"[53]

---

52 When the other Cyclopes ask Polyphemus if anyone is assaulting him, there is a play on words with a term often used to describe Odysseus' main character train of cunningness, shrewdness, and scheming.

53 The other Cyclopes must have heard this as "No man" through the cave walls.

The other Cyclopes, confused, said, [410] "If no man is assaulting you, you're probably just sick. If you are sick by Zeus' will, there's not much you can do, try praying to your papa Poseidon." Then they left.

Escape from the Island

I chuckled inside that my craftiness had worked and the Cyclops, screaming and crying in his pain, felt around and found the stone door, moved it out of the way, and then sat there reaching out with his arms trying to catch us escaping, as if we'd be stupid enough to just run out. [420] But I did need to figure out a plan for how I could save my life and the lives of my comrades. I mulled it over and over as one would do when their life was at stake, for the danger was very real. Here's the plan I devised. The Cyclops' rams were sizable, and each had a thick, black fleece. I silently tied them in groups of threes, side by side, using the twigs that the evil monster used as a bed. We were going to put a man under each of the middle sheep so that the [430] sheep on each end would provide a buffer, so there were three sheep for each man. I used the best of the rams for myself, and facing up I snuggled into his belly fleece, and held on tightly and steadily.

Fig. 73: Small Archaic bronze statuette of Odysseus under the belly of a ram (Archaeological Museum of Delphi; ca. 550-500 BC)

We waited with fear until Morning and when her child, the rose-fingered Dawn, appeared. It was time for the rams to go outside to graze while the ewes, [440] their udders full, re-

*Fig. 74: Odysseus in the cave of Polyphemus
(Pushkin Museum of Fine Arts; 1630-35)*

mained inside bleating in expectation of being milked. As the flock departed, their master put aside his pain to touch each of their backs but did not think to check for the men hidden underneath. As the ram departed last, heavy with his own fleece and with my weight, Polyphemus grabbed it and said, "Why are you last in line today, my favorite ram? You don't usually let the females go first, but instead lead the flock [450] running to the meadow or flowering stream, and you rush home in the evening; but at this moment you lag behind. Maybe it is because you sense that I've been blinded by Norman and his comrades - they tricked me with drink! I will kill him! If only we could communicate, I know you'd tell me where that sneaky No'man is hiding. If I catch him, I'll bash his skull against the floor, spreading brains everywhere. [460] That's the only way I'll feel better about the devastation he has caused me."

As the Cyclops said this, he still drove the ram out of the cave along with the rest of the flock. Once the ram and I had made it a little away from the courtyard, I let go of the ram's fleece and then freed my men. We drove the fattened sheep down to our ship. The rest of our comrades were thrilled to see us but they cried for the men that the Cyclops had killed.

But I hushed them with a frown and a shush[54] and [470] urged them to drive the sheep onto the ship and to start rowing. So they hopped on board, sat at their rowing benches, and struck the ocean's waves with their oars. When we were far enough away but close enough for my voice to reach the shore, I started mocking the Cyclops.

I shouted, "Cyclops, you didn't realize whose men you were eating in your cave. You bastard! Eating visitors to your cave?! Zeus and the gods have punished you for your crazy violence."

[480] The Cyclops' rage exploded, and he broke off a piece of stone from the mountain and hurled it into the sea, splashing just in front of our ship, nearing hitting it. The force of the rock sent us surging back toward the shore, nearly grounding us, but I pushed us off with a pole and [490] signaled to my men to row as if their lives depended on it, and row they did. When we were double the distance from shore as before, I wanted to mock the Cyclops again but my men pleaded with me to hold back.

Fig. 75: Odysseus and Polyphemus
(Museum of Fine Arts, Boston; 1896)

"Please contain your anger," they shouted, "and don't provoke the monster again. He already attacked us with one stone, which drove us back to shore - we almost died! If he had heard us near the shore, he would have smashed our heads and our ship into pieces with another stone - you saw how well he can throw."

---

54 Odysseus is very expressive with his face and can seemingly give orders to his men silently.

[500] I refused their pleas and called out to him again in anger, "Cyclops, if someone asks who it was that stabbed out your eye, making you ugly, you can tell them it was the hero Odysseus, son of Laertes, from Ithaca."[55]

Hearing my words, the Cyclops replied, "Then the prophecy is coming to fruition! Once long ago a seer named Telemos, son of Eurymos, visited here. He was strong and brave, a great seer, and he shared all of his visions with the Cyclopes [510] until old age. He told me this would happen: that a man named Odysseus would blind me. But this whole time I was expecting an impressive looking, muscular man, but you're just an ordinary, puny, little man, and you took advantage of me with wine in order to blind me. Come back, Odysseus, so I can show you my true hospitality and encourage the god Poseidon to aid you on your journey. Poseidon is my father, and if he chooses to, [520] he can heal me, which no other man nor god could do."

And I said to him, "I'm as sure of the fact that I want to come back and murder you and send your soul down to Hades as I am that not even Poseidon himself can heal your eye!" The Cyclops then raised his hands to the heavens and proclaimed, "Poseidon hear my prayer! If I am truly your son, [530] make it so that Odysseus never reaches home. But if he does, may he be delayed, may his comrades all die along the way, may he arrive in another man's ship, and may his home be in shambles!" Poseidon heard his words.

The Cyclops then broke off another piece of rock from the mountain, significantly bigger than the first stone, and whipped it at us with exceptional strength. [540] It crashed into the sea, again nearly hitting us, this time at the back of the ship. The sea swelled up and the massive wave pushed us away from the Cyclops toward the shore of the island.

Once we reached the island, we found the other ships and our comrades worried about us and waiting for us to return. We beached our ships, disembarked, and unloaded the Cyclops' sheep, which we divided up equally among the men so no one

---

55 Odysseus can't hold back from putting his name to his craftiest victory, a defeat over great size and strength using cunning and wits

would feel cheated. [550] But my men agreed that the special ram should be given to me, separate from my allotment. I sacrificed him right there on the beach and seared the thigh bone as an offering to the lord of all things, Zeus. But Zeus was not attentive to my efforts and was thinking only of how he would eventually wreck my ships and kill my comrades.

We feasted on meat and drank all day until the sun went down and then camped and slept on the beach. [560] When rose-fingered Dawn arrived, I ordered my men to board the ships and untie them from the shore. They sat on their benches in order and slapped the sea with their oars. We sailed onwards, happy to be alive but in grief at our fallen brothers.

The Rest of the Story

Things get worse before they get better for Odysseus, although we have some indication of this already since Odysseus is now alone on his journey. The story he tells in King Alcinous' hall continues across Books 10-12. Odysseus meets Aeolus, the king of the winds, which seems good since Aeolus gives him a gift of all the non-favorable winds in a tied-up sack, but Odysseus' men open the bag, releasing a storm of winds,

Fig. 76: Kylix (wine cup) depicting Odysseus' men turned into animals by Circe receiving the antidote (Museum of Fine Arts, Boston; ca. 550 BC)

which send his ships dramatically off-course again. Odysseus loses 11 of his 12 ships to the Laestrygonians (giant man-eaters who destroy his ship by throwing rocks from the shore, sound familiar?). Odysseus then lands on the island of Circe, a witch goddess, who turns Odysseus' men into pigs (Odysseus himself is saved when Hermes gives him an herb that counteracts the spell). Odysseus gets Circe to change the pigs back into men, but is seduced by Circe and stays on the island for a year. Odysseus is eventually allowed to leave but next visits the land of the dead where he meets his mother and learns about what is happening back home on Ithaca. He is further tested, passing the island of the Sirens with their devastatingly beautiful song, which his ship is able to sail past since Odysseus is tied to the mast of his ship and his men plug their ears with wax.

Fig. 77: Athenian red-figure stamnos (storage container) showing Odysseus and the Sirens (British Museum; ca. 475 BC)

They also manage to make it through Scylla (a six-headed monster) and Charybdis (a deadly whirlpool) although not without losses. On the next island they stop at, Odysseus' men eat some cattle sacred to the god Helios (Sun) that they picked up on their journey to the underworld, even though they had been forbidden to, and are punished by Zeus with a shipwreck. Odysseus is the lone survivor, washing ashore on Calypso's island, which completes the loops for us, since it was from Calypso's island Odysseus was escaping when he eventually washed up on Alcinous' beach.

Over the course of the remaining 12 books, Odysseus is delivered to his home island, asleep and in the dark, by Alcinous' sailors. Athena helps Odysseus by disguising him as an old beggar and, in an episode of *Undercover Boss*, he meets a swineherd Eumaeus, who has good things to say about Odysseus and who will help Odysseus (as the old man) get into the palace. Odysseus reunites with his son Telemachus, the dog he had left behind as a puppy, Argos, and his wife Penelope. In disguise, he tests Penelope's faithfulness. Satisfied, he begins to devise a way to get rid of the suitors, who had mocked the disguised Odysseus on his arrival to the palace. With Athena's help, an archery contest is arranged to determine the winning suitor in which the winner must string a very heavy bow and shoot an arrow through 12 ax heads. Odysseus is the only one strong enough to do so, and he uses the remaining arrows and other weapons to kill all the suitors.

Fig. 78: Attic red-figure skyphos (wine cup) depicting Odysseus slaying the suitors (Altes Museum in Berlin; ca. 440 BC)

Telemachus hangs 12 maids who had either betrayed Penelope or had sex with the suitors. Odysseus reveals himself to Penelope and proves his identity by referencing the construction of their marital bed. The story ends when Athena and Zeus stop a battle from taking place between Odysseus and Ithacans who were seeking vengeance for the slain suitors.

CHAPTER III

Golden Age of Greece

We saw that the Archaic Period in Greece (ca. 800-479 BC) saw the origin of many of the things that we consider quint-essentially "Greek": democracy, the Olympics, classical architecture, vase painting, sculpture, and philosophy, just to name a few. If that's the case, then the Classical Period in Greece (479-323 BC) saw many of these features reach their pinnacle. If large stone temples got their start in the Archaic Period, they were perfected with the Parthenon in the Classical Period. If philosophy took its first step with the natural philosophers of the Archaic Period, then it took a giant leap forward with Socrates and Plato during the Classical Period. In short, you might say that Greece was invented during the Archaic Period and perfected during the Classical Period.

The Persian Wars

The revolutionary accomplishments of the Classical Period, however, almost never got off the ground. At the end of the 6th century BC, the Greek world was thrown into chaos: Sparta was on the verge of attacking Athens; Athens had just tried to assassinate their own political leaders; and in the midst of all this, the Athenians had reached out to the mighty Persian Empire for help against their Spartan foes.

At this point in time, Greece was nothing more than a blip on the radar of the sprawling Persian Empire, which stretched from the borders of India to the shores of the Aegean. It had more than 50 million inhabitants living in its lands, compared with the less than 10 million of the Greek world at the time. And militarily, the Persians had essentially never lost a war: the Medes, the Lydians, and even the Egyptians all fell to Persian armies. So when they set their sights on the small, independent city-states of the Greek world, no one thought the Greeks had much of a chance.

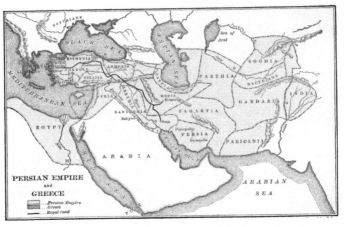

Fig. 79: Map of the Greek city-states and the Persian Empire
around 500 BC

The way this began was a bit of a fluke. Shortly before 500 BC, when the Spartans were planning an invasion of Attica (the peninsula that contains Athens), the Athenians sent to Persia for help. The Persians said they would help if the Athenians made them a gift of "earth and water." Now to the Athenian envoys, this didn't mean anything, so they went ahead and did it. To the Persians, however, this was a sign of submission to Persian rule. Unbeknownst to the messengers and citizens back home, the Athenians had just subjugated themselves to the Persian Empire.

Fast forward a few years, and the Greek city-states of Ionia (the west coast of Turkey) were running into problems with the Persian Empire. Every year they were taxed more and more until finally they decided they'd had enough. In 494 BC, the Ionian Greeks revolted against the Persians, marching upon the provincial capital at Sardis and burning it to the ground. A few other Greek city-states, like Athens, joined in the revolt as well.

The Persians were furious. And in response, they marched up and down the coast burning Greek city-states as they went. Then they set sail across the Aegean, laying waste to some of the islands along the way. In 490 BC, their boats ended up in the Bay of Marathon, about - you guessed it - 26.2 miles from the center of Athens. The Athenians could only muster about 9,000 troops to put up a defense against the Persian force of more than 30,000. Using their unified phalanx-style of warfare, however, they were able to defeat the Persian invaders. A man by the name of Pheidippides then ran from Marathon to Athens to deliver the good news and encourage the citizens to continue the fight. He then died on the spot of exhaustion.

Fig. 80: Reconstructed drawing of the Battle of Marathon from the Stoa Poikile in Athens (Athens, Greece; 5th century BC)

Ten years later, Persia showed up to take revenge. This time they didn't mess around with a measly force of 30,000 troops. Instead, as Herodotus notes, they brought with them the largest army the world had ever seen - 5,000,000 soldiers in all. Most modern (and even ancient) historians think that's a bit overblown, but it was still the greatest challenge Greece ever faced (and possibly the biggest army ever assembled).

The early days of the war looked ominous. In one of the most famous and heroic battles - that of Thermopylae in 480

141

Fig. 81: Attic black-figure lekythos (oil container) depicting the Battle of Marathon. Three Persians identifiable by their pants, shirts, and hats attack a lone Greek hoplite. (National Archaeological Museum of Athens; 5th century BC)

BC - the small contingent of 300 Spartans and a few thousand allies were eventually defeated by the overwhelming numbers of Persia's army. In the aftermath, the Greeks fled Attica, retreating to Corinth, the gateway to the Peloponnese. This left Athens completely unguarded, and later that year the whole city, acropolis and all, was burnt to the ground .

The Greeks eventually turned the tides. They sent a spy into the Persian camp, falsely claiming that the Greeks were ready to give up. One more military defeat, and they were ready to surrender to Persia. The Persian general bought into the ruse, and ordered to strike the final blow to the Greeks at the site of Salamis. Little did he know, the entire Athenian navy was laying in wait, hoping for this attack. When the moment came, they launched their fleet broadside into the Persian ships, sinking many and sending thousands of Persian troops into the depths of the Aegean. The Persian supply lines were broken, and the assault ground to a halt. The following year, in 479 BC, the Greeks won decisive land battles at Plataea and Mycale to kick the Persians out of Greece for good. It was an upset of unfathomable proportions, and it launched Greece from the Archaic into the Classical Period.

The Golden Age of Athens

The Greek victory over the Persians is usually the starting point for what scholars call the Classical Period of Greece. During the war, the entire city of Athens was burnt to the ground, but in the aftermath of the fighting, this provided a new, blank canvas for the Athenians to build upon. Much of this building was led by the Athenian politician and general Pericles, who rose to power in the aftermath of the Persian Wars. Pericles did two things particularly well - raise money for Athens and use that money to fund innovative projects.

To raise money, Pericles relied upon the same naval fleet that had defeated the Persians at the Battle of Salamis. While the Persians had been kicked out of Greece, their Empire was still many times the size of all the Greek city-states put together. So Pericles devised what was called the Delian League, an alliance of Greek city-states that would work together to defend against any future Persian invasions. To fund the league, each city-state had to contribute either ships for the fleet or money in place of ships. Most found it easier to give money than ships, and the treasury for the alliance grew substantially and was kept on the island of Delos (hence the Delian League).

Because the Persians did not end up invading again, the money raised by the Delian League continued to grow, and soon the treasury was moved to Athens and funds began to be used for specifically Athenian purposes. Most famously, the Athenians used their new wealth to rebuild the acropolis. The former Archaic Period Temple of Athena which sat atop the acropolis had been destroyed during the Persian Wars, and now Pericles set about rebuilding the religious center of the city. Four new buildings graced the rocky outcrop. The Propylaea stood as a monumental gateway to the the acropolis. The Ionic Temple of Athena Nike jutted out from the southwest. The Erechtheion - a temple to Athena and Poseidon and the early kings of Athens - sat to the north. It's famous today as the site of the mythological contest for Athens and for its caryatids, columns carved into the shape of women. Finally, at the center of it all, was the Parthenon.

Fig. 82: The Parthenon (Athens, Greece; built 447 - 432 BC)

The Parthenon, also known as the Temple of Athena Parthenos (or Athena the Virgin), stood as the largest, most elaborate temple the Greek mainland had ever seen. It was built in 15 short years, from 447 to 432 BC, and it stood over 200 feet long by more than 100 feet wide. Inside, the sculptor Pheidias had constructed a chryselephantine (i.e., gold and ivory) cult statue of the goddess Athena that soared more than 40 feet into the air.

Fig. 83: The Varvakeion Athena, shown above, is a Roman copy of the 5th century BC cult statue of Athena Parthenos. (National Archaeological Museum of Athens; 3rd century AD)

144

The outside of the temple too was covered with sculptures, many of which are considered the peak of Classical Greek sculpture. The pediments - the triangular areas on the front and back of the temple facade - bore deep relief sculptures that told the stories of the Contest for Athens and the Birth of Athena. The metopes - the small squares above the columns that surrounded the temple - depicted the Greeks defeating a series of barbarians: Trojans, centaurs, Amazons, and giants. Then, inside the outer columns, and running continuously around the temple, a sculptural frieze illustrated the Panathenaic procession, the religious ritual that celebrated the birthday of Athena and the delivery of her new gown to her cult statue inside the Parthenon. Today, these decorative elements are celebrated for their fluidity and idealistic beauty, which stand as the hallmark of Classical Greek sculpture.

Fig. 84: Part of the Parthenon frieze showing equestrian riders
(British Museum; 5th century BC)

Innovation was happening outside the realm of religion as well. The 5th century saw the emergence of Socrates as a major figure in Athens, and his student Plato (who we can thank for recording what we know about Socrates), went on to build his academy in the early 4th century BC. The philosophers of the Archaic Period were primarily concerned with finding out how the world worked, explaining natural phenomena without having to invoke the magic of the Greek gods. This new group of philosophers, however, was more interested in the behavior of people. They tried to answer questions like, "What does it mean to be a good person?" The answer to a question like this is obviously complex and debatable, but one of the things that we take away from these philosophical debates is their mode of inquiry - the Socratic method. We still find it useful, even in today's society, to try to understand the world by asking a series of questions, the answers to which always lead to more questions.

Figs. 85 (left): Bust of Socrates (Louvre Museum; Roman copy of a Greek original from the 4th century BC)

Fig. 86 (right): Bust of Plato (Vatican Museums; Roman copy of a Greek original from the 4th centuy BC)

Exciting things were happening in the world of entertainment as well. During the Classical Period, especially in Athens, we get the emergence of dramatic performances. These took place as part of a set of contests meant to worship the god Dionysus. Playwrights would submit to one of two categories: tragedies or comedies. Tragedies, as the name implies, tended to end on a rather down note. They centered on the gods and heroes of Greek mythology and often taught moral or ethical lessons through their narratives. Comedies, on the other hand, tended to have a much more pleasant ending. Rather than focusing on the gods, comedies commonly centered on everyday life. They could even be used as a way to critique the actions of political leaders, something that was relatively rare in the ancient world. For example, Aristophanes, the most famous of the Greek comedians, wrote the *Lysistrata*, in which the

*Fig. 87: The Theater of Epidaurus is nearly acoustically perfect.
You can hear person talking down in the orchestra all the way up
in the top row. (4th century BC)*

women of Athens go on a sex strike until the men of the city
put an end to the Peloponnesian War.

The Peloponnesian War & 4th Century BC

Speaking of the Peloponnesian War (431-404 BC), not everyone was particularly happy with how rich Athens was getting and with how much power they were exerting throughout
the Aegean. Sparta, especially, found this a tough pill to swallow, and by the end of the 5th century BC, they had made plans
to attack. Using Athens' mistreatment of Spartan allies as an
excuse, Sparta marched their army north and surrounded Athens in 431 BC, launching the start of the Peloponnesian War.

There wasn't much actual fighting between Athens and
Sparta in the early years of the Peloponnesian War. As Sparta
laid siege to the city, Athens continued to feed its people using
its "Long Walls," a series of fortifications nearly 10 miles long,
to reach the port of Piraeus and receive food supplies from
other parts of the Mediterranean. Things weren't easy for the
Athenians, however, and a plague broke out in 430 and then
again in 429 and 427, devastating much of the population.

After ten years of this going on, the Spartans and Athenians agreed to a 50-year truce in 421 BC. This, of course, did not last nearly as long as intended. The Athenians, under the influence of the colorful character Alcibiades, were convinced to set sail for Sicily, under the logic that conquering the island would give them the resources they needed to defeat Sparta once and for all. The Sicilian Expedition, however, was a complete disaster, wreaking havoc on the army, navy, and finances of the Athenians. They were almost utterly destroyed.

Fig. 88: Attic black-figure vase depicting two Greek hoplites in battle (National Archaeological Museum of Athens; 6th century BC)

Sparta, now allied with Persia, decided that this was the perfect opportunity to attack. The Athenians were truly desperate, so much so that they melted down the statues of their gods, using the proceeds from the melted metal to fund the construction of a new fleet. To everyone's surprise, they were able to soundly defeat the Spartans in 406 BC. So bad was the defeat that the Spartans sued for peace. Athens, foolishly, declined. Two years later, as Athenian ships sailed towards the Black Sea to secure their food supply routes, the Spartans laid siege to them at the site of Aegospotami. Now it was Athens' turn to suffer a devastating defeat.

This battle, in 404 BC, brought the war to a close with the Spartans as victors. Yet Sparta was never able to consolidate power over the rest of Greece, and during much of the 4th century BC, multiple city-states (especially Sparta, Athens, and Thebes) all vied for supremacy. The problem was, however, that any time one city-state seemed primed for dominance, the other city-states would ally together against them. And while all this was going on, a new power - the Argead dynasty of Macedon - was growing in the north.

Alexander the Great & Hellenistic Greece

While Athens, Sparta, and Thebes were battling for dominance of mainland Greece, the region of Macedon was growing more powerful in the far northern reaches of the Hellenic world. Originally it had been little more than a backwater, something on the outskirts of the Greek core centered on the Aegean. But the Peloponnesian War, and the alliances that resulted from it, drew them more in touch with Greek culture, warfare, and politics.

In the middle of the 4th century BC, the leader of Macedon was a man by the name of Philip II. He had adopted traditional Greek-style battle tactics, and his Macedonian troops had become some of the best fighters in all of Greece. In 338 BC, Philip II marched his troops against an alliance of Athenians and Thebans, the best defense mainland Greece could offer, and he soundly defeated them. It is said that in the aftermath of his victory, Philip got obliterated on wine and danced on the bodies of the dead.

Having defeated Athens and Thebes, Philip then consolidated power over all of mainland Greece; the formerly independent city-states now had to answer to a single ruler. He then set his sights on an even bigger target: the Persian Empire. His goal was to seek vengeance for the Persian invasion of Greece 150 years earlier. Just one task remained before he could set out; he needed to secure a marriage alliance (his fourth) to ensure all of Greece would remain calm while he was away in the east. At the wedding, Philip II was literally stabbed in the back and killed.

Fig. 89: Bust of a young Alexander the Great
(Capitoline Museums; Roman copy of a Hellenistic original from
the 3rd - 2nd century BC)

That year, in 336 BC, the teenage son of Philip, a young man by the name of Alexander III, took over control of Macedon. After quickly pacifying the Greek city-states that were roused as a result of Philip's assassination, Alexander set out to accomplish his father's goal of bringing the Persian Empire to its knees. Despite (or perhaps because of) his youth, Alexander had a knack for showing his bravery, skill, and cunning in battle. He often led the charge himself, rather than hanging back behind the lines, and his tactics consistently allowed his outnumbered army to triumph in the face of overwhelming odds.

Alexander's military accomplishments led him to be called Alexander the Great. He was the first of his army to set foot on Asian soil at the Battle of Granicus. A year later at the Battle of Issus, Alexander was able to defeat the Persian King, Darius III, despite at least a 2:1 deficit in his number of troops. At Gaugamela, he engineered a reverse pincer move that allowed him personally to charge at the Persian king. Darius III fled, and Alexander captured the royal tent. Later that night he was said to have donned the royal purple robes himself and bathed in the golden bathtub of Darius.

Fig. 90: Silver coin depicting Alexander the Great (333 - 327 BC)

The legend that grew around Alexander was just as impressive as any of his military deeds. When he arrived in the town of Gordian, he encountered the famed "Gordian Knot," a knot so complicated that no one could untie it. It was said that whoever could do so, would one day become Lord of Asia. Alexander, having no time for games, simply pulled out his sword and sliced through the knot, proclaiming himself to have fulfilled the prophecy. Years later, after having taken Egypt without having to even draw his sword, Alexander ended up in the western desert at the Siwah Oasis. There, he entered the Temple of Amun, consulted the god, and then told his troops that the Amun had indeed confirmed he was descended from the gods.

After defeating Darius III and the Persian Empire once and for all, Alexander continued his march east, much to the dismay of his troops. He married the local princess Roxana from Bactria and Sogdiana (an area that overlaps with Afghanistan Tajikistan and Uzbekistan), and he eventually marched his army all the way to India. There, he fought one final battle against King Porus and his war elephants. Alexander was again victorious, but this win came at a cost. Alexander himself was wounded, having caught an arrow to the shoulder. More than that, his troops had had enough, and they threatened to mutiny.

Alexander was forced to begin his march back to Greece. He unwisely chose a more direct route through the Gedrosian desert, losing half his troops to the harsh conditions. When he

Fig. 91: The Alexander Mosaic from the House of the Faun at Pompeii depicts his victory over Darius III at the Battle of Issus in 333 BC (National ARchaeological Museum of Napeles; ca. 100 BC)

reached the city of Babylon, Alexander took ill. Scholars debate the exact reason - infection from his arrow wound, excessive drinking, or perhaps poison - but whatever it was, he now lay on his deathbed. Alexander was still only in his early-30s, but he had built the largest empire the world had ever seen. His generals came to him as he lay dying, asking who would take over once he was gone. Alexander responded that he left his empire "to the strongest."

Fig. 92: The so-called "Alexander Sarcophagus" likely did not belong to Alexander, but it does show him victorious in battle (Istanbul Archaeoligical Museum; late 4th century BC)

While certainly dramatic, this was, of course, no help at all. Alexander's generals shot off to all corners of the kingdom, trying to stake their claims. His general Ptolemy even stole the body of Alexander himself, absconding to Egypt with it and using it as the basis for his claim to legitimate succession .

These successors to Alexander would go on to set up kingdoms that would last hundreds of years, incorporating lands far outside their home region of Macedon. As a result, we call this period the Hellenistic Period (323-31 BC), or the Greek-ish period, because it mixed the ruling Macedonian and Greek elite with local populations from all over Egypt and the Near East. The Ptolemies, descended from Alexander's general, would actually go on to be the longest-ruling dynasty Egypt had ever seen. In doing so, they explicitly blended Greek and Egyptian identities. Ptolemy and his successors were depicted both as traditional Egyptian pharaohs and as Greek aristocrats. Ptolemy II even took up the old Egyptian practice of royal brother-sister marriage, wedding his sister Arisinoe and gaining the nickname Philadelphus, or "sister lover" in the process. Even the gods became merged in a process known as syncretism, so that the Egyptian deity Amun was linked with the Greek god Zeus to form the hybrid Zeus Ammon.

Figs. 93 (left) and 94 (right): Ptolemy I Soter ("the Savior") depicted in both Greek and Egyptian styles (Louvre and British Museum; 305 - 282 BC)

For nearly 300 years, the successors of Alexander fought with each other to try to regain control of the empire he had built. No one, however, was ever able to put Humpty Dumpty back together again, for every time one side looked to take the lead, all the others would ally against them. While this was going on, a small power from the western Mediterranean had slowly been growing in size. First taking over Italy, then Sicily, then parts of Spain and Africa. Now in the 2nd and 1st centuries BC, it set its sights on these Hellenistic kingdoms - dividing, conquering, and picking them off one by one. The Greek world was coming to an end in the face of the mighty legions of the Roman Empire.

Fig. 95: Map of the kingdoms of Alexander the Great's successors
during the Hellenistic Period (ca. 300 BC)

Herodotus' *Histories*

The *Histories* was a ground-breaking document written
by Herodotus of Halicarnassus in classical Greek that covers
events that took place just before and during Herodotus' life
in the 5th century BC in the Aegean and Mediterranean world,
including Greece, Persia and Egypt. Herodotus lived from approximately 485 to 425 in the Greek city of Halicarnassus, in
Ionia (modern day western Turkey) which was then part of the
Persian Empire. This would give Herodotus a unique view of
events and the ability to look at things from both sides of the
story. The *Histories* is considered to be the first major work of
history as a genre in the Western tradition and Herodotus is referred to as the "Father of History" for this reason (by Cicero,
a Roman politician living 400 years later).

The *Histories* was a wide-ranging text that covered politics, geography, war, culture and biography. It starts with a re-
flection on the cause of the Trojan War (to Herodotus the start
of conflict between Asian and Europe), covers the rise and early
history of various city-states, deviates for an entire book to talk
about Egypt (what he calls "the Gift of the Nile"), and tracks
the burgeoning strength of Persia and its wars with Greece.
Herodotus did have historical predecessors, but it seems that
none matched his breadth and style. He is a great story-tell

155

Fig. 96: Bust of Herodotus from Athribis in Egypt
(Metropolitan Museum of Art; Roman copy of a Greek original)

er, although the line between history and historical fiction can seem a bit blurred, with some of his stories appearing quite fanciful. Other ancient writers called Herodotus' reliability into question, and it seems obvious to readers that Herodotus preferred to entertain than simply give dry facts. Yet he is still the best source on the Persian Empire from the western perspective and for this period of time in the eastern Mediterranean.

Why did Herodotus set out to "write history"? Herodotus begins his work by saying, "This is the inquiry of Herodotus of Halicarnassus, written so that the actions of men will not be forgotten, and so that great achievements by Greeks and Barbarians will not forfeit their fame, and in particular so that the causes of war between these people will be remembered." Here the word "inquiry" is a translation of the Greek word *historia*, from which we eventually get our own word "history." Herodotus' inquiry into the past supports his further motivation to memorialize events. But Herodotus approached his material analytically, trying to explain, compare and analyze.

He tried to establish cause and effect and there are times when we see him weigh various viewpoints and facts to establish an opinion of what really happened (we will see this in the selection below).

Herodotus' work grapples with themes that continue to be relevant to modern audiences 2,500 years later. What is the power of freedom and what does it mean to be free? What explains the rise and fall of empires? What are the cultural, geographic and political differences between the "eastern world" and the "western world" that have given rise to conflict? These same questions are asked by professional historians and political theorists today.

Fig. 97: Fragment from Herodotus' Histories, Book VIII on Papyrus Oxyrhynchus 2099 (Sackler Library; early 2nd century AD)

As mentioned in the introduction to this period, Greece at this time was not a unified nation. In fact, the word "Greek" was not used until Roman times. The "Greeks" referred to themselves by their city citizenship or sometimes collectively as Hellenes, from Hellas. The region, including the Greek mainland, many of the Greek islands and the east in Ionia, was composed of *poleis* (singular: *polis*), which we will translate as city-states. Examples are Athens, Sparta, Thebes, etc. A *polis* was self-governing but could take various approaches to government (aristocracy, oligarchy and even democracy). These city-states had various amenities including gymnasia, temples, theaters, and the agora which acted as the social and commercial center. *Poleis* created treaties for regular peace and trade but there was frequent warfare between them.

The main story-line in Herodotus' *Histories* is that of the Greco-Persian Wars in which the Achaemenid Persians attempted to subjugate the city-states in present day Greece. Some of these city-states had aided a rebellion against the Persians by Greeks living in Ionia, present day western Turkey. It is relevant to the upcoming reading to understand that the Greeks were not united in their plans to defend themselves from Persian invasion. Some city-states pledged allegiance to Persia and others stayed neutral. Regardless, the Persians under Darius vowed to crush Greece, but the first attempt was thwarted by the Athenians at the Battle of Marathon, as narrated in the above Historical Context section. In Book 7, you will read about a brief but decisive moment in the Greco-Persian Wars in 480 BC. Xerxes, son of Darius, has invaded Greece with a massive army and the Greeks have sent forces from various city-states to try to prevent or even slow down the invasion, which has already taken Thrace and Macedonia to the north. They race to a defensive position at Thermopylae (literally, the "Hot Gates"), where they attempt to block the narrow pass between the mountains and the sea, but are vastly outnumbered (something like 4,000 - 7,000 against 120,000 - 300,000). The report by Herodotus of the events at Thermopylae follows.

Words of the Ancients

Herodotus' *Histories*

The Battle of Thermopylae (Book VII.201-228)

[201] Xerxes and his troops set up camp in Malis in the region of Trachis, and the Greeks did so within the pass itself in an area that most Greeks call Thermopylae but which the locals call Pylae. This is how both sides were laid out, with one controlling all the land to the north of Trachis and the other side controlling everything south.

THE 300 SPARTANS AND THEIR ALLIES

[202] The Greek contingent that was camped here and awaited battle with the Persians was composed of 300 Spartan hoplites, 1,000 soldiers from Tegea and Mantinea (half from each), 120 men from Orchomenos in Arcadia, 1,000 from other places in Arcadia, 400 from Corinth, 200 from Phlius, 80 from Mycenae. The above were from the Peloponnese and then from Boeotia there were 700 Thespians and 400 Thebans.[1]

[203] On top of those numbers, the Locrians of Opus had heeded the call to bring their entire army, and 1,000 Phocians as well. The other Greeks had sent messengers to them saying that they were merely an advanced force and that more Greek armies would arrive each day; moreover the sea was well-guarded by Athens and Aegina and others whose task it was to guard the water.[2] The messengers said that there was nothing to be afraid of: Xerxes was not a god, just a man, and there had never been a man - nor would there ever be one - who

---

1   The Peloponnese is the southern 'half' of Greece, below the isthmus of Corinth. Boeotia is north of that, above Attica where Athens was, and would be first overrun if the Greeks lose the Battle of Thermopylae.

2   Simultaneous to the Battle of Thermopylae was the naval battle at the Straits of Artemisium which had the same strategy in place of blocking the Persian navy. The allied Greeks fought bravely and had some luck with a significant component of the Persian navy being destroyed by stormy weather, but once they heard about the defeat at Thermopylae they retreated to Salamis. There was no point in controlling the sea if they lost the land.

could avoid bad luck forever. The bigger the man the greater the chance for misfortune. Hearing this, the Locrians and the Phocians gave their support to the men at Trachis.

[204] There were plenty of leaders present at Thermopylae, commanders from each city, but the one who was most respected and was leading the alliance was the Spartan leader Leonidas. He could trace his lineage back to Heracles through his father Anaxandrides, son of Leon, son of Eurycratides, son of Anaxander, son of Eurycrates, son of Polydoros, son of Alcamenes, son of Teleclos, son of Archelaos, son of Hegesilaos, son of Doryssos, son of Leobotes, son of Echestratos, son of Agis, son of Eurysthenes, son of Aristodemos, son of Aristomachos, son of Cleodaios, son of Hyllos, son of Heracles.

Fig. 98: The Spartan Mother by Louis-Jean-François Lagrenée.
Spartans were supposed to return from battle with their shields or
on them (dead); that is, it was shameful to retreat.
(The National Trust, Stourhead; 1770)

[205] Leonidas' rule was surprising and unplanned because he had two older brothers, Cleomenes and Dorieus. Cleomenes had died with no male heir and Dorieus had fought and died in Sicily, so the throne passed to Leonidas. He was older than Cleombrotus, his father's youngest son and was married to Cleomenes' daughter.[3]

Fig. 99: Statue of a hoplite known as Leonidas, found in the Sparta (Archaeological Museum of Sparta; 5th century BC)

He had hand-picked the 300 men whom he had taken to Thermopylae, all men with sons.[4] He also took with him the Thebans I mentioned above in the count, who were led by Leontiades, son of Eurymachus. Leonidas was keen to take the Thebans with him out of all the Greeks because they'd been accused of sympathizing with the Persians, so he called on them to join him to determine whether they would even send troops or whether they would plainly declare their allegiance to the Persians. They sent troops but had ulterior motives.[5]

---

3   Yes, his niece.

4   This way if the soldiers died, they would have heirs.

5   Leonidas suffers no apparent negative consequences from this decision

[206] Leonidas and his 300 troops had been sent out from Sparta as an advanced guard. They meant to put on a show, demonstrating to the other Greeks that they were ready for a fight and dissuading them from flipping over to the Persians. The plan was to send more troops after the Carneia festival (which they had to respect) leaving behind in Sparta only a small force for defensive purposes.[6] The other cities had the same plan, since the Olympic festival was taking place at the same time. They had not anticipated that the battle at Thermopylae would be over so quickly, hence why they only sent these small advance forces at first.

XERXES AND THE PERSIAN HORDES

[207] Such were their intentions. But the Greeks who were already at Thermopylae were terrified when they saw the Persian army approaching the pass and considered whether they should retreat. The Peloponessian cities felt that they should retreat to the isthmus and defend that position.[7] The Phocians and Locrians were holding firm to this decision, but Leonidas argued that they should stay and send word to a few of the city states to send more support because their existing force would not be able to resist the Persians.

[208] While the Greeks debated, Xerxes ordered a scout on horseback to see how many soldiers the Greeks had and how they were preparing. When he was in Thessaly, Xerxes had heard that the Greeks were holding this position with a small contingent led by the Spartans and their king Leonidas, descended from Heracles. When the scout reached the Greek

---

though it did not seem a good strategic move.

6   The Carneia festival is the reason the Spartans only sent 300 troops instead of their full force to Thermopylae. It was an agricultural and military festival dedicated to Apollo that took place for a week each August, and during that time, all military activity was supposed to stop.

7   The isthmus referred to here connects the Peloponnese to the rest of Greece. The city of Corinth sits just south of the isthmus as the gateway to the region. Not all of the Greek allies lived south of the isthmus, so if they went through with this strategy, it would allow the Persians to destroy Thebes, Eretria, Athens and a number of other cities.

camp, he could not find a position to see the full force and could only see those on top of a fortification that the Greeks had repaired and those who were on guard outside the wall. By chance at that moment, it was Spartans who were outside the wall, and they were practicing sports and combing their long hair. The scout watched all this with amazement, took the best count he could, and then rode back to the Persian camp unbothered by the Greek force who seemed completely disinterested in his presence. He reported everything he had seen to Xerxes.

Fig. 100: Young Spartans Exercising by Edgar Degas
(National Gallery, London; ca. 1860)

[209] When he heard the scout's report, Xerxes could not make sense of it. The Spartans were actually getting ready to kill their enemy and die if necessary, but to Xerxes it sounded bizarre, so he summoned Demaratos, son of Ariston, from the Persian camp. Xerxes questioned Demaratos repeatedly about what the scout had seen, trying to explain their behavior. Demaratos said, "I told you about the customs of my people back then, when you initiated the war against the Greeks, and at the time you made fun of me, even though I tried to warn you what would happen. I have only ever strived to give you the full truth, Great King. So hear me when I say this, the Greek soldiers intend to fight for the pass - that is what they are get-

ting ready for. By their customs whenever they are in danger for their lives, they tend to their hair. If you are able to defeat these soldiers and the remaining Spartan soldiers left behind in their city, no other group will fight you or dare to take up arms to defend against you, O King. Your army is facing off against the best city in all of Greece and their best fighters." Xerxes thought this was absurd and asked yet again how so few would actually try to fight against his forces. Demaratos replied, "Great King, if in the end my words ring false, punish my lies!" Xerxes still did not believe Demaratos and so he waited four days to see if the Greeks would flee.

SPARTANS HOLD THE PASS

[210] On the fifth day when Xerxes saw that they persisted in their stubbornness, determination, and foolishness (so he thought), he angrily ordered the Medes and the Kissians to charge into battle, take the Greek soldiers as prisoners, and deliver them to him.[8] The Medes kept pressing the assault against the Greeks but they took heavy losses, wave after wave, and did not retreat. But it was clear to everyone, especially to Xerxes, that many enlisted soldiers could be beaten by a few well-trained men. They fought throughout the day like this.

[211] The Medes were being badly beaten and finally retreated to be replaced by a Persian contingent called "The Immortals" with Hydarnes as their commander. They attacked, assuming they would make better progress, but they won no more than the Medes. They were fighting in too narrow of a place with shorter spears than the Greeks and thus were not able to utilize their strength in numbers. The Spartans truly put on display their superiority and training against men who were untrained. They would even make a ruse of turning tail and pretending to retreat to draw the Barbarians[9] into an excited

---

8   The Medes and Cissians are both ethnic groups living within the larger Persian Empire. The Medes were actually the previous rulers of the area, and it was Cyrus the Great's defeat of the Medes that gave rise to the Persian Empire.

9   The Greek enemy is variously called Persian, Mede, and Barbarian in the

chase with yelling and banging of their weapons, only to circle around and cut them down in massive numbers. A few Spartans did lose their lives. The Persians had gained no ground at all by attacking the pass with their various armies and strategies and so they retreated back to their camp.

Fig. 101: Corinthian style helmet found at Sparta
(British Museum; ca. 550-500 BC)

[212] While the Persian army had been attacking the Greeks, it is recorded that Xerxes jumped out of his chair three times dreading the losses. The next day, the Barbarians gave the same effort and got the same results, for the Persian soldiers expected the Greeks to fail eventually since their forces were so small. The Greeks, though, were well ordered in their ranks, by city, and they took turns fighting. The Phocians guarded the path through the mountains in the meantime. Again the Persians retired at the end of the day, just as the day before, without any gains.

---

text. The latter term refers to those that do not speak Greek (it sounded to them like "bar bar bar") but also emphasizes that they are not citizens of city-states.

TREASON OF EPHIALTES

[213] Once Xerxes was at a loss as to what to do next, a Malian[10] man named Ephialtes, the son of Eurydemos, went to talk to Xerxes in hopes of great riches from the king in exchange for his information. He told the king he knew of a path through the mountains that would loop around to Thermopylae, which would thus mean the end for the defending Greeks. Later, Ephialtes took off to Thessaly for fear of retribution by the Spartans and indeed when the Amphictyons assembled at Pylaea the leaders put a price on his head.[11] He was eventually killed in Antikyra by Athenades from Trachis. Actually Athenades killed him for another reason entirely - I'll get to that later in my history - but the Spartans still honored Athenades for his action.[12]

[214] Indeed, Ephialtes was killed after the events at Thermopylae but there is an alternate version of the story in which Onetes, the son of Phanagoras, from Carystos and Corydallos from Antikyra were the ones who taught the Persians about the mountain path, but I do not accept this version. The first piece of evidence against this version is that the leaders of the Amphictyon did not put a price on the heads of Onetes and Corydallos but instead on that of Ephialtes the Trachinian,[13] and they must have had the best information at the time. Second, why else would Ephialtes have fled his native lands to avoid punishment? Sure, Onetes may have known the secret path, despite not being a Malian, if he had spent much time there. But Ephialtes was the one who showed the Persians the path himself and so I find him guilty of the treacherous act.

[215] Xerxes was glad to hear Ephialtes' information and

10 No, he's not from the country of Mali. Malis was a region near Thermopylae, and thus the Malians knew the area well.

11 Amphictyons were assemblies of groups of city-states who had a common purpose and arranged for common trading, religious practice and defense.

12 Herodotus never gets back to the fate of Ephialtes in his *Histories*.

13 Trachis is the main city in Malis, so Ephialtes is both Malian and Trachinian.

sent Hydarnes and his men out of the camp at around the time the lamps were being lit. The mountain pass in question was known to the Malians who live in that area and in the distant past they had led the Thessalians through the path to fight the Phocians. So, the Phocians had fortified the path with a wall to reduce the risk of an attack. The Malians had long since ignored the path which takes the following route: [216] it starts at the river Asopos, goes through the ravine, along the ridge of the mountain and then finishes in Alpenos, at the stone referred to as Black Butt and where the Cercopes[14] are from. Alepnos is the nearest Locrian town to the Malians. The name of the mountain and the path is the same: Anopaia.

[217] As the night stretched on, the Persians crossed the Asopos and followed the path, staying between the mountains of the Oitaians on the right and the Trachinians on the left. At dawn, they reached the bottom of the mountain Anopaia. You may recall that the path was guarded by a thousand Phocian hoplites, who were also thus defending their homeland. So whereas the other Greeks guarded the pass below, the Phocians guarded the mountain path, which they had volunteered to do for Leonidas.

[218] The Persian troops were invisible to the Phocians as they climbed the mountain with its oak-tree forests. The Phocians eventually heard the Persian troops coming because it was a quiet day and the Persians made a good amount of noise rustling through the leaves under their feet. So the Phocians jumped to attention, grabbing their weapons, but the Persians were on them quickly. The Persian soldiers, for their part, were surprised to find the Phocians arming themselves because they were not expecting to find anyone guarding the path, and now they were facing an army. Hydarnes was worried that the Phocians were Spartans but when he asked Ephialtes to which city-state these troops belonged and heard they were Phocians, he lined his men up for battle. The Phocians, under a barrage of

---

14 Within Greek mythology, the Cercopes were a couple of jokester thieves. Heracles once trapped them, but found their jokes so funny, he just let them go. Later, they offended Zeus and he turned them into monkeys.

arrows, retreated up into the mountain ready to face their fate, assuming that the Persians would chase them. Hydarnes, Ephialtes, and the Persian army completely ignored the Phocians and kept going down the mountain as quickly as possible.

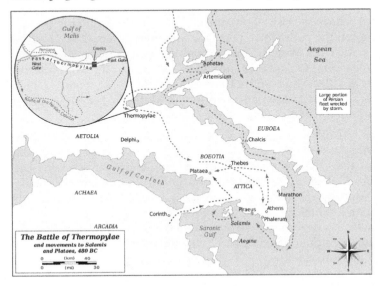

Fig. 102: Map of the Battle of Thermopylae (480 BC)

LEONIDAS' LAST STAND

[219] Meanwhile amongst the soldiers stationed down at Thermopylae, the soothsayer Megistias was reporting that he had analyzed the victims of the sacrifice[15] and that death would meet them at dawn. Soon after that, while it was still dark, Phocian defectors arrived with news that the Persians had taken the path around. Lastly, a third report came from the day watchmen, having come down from their posts in the mountains once the sun arose. At the news, the Greeks debated and

---

15 Seers, soothsayers, prophets, and oracles were all religious people who predicted the future or divined the will of the gods. They did this in a variety of ways, many of which involved interpreting natural phenomena. Readings the innards of a sacrificed animal was one of those strategies.

were of two minds as to how to proceed. Some felt that they should do their duty and fight to the end but others disagreed. Their assembly broke up and some city-states left with their troops, but the rest stayed to fight with Leonidas.

[220] Others say that Leonidas sent the other Greeks away out of concern for their lives. But Leonidas knew his duty and that the Spartans themselves had arrived first and it would be unbecoming of them to leave. I believe this second version of events, that Leonidas could sense that his allies could not muster the courage to face the battle until the very end and so he encouraged them to leave, but kept the Spartans there so that he would not degrade the Spartan reputation. On the other hand, Leonidas knew that if they stayed, he would achieve renown, and Sparta would not be destroyed. When the Spartans had asked the Pythian prophetess[16] of Sparta about the war when it first started, her oracle reported that either the Spartans would be crushed by the Persians or the Spartan king would die. She had given this oracle in the following verse:

> Oh ye men who reside in wide-open Sparta,
> Either the children of Perseus shall sack your remarkable city,
> Or, if that does not come to pass, then Heracles' descendent
> Shall die and all of Sparta shall lament;
> Neither raging bull nor mighty lion stays him
> Who has the force of Zeus and can't be stopped
> Until one of these is dispatched.

So I believe that Leonidas sent the other Greeks away to achieve fame for himself beyond all other Spartans, and not that the other Greeks left erratically because of a difference of opinion on strategy. [221] This proves it for me: Leonidas is said to have tried to send away the soothsayer Megistias the Acarnanian, a descendent of Melampus, so that he wouldn't be killed with the rest, after he had predicted future events from the sacrificial victim. Megistias would not leave, though he did send home his son, a soldier in the army, his only heir.

[222] The Greek allies of the Spartans all left, heeding Leo-

---

16 The "Pythian prophetess" was also known as the "Oracle of Delphi." She was known as the Pythia, because Delphi is where Apollo slew the Python, which had chased his mother since the time of his conception.

nidas' command, but the Thebans and Thespians stayed back. The Thebans stayed not out of choice but because Leonidas kept them as hostages. The Thespians stayed voluntarily, saying that they could not abandon Leonidas and the Spartans, so they stayed behind and died with them under the leadership of Demophilos, son of Diadromes.[17]

[223] In the morning, Xerxes made libations to the sun and then waited to attack until the time of day when the marketplace normally fills up. Ephialtes had recommended that timing because the descent down from the mountain was shorter and faster than the climb.[18] The Persians began their attack, and the Greeks under Leonidas, anticipating death, marched out into the wider portion of the field, further than they had previously while defending the wall, when they kept to the narrowest part of the pass. Now the Greeks were fighting out in the open, massacring many Persians who were being whipped from behind by the leaders of each division, pushing them forward. Many Persians were herded right into the sea to their death and even more were crushed alive by the stampede of their comrades, to the point where the losses were innumerable. The Spartans expected that death was coming from the mountain path so they fought against the Persians with peak performance of strength and bravery, oblivious to risk and incredibly daring.

[224] At this point in the battle, many of the Spartans had broken their spears on the enemy and were cutting down Persians with their swords. In the fray, Leonidas died, having proven his grit, along with many other Spartans whose names I rightly know for their bravery. In fact, I have studied all three-hundred names. Some famous Persians died that day as well, including two sons of Darius, brothers of Xerxes, Habrocomes and Hyperanthes, born to Darius by Phratagune the daughter of Artanes. Artanes was Darius' brother and Hystaspes' son, who was the son of Arsames. When Artanes

---

17 Sorry for the spoiler, but it is in the original text.

18 In other words, Xerxes was trying to time his attack to match up roughly with the appearance of the troops who had taken the path through the mountains.

Persian Median Elamite Parthian Arian Bactrian Sogdian Choresmian Zarangian Arachosian Sattagydian Gandharan Hindush Saka haumavarga

Saka tigraxauda Babylonian Assyrian Arab Egyptian Armenian Cappadocian Lydian Ionian Ovrnwn Saka Skudrian Ionian Libyan Ethiopian
with shield-hat

Fig.103: A section of Xerxes I's tomb showing soldiers from various ethnicities, representing the massive size of the Persian Empire (Naqsh-e Rostam; ca. 465 BC)

gave Phratagune, his only child, to Darius, it was his whole livelihood.[19]

[225] There was a fight over Leonidas' corpse between the Persians and the Spartans, but the Spartans drove back the Persians four times, eventually pulling Leonidas' body away. [20]They continued this way until the Persian men with Ephialtes arrived, which caused the Greeks to retreat back into the narrow part of the pass, back behind the wall, all together (except for the Thebans) on a hill. On this hill now stands a statue of a lion to honor Leonidas. The group enmassed on the hill fought with everything they had - daggers, hands, teeth - until they were overpowered by arrows. Some of the Barbarians had chased them through the wall and destroyed it and others had moved in and surrounded them.

[226] This is how the Spartans and Thespians affirmed their heroism, although one Spartan in particular demonstrat-

---

19 Apparently both Leonidas and Xerxes had kids with their nieces.

20 This scene is reminiscent of a scene in the *Iliad* in which the Greeks and Trojans fight over the body of Patroclus, Achilles' close friend (and possible lover), who went into battle wearing Achilles armor, fought bravely, but was killed by Hector. Patroclus' body was fought over, with Achilles finally reclaiming it. Unfortunately, after the battle, Xerxes ordered Leonidas' head to be removed and put on a stake, a decision that signified to Herodotus Xerxes' extreme hatred of Leonidas.

171

ed his singular valor. Dienekes was his name and they say that before the battle with the Persians one of the Greek soldiers of Trachis noted that when the Barbarians shot their arrows, the volley was so thick it blocked the light from the sun, but Dienekes, not overwhelmed by the size of the Persian contingent, said "Excellent, then our battle will be fought in the shade!" This comment, among other quips, help us remember the glory of Dienekes the Spartan.[21]

Fig. 104: Leonidas at Thermopylae by Jacques-Louis David
(Louvre Museum ; 1814)

[227] After Dienekes, two brothers Alpheos and Maron, sons of Orsiphantos, were most courageous among the Spartans. Amongst the Thespians it was Dithyrambos, son of Marmatides, who found the most fame. [228] All the men who died during the battle were buried on site. For these men and for those who fell before the majority of the Greek army was sent away by Leonidas, a monument was raised with the following inscription:

---

21 Unfortunately, we will never know what other great jokes we have missed.

> *On this spot, a mere four thousand Peloponnesians did endure*
> *an enemy force three million strong.*[22]

That inscription honored the full force, but the Spartans received a special epitaph:

> *He who reads this inscription, pray tell the Spartans: we who*
> *are buried here maintained our code.*

> That's the testament to the Spartan dead, and specifically for
> the soothsayer it read:

> *Here lies famous Megistias, killed by the Persians on the banks*
> *of the Sperichos. He knew death was his fate but did not aban-*
> *don his comrades.*

The Amphictyons were the ones who set up the monument on the hill, but the one for Megistias was arranged by Simonides, son of Leoprepes, based on their friendship.

The Rest of the Story

For readers curious about how the Greco-Persian Wars ended: After Thermopylae the Persian army burned down Athens and conquered most of northern Greece. As they invaded south, though, they lost a major naval engagement at the Battle of Salamis, which allowed the Greeks to maintain control of the Peloponnese and have a little breathing room to regroup. Most of the Persian army retreated but a smaller force was defeated by the Greeks at the Battle of Plataea, which was the end of the Persian invasion. Over the next few decades, the Greeks from the mainland were able to assist the Ionian Greeks out of Persian rule. About a century later, Alexander the Great would get revenge on the Persians by defeating the Persian hosts on their own turf and taking over their empire.

---

22 We do not know how reliable Herodotus' reports of army sizes were, although here was clearly closer to the real number of Greeks, even though another ancient writer reported a slightly larger Greek contingent. The Persian army was undoubtedly not 'three million strong'. Modern estimates are between 120,000 and 300,000, still one of the largest armies assembled to that date in history, perhaps the largest.

CHAPTER IV

Rome's Earliest Days

When we think of Roman history today, we imagine an empire stretching across the Mediterranean, from the modern countries of Britain to Egypt, from Morocco to Azerbaijan. We imagine big marble buildings and arches, statues, roads, bridges, a strong military tradition, and a culturally and linguistically diverse set of citizens. Despite the fact that Rome was destined for glory, it did not start out that way, of course. Rome began as a small settlement in central Italy along the banks of the Tiber River. There is actually evidence for settlement in this area of the world, and specifically within the Roman city, from approximately 14,000 years ago. From about 1000 BC, settlers we call the Latins, lived in Rome and they did have diverse backgrounds as we can see from burial techniques and approaches to pottery. Rome itself was a great place for a city: it had a river with an island that would make it easier to cross. It had seven hills that could be used for defensive purposes, and it offered relatively good agricultural resources. At the time of Rome's "founding" there were many other similar settlements in the area, including some belonging to the Etruscans, a reasonably powerful and culturally rich civilization.

*Fig. 105: Map of Italy showing the expansion of Roman power
during the Monarchy and Early Republic*

The Roman Monarchy

The earliest period of Rome's history is called the Monarchy because, according to tradition, Rome was led at first by seven kings who reigned from approximately 753 BC through 509 BC including the first king, Romulus, the city's eponymous founder. Take these dates with a grain of salt, as various ancient authors date Rome's founding variously from the late 9th century into the middle of the 8th Century. We do have archaeological evidence of fortifications on the north slope of the Palatine Hill dating to the middle of the 8th Century BC, but we also know that people had been living there before. Livy himself recognized that the events he was recounting from this period were too distant to fixate on historical accuracy and acknowledge a poetic nature to his writing.

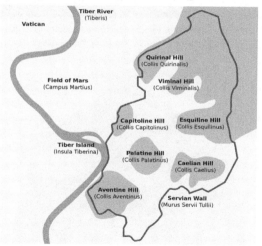

Fig. 106: The Seven Hills of Rome. The line around the hills represents the Servian Wall, an early 4th Century BC defensive construction.

During this period, elected kings ruled Rome and were invested with the highest level of executive, religious, judicial, and military power for life. The first king was Romulus (we'll read about him below), and then six more including Numa Pompillius and the final king Tarquinius the Proud. These kings

177

Fig. 107: Archaeological remains of the so-called hut of Romulus on the Palatine Hill (Rome, Italy; 8th century BC)

Fig. 108: Iron Age house-shaped funerary urns like this give a sense for what the hut of Romulus may have looked like (Walters Art Museum; 8th century BC)

(supposedly) created and embodied various areas of Roman culture that would be natural to Roman leaders for the next few centuries: warfare and expansion, religious institutions, economic growth, political developments, and defense, just to name a few. Most were said to have helped Rome gain control over their region of central Italy, Latium. Many of the institutions that Rome held dear, like the division between *patrician* and plebeian, the senate (albeit in weakened form at this time), religious ceremonies, and the 12-month calendar are attributed to this period. A number of building projects like the Temple of Jupiter on the Capitoline, aqueducts, and the Cloaca Maxima, a massive sewer system to drain the swampy area that would become the forum, are also said to have been initiated during this time. In Livy's account, the Monarchy is said to have ended when the final king, Tarquinius the Proud, raped a noble woman and was overthrown and exiled by a group of *patrician* men, including Lucius Junius Brutus (the ancestor of Marcus Junius Brutus, who participated in the assassination of Julius Caesar).

The Roman Republic

What the Romans established in its place was the Republic, which, as a form of government, would last for the next approximately 500 years. During this period, Rome would go from a city of seven hills along the Tiber to a vast empire, the dominant force in the Mediterranean. Instead of a king, the Republic created a system of representative government, we might even call it a representative democracy. The new head of state would be called the *consul*, but actually there would be two at the same time. *Consuls* held similar powers as the elected kings but were only elected for one year, and they provided a check on each other since both had veto power. Over time, other government officials were created that continued to diminish consular power, such as the censor, the *praetor* and the *pontifex maximus* who controlled the appointment of magistrates, the chief judicial responsibilities, and religious high office, respectively.

The senate is the most famous of the elements of the

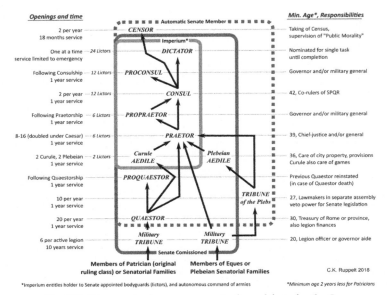

Fig. 109: Diagram to showcase career paths and facts for the Cursus honorum in the time of Caesar's career (1st century BC)

Roman constitution from the Republic and was composed of landed aristocrats. The senate could not technically pass binding legislation, but because of the respect and esteem that people had for the senate, they were very powerful and also controlled budgetary and military affairs. They would issue advisory decrees to the *consuls* and other magistrates, with a special focus on foreign policy (very important during these years of massive growth). There were various other legislative assemblies, committees, and councils, as well as a slew of magistrates controlling everything from the census to diplomacy, and others who would manage Rome's provinces as it began to grow.

The basic political unit in Rome was the citizen. The Roman citizen was afforded the right to conduct business with contracts, marry, vote and thus elect their assemblies. But, right from the beginning, there was class conflict and social inequality, including a division between *patricians* and *plebeians*. *Patricians* were aristocrats who could trace their family lineage back to the time of the founding of Rome. This group had higher status and originally held all of the magistracies. Below we will read in Livy's account that he created a senate of 100 men and that these became *patricians*. Yet most of the population was composed of *plebs* or *plebeians*. The *plebeians* gained political ground in the 4th century BC and were able to achieve nominal political equality with the *patricians* through a series of social struggles including various secessions during which they would withdraw their labor. They gained access to written laws and the political process, including an elected representative called a tribune who could veto senatorial decisions and who was protected from harm by law. Later they were able to make binding legislation and control important elected positions. The importance of the division between the classes waned toward the end of the Republic, especially since many *plebs* were gaining vast family fortunes.

Fig. 110: The Roman Senate by Cesare Maccari
(Palazzo Madama; 1899)

Roman Expansion through the Punic Wars

The history of the Roman Republic is rife with warfare and expansion. We will look here at the period from the end of the Monarchy (ending in 509 BC) through the Punic Wars (264-146 BC). We hardly have space for a brief summary of these events, nevermind a battle-by-battle retelling. The important thing to understand is that Rome kept the war machine going, and even though they sometimes suffered considerable losses, they were able to innovate and conscript their way to victory.

During the Monarchy (and even during Romulus' reign as we will read below), the Roman state (just a large town at the time) started beating, annexing, and unifying some of the other small towns in Latium. Over the course of the next approximately 100 years, the Romans fought a people called the Samnites, who controlled other parts of central Italy, until finally subjugating them by 290 BC. The Roman city was sacked in 387 BC by an incursion of the Gauls but despite this, the Romans rallied and defended themselves successfully. The last hold out in their control of Italy was the city Tarentum, which was receiving support from Pyrrhus of Epirus in the east, which again provided the Romans with some setbacks which were again temporary. Rome held the entirety of the Italian peninsula by 218 BC.

The major and most famous set of wars that took place during this period were the Punic Wars, which started in 264 BC and lasted, on and off, until 146 BC. As Rome conquered the Italian peninsula, the closest rival power was that of Carthage, located in modern Tunisia in Northern Africa. Carthage was a significant regional power and had a sphere of influence that included Sicily, southern Spain, and most of North Africa. The First Punic War (264-241 BC) started when Rome intervened in Sicily in a dispute between Carthage and its former allies on the island. This gave Rome the excuse to violate an existing treaty with Carthage. The Romans realized they could not win the war on land, given that they were fighting on an island against a power located across the Mediterranean and so they built a large navy from scratch in a short period of time, modifying the ships to suit their advantages.

The First Punic War lasted 23 years after much back and forth, especially at sea, and the resulting treaty was very harsh on Carthage, which led to the Second Punic War (218-201 BC). The Carthaginians wanted to make up for their loss of Sicily by expanding into Spain and it was then that Hannibal decided to cross by land from Carthage into Italy, losing most of his elephants and approximately half his army while crossing the Alps. Hannibal was a cunning commander and won a series of pitched battles against Roman armies, including the Battle of Cannae (216 BC), which was the deadliest in Roman history in which the Romans lost about 60,000 men. However, the Romans soon adopted a new policy in which they would simply not engage Hannibal, basically waiting him out, which eventually worked and the Romans applied an even stricter penalty on Carthage in the second treaty.

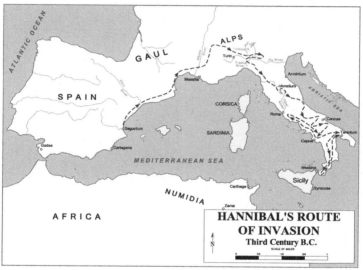

Fig. 111: Hannibal's route of invasion across the Alps and into Italy (3rd century BC)

During the Third Punic War (149-146 BC), the Romans found an excuse to go to Carthage and lay siege to the city. They said that if the Carthaginians opened their gates and gave up their weapons, they'd let them peacefully surrender. But when Carthage did just that, laying down their arms, Rome burned the now-defenseless city to the ground. They then salted to the earth, just to make sure nothing would ever grow there again. Soon, however, they established a Roman colony nearby that would be the capital of its new province.

183

Meanwhile, the Romans were winning further territorial wars in the east, in Macedonia, and against the Seleucid Empire, which controlled much of the empire conquered by Alexander the Great. And Greece was eventually made a Roman province in 146 BC. Thus, by that year, Rome controlled a significant portion of the Mediterranean basin, becoming the most powerful actor in the region and setting itself up for future expansion. Some scholars believe that the model of the empire, with its rapid expansion of land and labor force, negatively affected social cohesion and order. Regardless of the causes, a series of civil wars were on the horizon.

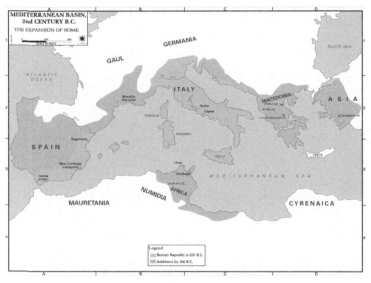

Fig. 112: Map of Roman territory during the 2nd century BC

Roman Social and Economic Life

While the citizen was the basic unit of political life, the *pater familias* was the basic unit of social and economic life. The *pater familias* is the oldest male of a citizen family and had full authority within his own family and household, even including the authority to execute family members if needed. He

184

was responsible for making sure that his family upheld Roman law and Roman moral codes as well as carrying out important family religious ceremonies, such as maintaining rites for the ancestors of his own family. The *pater familias* had ultimate control over his wife (who was generally required to have a male attendant in public) and could decide whether to expose his children, ie. leave them to die after birth if they were deformed, not the right gender, or simply one-too-many. Children were expected to have respect for their elders and execute their duties.

Roman families, especially *patrician* and other rich families, would have many connections to other citizens and non-citizens who would be associated with their family. This included friendships and alliances between the *pater familias*, acting as patron, and a slew of men, called clients. The clients would support the patron by attending him around the city, fighting alongside him if called to war, and voting as a block. The patron would offer protection and sponsorship for clients, who might even be of the same rank in society, but who would be less wealthy or less powerful. Especially as Roman power and influence grew, and territories were conquered, many wealthy families owned slaves. The Roman slave system was not built on race, but rather on power and status. Roman slaves performed a great variety of duties, from tending to the entire house (like in a middle class family who owned only one slave) to things as specialized as folding clothing.

The Roman economy was powered by agriculture, in particular the growing of various grains. This was the main business of the Roman elite, who built up massive estates reliant on slave labor (slaves are estimated to have been about 35% of the population in Italy in the 1st century AD). Agriculture, however, was also the job of most of the lower classes of Roman society, especially in the countryside. In both cases, good years could lead to surpluses but ancient farming, just like modern farming, could be risky business year-to-year. Farms would grow grains like millet, emmer, and spelt (all varieties of wheat); legumes such as lentils, peas, and beans; cash crops like olives or grapes for wine; and of course a variety of fruits, vegetables, and spices. There were also of course plenty of other jobs like fishing, merchant, smith, builders, entertainers, and clothing makers.

*Fig. 113: The Aqua Claudia aqueduct south of Rome
(1st century AD)*

Romans throughout the lands of the Republic were taxed, whether for money or grain, on various activities, including land taxes, poll taxes, customs and trade taxes, inheritance, and a variety of others. The Roman state used this money primarily to fund its military operations but also to improve its empire through investment in economic infrastructure like ports, roads, and aqueducts, which strengthened trade and intensified agriculture. Goods, such as clothing, wine, grain, metal, glassware, pottery, papyrus, and timber flowed from one end of the Mediterranean to the other, and even beyond that: Roman artifacts have been found as far away as India and China. All of this economic strength allowed the Roman state to experience per capita economic growth, highly unusual for any society before the Industrial Revolution.

Roman Religion

The Romans practiced a polytheistic religion which combined local deities, family spirits, imported gods from various parts of the empire, and the major gods that we associate with Rome such as Jupiter, Mars, Mercury, and Minerva. The Romans considered themselves very pious and viewed their piety as a major factor in their success. But Roman religion was not based on beliefs or even really ethics in the modern sense. Rather, it centered on the practice of rites and rituals that had to be done properly. Vows should be worded properly, rites should be performed in the right order and in the right way, and sacrifices and other rituals could be performed to secure favor. This favor could be for anything we might pray for now (health, farm yield, money), but on the level of the state, it was often applied to military success.

The Roman calendar was packed with religious festivals which were celebrated with sacrifices, festivals, games, and feasts. Religious figures such as priests and augurs overlapped with magistrates in the sense that both were held by the elites. Roman religion, the Roman family, and the Roman state were intricately tied together, as opposed to our notion of a separation of church and state. For instance, the Vestal Virgins were a state-run cult of female priestesses who would maintain a hearth flame in Rome, which was the state's version of the same practice that would be done inside the household. Under the empire, the emperors themselves would be accepted into the pantheon of gods after their deaths.

Roman religion was influenced by its neighbors, first locally by the Etruscans and by the Greeks (who had a presence in Italy). Later, Roman religion would come to include the gods, cults, and religious practices from the vast reaches of the empire. The Roman Empire's general religious policy was inclusionary: they would accept and absorb external gods and practices into their society, rather than attempt to subjugate them, as long as local peoples were willing to honor the basic tenets of the state religion. But the Romans also spread their state religion throughout the territories, building temples and other religious structures in town centers around the empire. Cults from around the empire grew in popularity and spread, including the Bacchanalia from Greece and the cult of Isis from Egypt. There is even evidence for a Jewish synagogue in the main Roman port from around the 1st century BC. In a section of his *History of Rome*, Livy blames the losses at the beginning of the Punic Wars on the growth of cults, poor augury, and the increased rejection of the state gods.

It is in this context that Christianity grew within the empire, benefiting from the unity of the empire and its accepting

Fig. 114: Statue of the god Mithras; Mithraism was originally a derivative of the Persian religion of Zoroastrianism and was brought into the empire by the Roman army
(Louvre Museum; 2nd century AD)

policy of outside religion, including some others that preached the rejection of possession and a fixation on life after death. This is true despite the fact that the empire had made efforts to stamp out Christianity, since it appeared to the Romans as atheistic, and Christians refused to respect Roman state religion. Christians were frequently persecuted during the first few centuries of its growth, right up under the conversion of Constantine at the beginning of the 4th century AD. Christianity kept on growing and eventually became the state religion by AD 380 under the emperor Theodosius.

Livy's *History of Rome*

Livy (Titus Livius) was a Roman historian who lived from approximately 59 BC to AD 17. He is known for one major work, his *History of Rome*. His overall chronicle traced the rise of Rome from its very origins up until Livy's present day, including how it conquered Italy and eventually how it conquered the entire Mediterranean. He also describes Roman values and virtues that supported this growth. Below this introduction we've supplied our version of the first quarter of Book 1 which includes Livy's preface reflecting on his role as historian and on the history he has produced.

Fig. 115: Bronze bust of Livy (Titus Livius) by Andrea Riccio (National Museum of Warsaw; 15th century)

Livy was born and raised in a town called Patavium in northern Italy, which was known for its conservative values. He lived and was writing at a time of incredible tumult. The period right before Livy's birth had been filled with slave uprisings and wars with Rome's former Italian allies who were pushing for citizenship (eventually granted to all of Italy in 87 BC). Livy would have been a young man, likely about 10 years old, in 49 BC when Julius Caesar invaded Rome after conquering Gaul (modern day France). The next two decades were filled with dictatorship under Caesar, his assassination, and then civil wars vying for control of Rome. He was writing his work just as Caesar's adopted son, Octavian (later called Augustus), had finished consolidating power and had become the first emperor of Rome. Livy started spending time in Rome in the 30s BC and eventually ended up on friendly terms with the emperor Augustus. Livy clearly had enough financial resources to dedicate much of his life to his writing and seems to have been able to avoid military service.

The scope and size of Livy's work, *History of Rome*, is significant. It was composed of 142 books, stretching from the early origins of Rome all the way up until 9 BC, Livy's present day. Only Books 1-10 and 21-45 survive, with some gaps in some of the later books due to missing pages in a manuscript. There are additional snippets and summaries, the latter of which may not be particularly reliable. Livy was widely read in ancient times and his works were complete and accessible for four or five hundred years after they were produced. Livy used various literary and historical sources for his history, including previous historians such as Polybius, Sallust, and a handful of others. He generally relied on one source per section, supplementing with others when available. He did not consult official documents or much physical evidence in producing his work.

Livy's own preface lays out some of the major themes of his work. Throughout, he emphasizes Rome's greatness and indeed that feeling would have been in the air in Rome during Livy's adulthood, as Augustus firmly held power, prevented civil war, and spent state resources on major public work projects, everything from infrastructure to temples to public art. Rome's past moral virtue, according to Livy, was crucial to its success. However, Livy clearly feels that by his present time, Roman virtue and morality had declined, and he felt that directly led to the wars and political tumult he had learned about or witnessed. At the same time, even in the selection we present below describing the first decades after Rome's founding, Livy's work is full of murder, thievery, warfare, tricks, rape, fratricide, and exposure of babies. While you are reading, see if you can figure out what Livy's means by morality and virtue. You will likely notice significant differences from our modern conceptions.

Other themes to consider as you read include historical fact combined with mythological origins, the role of the gods, gender norms, the cycle of peace and warfare, the importance of

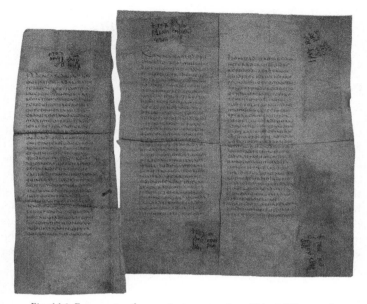

Fig. 116: Fragments of an ancient manuscript of Livy's History of
Rome *(Vatican Library; 5th century AD)*

religion, and what it means to be Roman. For instance, as you
will see, Livy admits right away that parts of his early books
may read more like poetry than history and he makes it clear
a few times that some of these stories may not be accurate but
that they are worth telling as tradition has passed them down.
Does it matter if the origin story of Rome includes both historical narrative and mythological elements? What does this mean
for the rest of the work, if anything?

The reader is advised that this section of Livy's *History
of Rome*, Book 1 contains acts of violence including scenes of
sexual violence.

Words of the Ancients
Livy's *History of Rome*
Book 1

PREFACE

[1] I am not certain whether I will be doing anything particularly beneficial or useful by laying out the history of the Roman people starting from the foundation of the city.[1] [2] It is common for historians to think that they are extracting new truths from old facts or that they can score style points over their predecessors. [3] Putting those considerations aside, I will feel fulfilled contributing a little bit to the story of my people, the best nation on earth. If my work fails to become famous and stand out among the many others who have covered the same topic, I'll at least take comfort in knowing that I have lost out to great competitors.

[4] The task at hand is a huge one. I will reach back 700 years into the past to our small beginnings. By the time we get to the modern age, our history is so expansive that it is hard to cover everything that is needed. Many readers may not even enjoy the earlier part of the account describing the beginnings of Rome and will want to speed read until they get to current events to understand how our system is now so self-defeating. [5] For me, writing about earlier times is relaxing and rewarding, since I am able to temporarily ignore and not be distracted by our current difficulties, even if in the end I must still tell the full truth.

[6] The stories we've inherited about the period before the city was built or even planned out are more like poetry than a true historical account, and so I will tell them without casting judgment. [7] Blending together the natural and the supernatural adds a level of dignity to the ancient past. If there are people who can claim a divine origin and godly blessings on their

---

1 Modern translations generally treat Livy's preface separately, so it has smaller numbered sections, whereas the rest of the Books are broken up into larger ones.

foundation, it should be the Romans. So when the Romans, so successful at war, say that Mars is their father and the father of their founder, their adversaries should accept that fact just like they must accept our rule.

*Fig. 117: Statue of Mars Ultor ("the Avenger") found in Rome
(Capitoline Museums; 2nd century AD)*

[8] Let's not worry too much about these small matters. [9] Instead, readers should pay serious attention to things like the types of lives our ancestors lived, how they expanded their empire (during peacetime and through war), and who was involved. They should consider how we declined morally, at first slowly, but then further and further until the present day when

we cannot face our wickedness nor handle the effort required to fix it. [10] A healthy and beneficial study of history allows us to analyze all the different ways we acted in lots of different scenarios, which then empowers us to duplicate the good things and to avoid the things which were deplorable in their design or in their outcome.

[11] It is possible I am biased, but I honestly think that compared to Rome, no country has been better, more moral, or offered more examples. Our history lasted a long time without wasteful opulence and greed. And for a long time we respected simple living [12] so that the less wealth we had, the less we desired it. Recently, new riches have led to more greed, and hedonism has made us self-destructive.

Such negativity is probably unwelcome, so let's hold off on more at least until we get through the beginning of this affair. [13] Instead, like the poets, let's start with prayer and good portents so that the gods will support this difficult endeavor.

BOOK 1

It is widely known that when the Greeks took Troy they showed cruelty toward the Trojans except toward Aeneas and Antenor. The Greek army went easy on Aeneas and Antenor because they had worked for peace and for the return of Helen, plus there were some long-held connections between them and the Greeks. After various adventures, Antenor joined forces with a group of Heneti who had been ousted from Paphlagonia and who had lost their king, Pylaemenes, in the Trojan War.[2] The Heneti were looking both for a leader and for a place to settle down. They arrived at a bay in the Adriatic Sea along the coast of Italy and drove out the Eugenei who lived between the sea and the Alps, taking possession of the land. This place where they settled they called Troy, the small region is called Trojan, and the greater region is called Veneti.[3]

---

2   The Heneti were a tribe from the region of Paphlagonia, located on the north coast of modern day Turkey.

3   This region of Italy is now called the Veneto, which is centered on the canal city of Venice.

*Fig. 118: Aeneas flees Troy with Anchises and Ascanius by Gian
Lorenzo Bernini (Galleria Borghese; 1618)*

AENEAS ARRIVES IN ITALY

It is also well known that Aeneas was driven out of his
homeland with similar difficulties, but fate would have him
found a great empire.[4] First, Aeneas landed in Macedonia and
sailed on to Sicily looking for a place to settle. From Sicily he
went to Laurentum. This place is similarly named Troy. When
the Trojans landed at Laurentum they had no possessions left
except weapons and ships, so they began to plunder the lands.
The original inhabitants and their king Latinus assembled an
army from their city and countryside to meet their new enemy.
There are two versions of the story at this point. In one, Aeneas
and the Trojan beat Latinus and his people in battle, and so

---

4   For the most complete account of Aeneas' journey from Troy to Italy,
     check out Virgil's *Aeneid*, commissioned by Augustus and published
     around the same time as Livy's *History of Rome*.

Latinus allied with Aeneas. In the other, the two sides lined up against each other for a pitched battle, but Latinus came forward to meet Aeneas in conversation, asking who they were, where they had come from, what had caused them to leave home, and why they had come to Laurentum. Latinus heard that the people were Trojans, that their leader was Aeneas, son of Anchises and Venus,[5] that they had left a burnt home and were looking for a place to build a new one. Upon hearing this, Latinus respected the high born origins of the people, their hero Aeneas, and their willingness to fight or find peace, so he offered Aeneas his hand as a future ally. Once their chiefs agreed, the Trojans and the locals acknowledged the accord. Latinus hosted Aeneas and gave him his daughter in marriage with his household gods as witnesses in order to seal the public agreement with a private one.

The Trojans had been wandering for a long time but this event solidified for them that they were now home. They built a town which Aeneas called Lavinium, named after his wife. Soon after that, Aeneas and Lavinia had a son, whom they named Ascanius.

[2] Later, the Trojans and the locals were attacked by Turnus, kind of the Rutulians. Turnus had been engaged to Lavinia before she had married Aeneas and Turnus was incensed that she'd been offered to a stranger over him. It did not end well for either side: the Rutilians were destroyed and the Trojans with their local allies suffered the loss of Latinus. Turnus and the Rutulians were weakened but fled to the sizable state of the Etruscans and their king Mezentius, who ruled the city of Caere,[6] which at that time was wealthy.[7] Right from the start,

---

5   Note that Aeneas is the son of the goddess Venus (Greek: Aphrodite). Later Roman leaders, like Caesar and Augustus, would not hesitate to highlight this divine lineage.

6   The Etruscan city of Caere is now called Cerveteri. It has some of the best preserved Etruscan tombs in all of Italy.

7   The Etruscans were a relatively powerful and advanced people controlling a region north of Rome, including a number of the cities mentioned in this excerpt of Book 1. They were probably also fairly recent foreign settlers, perhaps from Asia Minor, perhaps descended from other local tribes.

Mezentius had been suspicious of the founding of the new city Lavinium and he realized that they were growing too quickly and threatening his own security, so he quickly joined forces with the Rutulians.

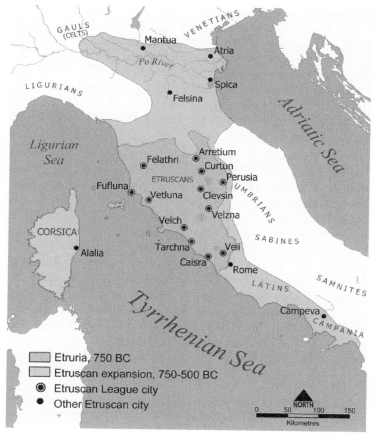

Fig. 119: Map of Etruria (ca. 750 - 500 BC)

Aeneas then made a move to ensure that the native people[8] would be ready to face the upcoming war. He gave the name

---

8   The "native" population here are the people fighting under king Latinus when Aeneas first landed in Italy. Now that Latinus is dead, the original population has joined forces with the Trojans.

of Latins to both people, the natives and Trojans combined. This way, they could have the same name and the same laws and customs and would grow stronger together. From then onwards, the natives matched the Trojans for their bravery and devotion to Aeneas. As the two grew closer each day, Aeneas led his forces onto the field, even though he could have gotten away with a defensive position. He did this despite the fact that the Etruscans were powerful and famous across Italy, from the Strait of Sicily to the Alps, for their military skill on land and by sea. This battle was the last living act of Aeneas and it was a victory for the Latins. Aeneas was laid to rest by the river Numicius and whether he was a man or a god, he is now called Jupiter Indiges.[9]

[3] Aeneas' son Ascanius was too young to rule so his mother Lavinia acted as regent and capably secured the kingdom of his father and grandfather.[10] But there is some doubt about whether this was the right Ascanius or whether it was actually an older one born back in Troy to Creusa and taken to Rome by Aeneas as he fled Troy (this is the same Ascanius who is nicknamed Iulus from whom the Julian family get their name).[11] The story is so old it is hard to be certain. Whichever Ascanius it was (Aeneas' son regardless), he eventually departed Lavinium since it was successful and bustling and left it in his mother's (or step-mother's) hands to found his own city in the Alban Hills. The town extended along a ridge and so was called Alba Longa. It was only about 30 years between the founding of Lavinium and the creation of Alba Longa, but

---

9 The "Indigenous" or "Native/local" Jupiter.

10 Remember that Lavinia was the daughter of Latinus who was ruling the area when Aeneas got there, so Livy is referring to him and Anchises here but then immediately muddies the waters.

11 Aeneas is often depicted carrying his father Anchises with his son Ascanius at his side. Such is the case in the *Aeneid*, the epic poem by Vergil describing Aeneas' flight from Troy and founding of Rome. A famous statue of this moment was sculpted by Bernini in the early 17th Century. Creusa was Aeneas' wife when he lived in Troy who died tragically as they were fleeing the city during its sack by the Greeks. The *gens Julia* (Julian Family) was at the time of Livy an ancient, rich and distinguished *patrician* family that included Caesar and then by adoption Augustus, the first emperor of Rome.

during that time, especially after defeating the Etruscans, Lavinium had become powerful enough that no one attacked it: not Mezentius nor the Etruscans nor any of their neighbors. This was true even right after Aeneas' death, during the regency of Lavinia and in the early years of the rule of young Ascanius.

BIRTH OF ROMULUS AND REMUS

There was a peace treaty between the Latins and Etruscans that set the Tiber River[12] (then called the Albula) as the boundary between the two. After Ascanius his son Sylvius, who was somehow or another born in the woods, succeeded to the throne.[13] He fathered Aeneas Sylvius who in turn fathered Latinus Sylvius who founded a number of colonies. From that point forward, all the rulers of Alba Longa took the name Sylvius. After Latinus, there was Alba, Alba fathered Atys. Atys begot Capys, from Capys came Capetus, and from him there was Tiberinus who drowned in the Albula River and gave it its now famous name. Next was Agrippa, Tiberinus' son, and after Agrippa, Romulus Silvius took the throne. He was killed by lightning strike and left the throne to Aventinus who gave his name to the hill in Rome on which he was buried.[14] Proca reigned after Aventinus and begot Numitor and Amulius. He gave the throne of the Sylvian family to Numitor, the eldest son, but Amulius forced him out and stole the throne, disrespecting his father's wishes and his brother's seniority. To further extend the list of his crimes, Amulius murdered Numitor's son and forced the daughter, Rhea Sylvia, to become a Vestal Virgin, undermining her ability to have any offspring.[15]

---

12 This is the river that still today flows through Rome.

13 *Sylva* is the Latin word for "woods". We use the word "sylvan" as an adjective meaning, "from or related to the woods."

14 Livy loves telling us the origins of place names. The Aventine Hill is Rome's southernmost, which ends up being associated with Remus. During the empire, the Aventine was a popular place to live for the richest of Rome's residents.

15 Vestal Virgins were a group of four to six priestesses that tended to the flame to Vesta (Greek: Hestia), the goddess of the hearth, located in the forum in Rome. They were young girls who had to take vows of chastity

[4] In my humble opinion, it was the Fates that led to the creation of our great city and to our empire, second only to the kingdom of the gods: The Vestal Virgin Rhea Silvia was raped and gave birth to twins. She claimed that Mars was the father; it is possible that she believed that, or it is possible that she felt she would feel less guilt by blaming a god.[16] But neither the gods nor men could protect the twins from the king's cruelty. He bound and jailed the mother and ordered that the boys be drowned in the river. As Fate would have it, the Tiber had flooded its embankments which made it difficult for Amulius' men to reach the river itself to drown the babies, so they put the babies in the flood water thinking that would suffice. This flood water location is where the Ruminal fig-tree (previously known as the fig-tree of Romulus) now stands. That location was unoccupied, wild land at that time.

Fig. 120: Marble statue of Rhea Silvia by Jacopo della Quercia (Santa Maria della Scala, Siena; 1414-19)

for the duration of their service, about 30 years from when they started as young girls.

16 Mars started as a local deity of plants and growing, but he ended up being associated with the Greek god of war, Ares. Moreover, the punishment for a Vestal Virgin breaking their vow of chastity was to be buried alive upside down. So there was a real incentive to put the blame on someone else, to say the least.

Tradition has it that when the flood water receded and the basket in which the children had lain hit a dry patch, a wolf came from the nearby mountains to drink, heard the babies crying, and allowed them to suckle at her breasts. The king's shepherd witnessed this scene. They say his name was Faustulus and that he carried the children home so his wife Laurentia could nurse them. It is also said that her name was Lupa among the other shepherds, since she was a common whore, and that explains the origin of this story.[17]

Fig. 121: The Capitoline Wolf (shown above) was originally thought to be Etruscan but now is dated to the medieval period (Capitoline Museums; 13th century AD with twins added in the 15th century)

That is the story of the twins' birth. Their upbringing involved not only working in the fields and taking care of the animals, but also hunting. So they grew strong enough to fend off wild animals as well as thieves, whose stolen goods they would later divide among the other shepherds. They made friends like this and kept up with their work and play.

---

17 In Latin, *Lupa* means both she-wolf and prostitute, thus the play on words. Which story seems more likely to you?

[5] Even that far back, the Palatine Hill (which derived its name from Palanteum, a city in Arcadia) hosted the Lupercalia festival.[18] Evander the Arcadian had held that territory in the past and had instituted the feast, with its young men running about naked causing mischief, in the honor of Pan Lycaeus (whom the Romans later called Inuus). During one particular festival, the thieves who were angry at losing their stolen goods set a trap for Romulus and Remus. Romulus defended himself and got away but they captured Remus. They brought Remus to King Amulius and accused him and his brother of assembling a pack of young men to raid Numitor's land. And so Remus was brought before Numitor for justice.[19]

Faustulus had always suspected that the boys he was raising were royalty. He knew that the king had ordered twins to be exposed and that he found them at about the same time as the decree. But he had not let anyone know this secret because the need had not yet arisen. Well the need had arisen, so he told Romulus the full story. With Remus in his custody, Numitor also started putting the story together too: he heard that the man he held was a twin, he figured out their age and he noticed that their spirits were not like lower class citizens, and so he began to think the twins might be his grandchildren. Romulus acted quickly. Realizing that he couldn't win an open-field battle, he told the shepherds to come by a different route and meet him at a set time. Remus fought with a group from inside the house, converged with Romulus's units and they killed King Amulius with this surprise attack.

[6] Before the battle, Numitor had recognized that the city had been invaded and the palace attacked ,and he had taken some of the Alban military to defend his fortress. Once he saw that Romulus and Remus were victorious and on their way

---

18 The *Lupercalia* was a festival that was celebrated annually on February 15. In it, young men, scantily clad if at all, ran around spanking women with pieces of goat leather.

19 Recall that Numitor is the brother of the current king, Amulius, who stole Numitor's throne, killed his son and made his daughter a vestal virgin but who apparently did not kill his brother and chief rival, a classic misstep.

to his fortress to congratulate him, he called a meeting of his people. There, he told his people about his brother's actions toward him, how he had taken and exposed his grandchildren, how they were born and raised, how their identity had been discovered, and how the king was dead by his command. When the twins came into the fortress and met the audience, they saluted their grandfather as king which was supported and confirmed with a shout from those assembled.

THE FOUNDING OF ROME

Once Alba Longa was held by Numitor, Romulus and Remus decided that they wanted to found their own city on the spot where they had been exposed and raised. There was an overpopulation of Albans and Latins, and the shepherds too would join them, so they imagined that their city would dwarf Alba and Lavinium. But their aspiration for power, which had also devastated their grandfather, would be their undoing. They began to argue. Since they were twins, neither had the seniority and so they left it to the gods to decide, through augury, who would rule the city they founded and whom it would be named after.[20] Romulus took up position on the Palatine Hill and Remus on the Aventine Hill to read the auspices.[21]

[7] They say that six vultures were seen by Remus first, and he sent a group to declare victory to Romulus who claimed to have seen twelve vultures afterwards. So one claimed the future city based on seeing the omen first and the other made his claim based on the number of birds. As their anger and jealousy turned to violence, Remus was struck and killed. It is more commonly reported that Remus jumped over the defensive wall of his brother's territory and that Romulus killed him for this offense, saying, "Any man who climbs the walls of my city shall

---

20 *Augury* is any practice with which you try to see the will or approval of the gods through some manifestation in the physical world. Its association with politics has crept into English through words like inauguration.

21 *Auspices* in Latin means the observance of birds but usually refers to diving the will of the gods and ends up being applied to observing other natural phenomena. The English word auspicious, meaning "favorable" derives from Latin.

suffer a similar fate." This is how Romulus came to rule the city by himself and when it was built, it bore his name.

Fig. 122: Etching of Romulus killing Remus by Giovanni Battista Fontana (British Museum; 1575)

As his first deed, he fortified the Palatine hill, where he had been raised. He made sacrifices to the gods: to the local gods according to the Alban rituals and to Hercules in the Greek way as started by Evander. The traditional story is that Hercules had come to this place after he killed Geryon, stole his cattle and herded them into the area.[22] He swam across the Tiber, the cattle in front of him, and weary from his trek he slept in some grasses along the banks of the river, while his cattle grazed.

A local shepherd named Cacus found Hercules asleep and full of food and drink. Coveting the attractive oxen and planning to steal them, he decided to pull the best of the cattle backward by their tails into his cave so that Hercules wouldn't be able to track their hoofprints.[23] Hercules woke up in the morn-

---

22 Retrieving the cattle of the three-headed giant Geryon was the 10th of Hercules' labors. Geryon lived in Erytheia, an island of the Hesperides, which (according to Greek mythology) lived in the very far reaches of the western Mediterranean - thus the need for Hercules to travel through Italy on his way back to Greece.

23 Truly a dumb plan. Did you not see the man's biceps? That said, Hercules

ing, studied his herd and noticed that there were some missing. He went immediately to the closest cave to see if their tracks would help him locate the cattle, but realized that the prints were facing out of the cave and in no other direction than from where he had come. So Hercules, confused, started to drive his cattle from the area. As they were departing, some of his cattle let out a low "moo", longing for their missing friends, and Hercules heard the missing cattle answering from inside the cave. Cacus attempted to stop Hercules through physical force and was killed with one blow from a club, even as he tried to get other shepherds to come to his aid.

Fig. 123: Hercules and Cacus by Henrik Goltzius
(Frans Hals Museum; 1613)

isn't known for his wit.

205

In those days Evander, having left the Peloponnese,[24] controlled the area through ability and influence rather than through force. He was respected for his ability to read which was a novel concept and unfamiliar to the uncultured, but even more so he was esteemed because his mother Camenta had been a divine character who was considered a prophet before the Sibyl was in Italy.

Evander saw the group of shepherds converging on the foreigner accusing him of murder and heard the story of what had happened and why. So he asked the foreigner his name, realizing that he was larger than life with a long stride. When Hercules responded with his name, that of his father, and his homeland, Evander said to him, "Greetings, Hercules, Jupiter's son. My mother, a prophet of the gods, foresaw that you would increase the number of our gods and that we would devote an altar in this location to you and in many generations from now it will be called the *Ara Maxima* (Greatest Altar) by the strongest people in the world." Hercules shook his hand and Evander proclaimed that he would follow through on the omen and the Fate's prediction. So he built and dedicated the altar. A sacrifice of a cow from the herd was offered to Hercules at this location for the first time.

The Potitti and the Pinarii, two nearby families who were the most famous families in the region, were invited to the ceremony and festival. The Potitti arrived on time and were served the entrails and the Pinarii arrived late after the entrails had been eaten. It was declared that from that time forward any subsequent Pinarii should not eat the entrails at a sacrifice.[25] On the other hand, the Potitti were given the honor by Evander of being priests at rituals for many generations forward, until their family died out once they had authorized public slaves to handle the responsibilities. This was the only foreign ritual that Romulus accepted into Rome's traditions, since he believed that immortality should be earned through deeds, something he was well on his way toward achieving.

---

24 The lower part of the mainland of Greece.

25 This may not sound like a punishment, but people did consume (and still do) these parts of the animal.

[8] So once Romulus had made the sacrifices, he convened the people and gave them a legal code, figuring that they were as unified as they could be without sharing the same rules. He gave himself symbols of power and dressed in a more dignified fashion, thinking that the laws would be respected by the common men if they looked up to him. For this purpose, he also assigned twelve men as lictors to help him with his responsibilities.[26] This number of lictors may have represented the number of vultures which had signified his ultimate rulership over Rome. I share the view of those who think that the idea of the lictors, their status and number was appropriated from the Etruscans, from whom we had also borrowed the throne and the robe with purple border. The Etruscans themselves had chosen the number twelve because they had twelve districts that elected the king and from each came one lictor.

The city itself also expanded, adding plots of land for more building, with a view to further population expansion. Like other ancient city founders, Romulus had pulled together a random assortment of men, pretending that the population had come from the very earth itself, but now he opened a sanctuary in Rome, located in an area of the city down by the two groves. Men from the region flocked to Rome's sanctuary, both slaves and freemen, anyone looking for a new life. This was a first step in their growth toward power. With the new population and Rome's strength growing, Romulus next began to organize. He promoted one hundred senators, either because one hundred was enough or there were exactly one hundred men who could identify their fathers. These men were called "Fathers" and their descendants became *patricians*.[27]

---

26 Lictors were minor public officials who acted as a show of force for kings and later *consuls*, carrying symbols of violence and power.

27 The Latin term *patricius* derives from pater meaning "father," hence the *patricians* being called "Fathers" and earning the position by being to identify their fathers. The *patricians* and *plebeians* struggled for power in Rome's earliest days. The *patricians* were aristocrats by birth, could trace their family's history, and had access to high offices and priesthoods. The *plebs* were everyone else. Eventually the *plebs* became a significant political body, had their own assemblies, and appointed officials. To advocate for more equal rights, they would sometimes threaten to secede (i.e., stop working) in order to highlight their importance to the city's

Rape of the Sabines

[9] Rome was now strong enough to defeat any of its neighbors in battle, but there was the small problem that there were no women among their ranks and so they would only last one generation. They certainly couldn't produce children at home (with no women to bear them) and they did not intermarry with their neighboring states. The Fathers advised Romulus to send representatives to their neighbors to propose that they join forces and also allow for intermarriage between the two groups. They said to Romulus, "All cities start small, but the cities supported by the gods and their own good deeds will become famous and powerful. Romulus, you know as well as anyone that Rome's start has been assisted by the gods and that we have earned our good fortune. We should feel no shame at all in mingling our blood with other mortals." But the ambassadors had no success with any of the neighbors because each of them hated Rome and feared that such a power was rising in their midst. The neighboring states declined the alliance, sending the ambassadors home and telling them they should open up their offer of asylum to women too, so they could find the spouses they deserved.[28] The Romans took this as an affront that could only lead to violence.

Romulus pretended not to be angry and instead pulled together a plan to achieve his goals at the right time and place.[29] He ordered the establishment of festival games to be held in the name of Neptunus Equestris which would be called *Consualia*.[30] The games were announced to all of the neighboring cities.

---

functioning.

28 This comment is meant as a diss rather than a policy suggestion. It is implied that men seeking asylum might be one thing but any woman wandering around the countryside by herself would not have been a quality spouse.

29 You may notice that in this scene, Romulus acts much more like Odysseus than some other heroes who would run headlong into battle. He bides his time, controls his emotions and lays his trap.

30 The *Consualia* became a long-lasting festival in ancient Rome, celebrated in both August and December. It was dedicated to Consus, god of the harvest and of stored grain, but Mars and the household gods were

They put full effort into making sure that the festival would be as spectacular as possible to ensure popularity and widespread attendance. Huge crowds came, both for the games and to see the newly founded city, with particularly large numbers coming from the Caeninenses, Crustumini and Antemnates. And almost the entire population of the Sabines attended, even the women and children. Everyone was incredibly impressed with how fast Roman power had grown once they saw the city's houses and defenses.

Once the event actually started, everyone was paying close attention to the festival when suddenly there was a commotion and a signal to the young Roman men who then grabbed the visiting women (all virgins) and ran off with them. The common men were responsible for rounding up multiple women, some of whom were beautiful enough that they would eventually go to the top senators. One woman of particularly good standing and good looks was taken by Thalassius' men, who shouted at anyone asking where they were taking her that they were "Taking her to Thalassius" and that is how that became a wedding ritual. The games had been completely disrupted and the parents of the women were furious, claiming that their rights as guests had been abused and that they had been manipulated into being there for religious purposes to honor Neptunus Equestris, just to be deceived. The women themselves were angry but equally without recourse.

Romulus went around saying, "We did what we did because of your arrogant fathers who refused us the ability to intermarriage. Nevertheless, you shall marry our men legally, partake in ownership and citizenship with them and have children together, the greatest joy we have as human beings." He asked them to calm their rage, put a smile on their faces, and to give in to their current possessors. He said, "Love and friendship can often come from a harmful start. Your husbands will be nicer to you now, and besides doing their marital duties, they must work extra hard to make up for your lack of home and family." The men embraced the women and explained their

---

also worshiped. These were festival "games" because they included ritual chariot races, later held in the Circus Maximus

Fig. 124: The Rape of the Sabines by Peter Paul Rubens
(National Trust, Antwerp; 17th century)

actions, saying they were driven by a lust and passion for the women, a justification that generally works on the fairer sex.

[10] The virgins themselves calmed considerably but their parents' sadness and anger grew. They did not merely mourn privately, but came from far and wide to the king of the Sabines, Titus Tatius. Other cities also sent their representatives to him since he had the highest authority around. The Caeninenses, Crustumini, and the Antemnates were raging and it seemed to them that Tatius and the Sabines were delaying their response. And the frustration of the Crustumini and the Antemnates was surpassed by the irritation and anger of the Caeninenses, who invaded the Roman territory on their own. They attacked in small groups and were met in the field by Romulus who taught them that the size of their army didn't match their anger. Romulus beat them and cut them down as they retreated, murdered their king, and immediately took their city with minimal effort.

He led his triumphant army back to Rome with his new-found fame. As he entered the city, he did so carrying in front of him the dead enemy general's armor attached to a fixture made for this reason. He placed the armor down at the trunk of an oak tree that was sacred to the shepherds and delineated the space for a temple to Jupiter. This Jupiter he called Jupiter Feretrius,[31] saying, "I, King Romulus, give to you, Jupiter Feretrius, this armor as an offering and commit to building a temple here. And in that temple which I've just delineated, all my successors shall deposit their own spoils of war when they too kill kings and generals, just as I have done." This explains the creation of that first Roman temple. Ever since then the gods have been pleased that the promises made by the founder of the temple were not made in vain and that the heirs of Romulus have delivered the spoils of war to that temple. Yet future actions did not lessen Romulus' victory and in the generations since, through all our wars, the honor of this highest level of war spoils has been won only twice.[32]

[11] In the meantime while the Romans celebrated, the Atemnates invaded the Roman state. The Roman army quickly gathered and surprised the enemy slowly making their way through the fields. They defeated the army of the Atemnates with their first yell and foray into battle and then took their town. As Romulus was returning to Rome, celebrating twin conquests, Hersilia, his wife, who had been begged by the other captured women, implored Romulus to forgive their fathers, grant them citizenship at Rome, and to bolster his own strength through a settlement. Romulus granted her appeal. Right away, he also brought his forces to bear on the Crustumini who were

---

31 As we've seen several times, gods like Jupiter can have various epithets or versions. "Feretrius" likely comes from the Latin *ferire* meaning "to strike" because he struck down the opposing king, or it could come from the Latin *ferre* meaning "to bring" because he brought the offering of armor to this place.

32 Livy is here describing the first triumph which is a procession of a Roman general back into the city after a major victory. The victorious general would dress lavishly, ride a four horse chariot, be attended by soldiers and leading captives and spoils of war. There would be a parade route going through the Triumphal Gate, through which only a triumphant general could enter. One wonderful detail is, because the triumphs were so splendid the Romans didn't want this getting into the head of the general, a slave would attend and whisper into the general's ear reminders that he was a mortal man, not a god.

also getting ready to fight but who saw what happened to their neighbors and offered little in the way of opposition. Romulus sent colonists to the various cities but more to Crustumium because it had quality arable land. Many people were immigrating into Rome from the region, especially some of the families of the stolen women.

TREASON OF TARPEIA

The Sabines were the last of the cities to go to war and they ended up being the toughest because they were smart about it, controlling their emotions and not giving away their intentions before acting. On top of their wisdom, they were also strategic: Tatius bribed with gold the daughter of Rome's citadel commander, a man called Tarpeius, in return for letting armed Sabines into the fortifications. She pretended to need to go outside the fortifications to get water for a ritual sacrifice. The men she admitted killed her, smashing and piling their weapons on top of her either to make it look like they had rushed the fortifications or to prove the point that you should never trust a traitor.

Fig. 125: Sculptural relief of Tarpeia killed by Sabine soldiers originally from the Basilica Aemilia
(National Museum, Rome; 1st century BC to 1st century AD)

This may be apocryphal, but it is also said that the Sabines customarily wore heavy gold bracelets on their left wrists and rings with valuable stones. Some say that, in exchange for her traitorous act, she had negotiated "what they had on their left hands." And so they gave her their shields instead of golden gifts. Others say that she had purposely negotiated their shields in asking for what was in their left hand and that she was killed by a gift of her own making after her treason.

[12] The Sabines held the citadel. The next day, the Romans marched in battle formation into the lowlands between the Palatine and Capitoline hills. The Sabines did not leave the citadel to meet them on the battlefield, so the Romans, growing impatient to retake their fort, assailed the enemy. The Sabine general Mettus Curtius was on one side and the Roman Hostus Hostilius was on the other side, leading their men. Hostus was fearless and gallant, fighting in the front of his men who were on unfavorable ground. When he was killed, his men broke ranks and were forced back to the Palatine gate. Romulus himself was overwhelmed and prayed to the gods with his hands in the air, saying "O Jupiter, based on your own signs, I built the foundation of the city here on the Palatine Hill. Through treachery the Sabines have taken the citadel and are already halfway here, armed and ready. O Father of gods and men, please prevent the enemy from taking the hill and dissolve the fear in my troops so they will stop retreating. If you save the city now, I will build another monument to your glory, dedicating a temple here to you as Jupiter Stator."[33]

Once he was done with his vows, Romulus believed his prayers would be answered and shouted to his men, "Romans, hear me! The unequaled sovereign Jupiter commands you to stop fleeing and attack!" The Roman soldiers stopped suddenly as if told by the god himself, and then Romulus led the charge at the front of the formation. Mettus Curtius, also leading from the front of the ranks of Sabines, routed the Romans into a retreat where the forum now stands. As he approached the gate of the Palatine, he yelled out, "We have beaten our deceitful and despicable enemies. Easy enough to defeat virgins, but a harder task to beat men." Hearing this arrogance, Romulus sallied forth with a group of his bravest men. Since Mettus was doing battle from his horse, the Romans beat him back easily

---

33 Jupiter the Sustainer.

and went after him as he fled. The other Roman soldiers saw their king's courage and with fresh energy pushed back the Sabine army. Mettus' horse was afraid of the noise of the soldiers and Mettus was knocked into a lake. The Sabines saw this and were disheartened. But Mettus, energized by his comrades calling out to him, was able to get out and escape. The battle wore on and the Romans started to win.

[13] At this moment in the battle, the Sabine women, the whole reason for the war, got involved. Their hair was messy and their clothing torn apart in their grief and fear at seeing the battle, but nevertheless they bravely rushed into the middle of the battle, men and weapons everywhere, right in between the two armies, to pacify both sides. They begged their fathers on the Sabine side and their husbands on the Roman side saying, "It is scandalous to draw each other's blood as fathers-in-law and sons-in-law and to inflict the horror of a dead father on each other's children or grandchildren. If you need to blame someone, blame us for the war rather than being angry at each other. If you need to punish someone, punish us, for we caused this damage, this bloodshed to our fathers and spouses. We'd rather die than be left widowed or fatherless."

The soldiers and generals all felt the moment and all fighting ceased while quiet overtook the battlefield. The generals met each other in the middle of the field to devise a peace treaty, but that treaty went beyond peace and formed a singular state. The Sabines acquiesced and gave their full governance over to Roman rule.

The size of the city doubled and the Sabines were called Quirites, from the word *Cures*, as a sign of respect for their actions. To commemorate the battle, they named the lake where Curtius' horse had gotten him stuck in the water the Curtian Lake. As a result of this reconciliation, the parents and husbands of the Sabine women, but especially Romulus, held the women in even higher esteem. He named the divisions of the people, the thirty curiae, after the Sabine women.[34] There were

---

34 *Curiae* were groupings of citizenry. Representatives of the *curiae* would meet to perform ceremonial or official tasks like finalizing wills and adoptions, presiding over induction ceremonies of priests and confirming elec-

undoubtedly more than thirty Sabine women and it isn't clear how the names of the curiae were selected, whether it was by age, the position of their husbands or by random chance. At this time there were also three centuries of Roman knights recruited, the Ramnenses named for Romulus, the Titienses, named after Titus Tatius and the Luceres, although we don't know where their name came from. After that, the two kings maintained royal power together, in agreement.

[14] A few years later, some of king Tatius' relatives beat up some representatives of the Laurentes. The Laurentes brought a suit under the law of the land and in making his decision, King Tatius showed favoritism toward his relatives, so he himself received the punishment due to his relatives, and he was killed in Lavinium by a crowd when he went for the annual sacrifice. It is said that Romulus wasn't quite as angry as he should have been about this incident, either because they weren't really getting along as kings together or because Tatius had deserved it. Romulus decided not to declare war, but he did reestablish the treaty between Rome and Lavinium so that the matter of the murdered king and the beaten ambassadors could be laid to rest. Unexpectedly, the treaty worked and peace reigned.

But, conflict was to break out closer to Rome, almost at its border. The Fidenates considered the growing power of Rome to be a threat and decided to declare war against them, before the strength of the Romans would reach its potential. A band of soldiers destroyed all the land between Fidenae and Rome. They followed the Tiber and continued marauding the land, terrorizing the local farmers. Word finally reached the city from the countryside and Romulus marched his troops forth, taking seriously a battle so close to home, and set up camp a mile from Fidenae. He left some troops guarding the camp and led the rest of his soldiers out, telling some of them to hide in an ambush in an area that was thick with brush. He took all the rest of his troops and all his knights and they attacked the fortifications of Fidenae like maniacs without battle order.

---

tions of other officials. This is derived from the word *Cures*, which was a Sabine town prior to the Sabine population being moved to Rome.

The enemy came out to meet him, which was Romulus' plan all along. The manner in which the cavalry fought would make their retreat, which they were about to fake, seem unsurprising because they seemed like they were hesitating, unsure of whether to fight or flee. The Roman infantry fell back, baiting the Fidenates to attack the Romans right where Romulus had placed the ambush. The Roman soldiers who were hiding popped up and struck against the flank of the enemy's formation. The troops who had been left behind in the camp also began to spill forth, standard held high, striking further fear. As a result of these mounting horrors, the Fidenates turned tail even before Romulus and his knights could reverse their horses and so men who had just been chasing the enemy were now themselves being driven quickly back to their town. The Roman soldiers, pursuing closely, burst in through the gates right alongside their enemy.

[15] The Veientes[35] were inspired by the war with the Fidenates and decided to support them, either because they were closely related (the Fidenates were Etruscans as well) or because of how close everything was to their own city. So they invaded Roman lands, mostly to maraude rather than to have a real pitched battle. They never built a camp or tried to face the Roman army but instead returned home with spoils. When the Roman army couldn't locate the Veientes, expecting a pitched battle, they crossed the Tiber River. The Veientes saw that the Romans were setting up a camp and decided to march out and face them out in the field, rather than wait to fight them from inside their battlements and their homes. Romulus was able to defeat them through sheer force, not even using any special tactics but relying on what was now a veteran force and the Romans pushed the enemy right back to their city. Romulus decided not to lay siege since the city was well guarded and naturally protected, so instead he ravaged, focused not on loot but on punishment. The Veientes, abased equally by their loss in battle and their destroyed land, sent representatives to Rome to request peace. The Romans took some of their land as a penalty but granted them a one hundred year armistice.

---

35 Veii was an important Etruscan town.

Apotheosis of Romulus

These were the main events that took place during Romulus' rule, both in peace and war. The story is compatible with his divine origins and the fact of his deification after death. He was able to reclaim his grandfather's kingdom and found and build a city which he bolstered through politics and fighting. So strong was Rome due to Romulus that it thrived without war for the next forty years. It should be said, though, that Romulus was better liked by the common people than the Fathers, but even more so he was loved by the soldiers. He kept three hundred soldiers with him at all times, during peace and war, who he called Celeres.

[16] These were the godlike achievements of Romulus. Then one day he brought together his soldiers in the field near Lake Capra for inspection. Suddenly a storm of thunder and lightning ensued, wrapped Romulus in a thick cloud, and Romulus disappeared, never to be seen again. When the storm cleared out and the sky was clear again, the soldiers looked up and saw that Romulus' throne was unoccupied and heard rumors from Fathers that the storm itself had carried Romulus to the sky.[36] The men were filled with sorrow that they were left leaderless and stayed silent for a long time. A few began proclaiming Romulus a god, son of a god, the king, and the father of the city of Rome, and the rest of the masses followed suit. They prayed for his benevolence and that he would watch over and support his children. I think that even back then, there were quiet rumors that, actually, Romulus had been ripped to shreds by the Fathers, but who knows. The respect that they had for Romulus, and their overwhelming sadness, encouraged everyone to believe the first story .

One man's report seems to support that story: Proculus Julius, a well-regarded man in important matters. While the people were depressed about their king and angry at the senators, he spoke to those assembled, saying, "Romans, the founder of

---

36 The word "apotheosis" means the elevation of someone to divine status, and in this story we see that happening to Romulus at the end of his life.

our city, Romulus, appeared to me this very morning, coming down from the sky. I was in complete shock and in awe of the apparition and begged him to let me see him up close. He said to me, 'Proculus, go tell the Romans that the gods decree that Rome will one day rule the entire world. The Romans shall learn warfare and shall know from generation to generation that no people can defend against Roman might.' As he finished, he transcended back up to the sky." Somehow with this speech, Proculus was able to sooth the anguish of the commoners and army about the loss of Romulus.[37]

Fig. 126: Etching of the apotheosis of Romulus by Giovanni Battista Fontana (Rijksmuseum; 1573)

The Rest of the Story

Livy's remaining work covers Roman history all the way from the start (which you just read) to near the end of the rule of Augustus in 9 AD. Book 1 goes through the rest of the history of the Monarchy, going systematically through each king and talking about the expansion or cultural advancements

---

37 This episode has parallels to the assassination of Julius Caesar by a group of senators and subsequent deification by his adopted son, Octavian on his way to becoming Augustus, first emperor of Rome.

during each reign. Book 1 ends with the overthrow of Tarquin the Proud, and then Book 2 covers the creation of the Republic, some local warfare, and the first time that the *plebs* secede. The remaining set of Books 3-10 cover conflicts between the *patricians* and *plebeians*, wars against Rome's neighbors (it would be weird if it didn't!), especially with the Samnites, and the development of Roman legal traditions. Books 11-20 are mostly lost with some fragments and quotes here and there giving us a clue as to what was contained there: the Pyrrhic War, creation of gladiatorial games, and most importantly, the First Punic War.

We have most of Books 21-45 which you'll be surprised to hear mostly cover warfare. Importantly, they focus on the Second Punic War against Hannibal and the Carthaginians, including many defeats for the Romans. This section also covers some engagements between Rome and the east (e.g., Macedonia, the Seleucid Empire). Unfortunately, the entire rest of the work is either lost or fragmentary, as it would have given us many details about the important period we cover in our Historical Context section about the social, economic and political upheaval of the 1st century BC. It would have been particularly useful to have another nearly contemporaneous account of Caesar's wars in Gaul (to compare with his own account!) and the civil wars that led to the eventual takeover by Octavian/Augustus.

CHAPTER V

From Republic to Empire

When we left off in the previous chapter, Rome had become the dominant power in the Mediterranean after defeating the Carthaginians and the Greeks over decades of warfare. With this expansion and growing power came massive changes to Roman politics and society: there were more lands and people to govern, there were incredible amounts of wealth flowing through the empire, and there were powerful armies and generals leaving Rome and gaining glory. The Republican system began to strain under its own weight. Over the next one hundred years plus, Rome would again be at war, which was not new, but this time against itself. When the dust settled, the new head of state would be an emperor - Rome would once again have a "king," for better or worse. But for this to happen, the Roman state would need to experience crisis after crisis, which it did.

Civil Disruptions

One civil disruption that arose was from slave uprisings. Recall that Roman expansion meant slaves gained from various territories, first brought in as captives and then raised from birth. So the slave population was ballooning. Between 135 BC and 71 BC, there were three large-scale slave revolts, called the Servile Wars (from the Latin servus meaning "slave"). The first started in Sicily with a small group of 400 slaves led by a magician/entertainer named Eunus. The revolt spread quickly and numbers grew to between 70,000 and 200,000 assembled slaves, which included women and children. It took a couple of years for the Roman army to put the revolt down. The Second Servile War also took place in Sicily and again took a few years to put down. The Third Servile War was led by Spartacus and took place on mainland Italy, starting with the escape of 70 gladiators in Capua. Their forces grew to 120,000 and gave the Roman military a lot of trouble. The two eventual victorious Roman generals, Pompey and Crassus, would use their glory to win further power later.

Further social upheavals were happening at the same time. By this time, it was less a conflict between the *patricians* and *plebeians*, since the *plebs* had successfully gained most of what they wanted. Instead, the conflict was now between the *optimates*, those who drew their power from the traditional aristocracy and senate, and the *populares*, those who drew their power from the masses of regular people.

In 133 BC a man named Tiberius Gracchus became the tribune of the *plebs* (the elected leader of the *plebs* who could veto other legislation and who was personally protected from violence) and started trying to push through reforms to the Roman system we might call "populist" (or even "socialist") today. As one of the *populares*, he wanted to limit how much land individuals could own and divide up public lands more fairly to benefit the regular people of Rom, but the law was vetoed and Tiberius was later assassinated. About 10 years later, his brother Gaius took up the helm and also conceived of reforms to support the *populares*, like subsidies for grain, citizenship for Rome's allies in Italy, updated juries, etc. Gaius was also killed but these ideas were gaining a footing and working up a lot of tension among the populace.

Fig. 127: Bronze statue of the Gracchi by Jean-Baptiste Claude Eugène Guillaume (Musée d'Orsay; 1848-53)

Civil Wars

In 91 BC, the Italian allies of Rome revolted in what became known as the Social Wars, whether they sought succession or full citizenship we are not exactly sure but they won citizenship and peace was obtained. Still, the war may have destabilized what it meant to be a Roman soldier. In 107 BC, Gaius Marius, a veteran of foreign wars (against one of the great ancient names: Jugurtha), was elected *consul* with the support of business interests and the lower class, as an adversary to senate corruption and incompetence. In short, he was the epitome of the *populares*.

In 88, Marius opposed the *consul* Sulla who was heading with his consular army to the east by assigning himself Sulla's army. Sulla actually marched his army on Rome and declared Marius and others exiles, but then went east again. Marius and his political ally Cinna got themselves elected *consul* and again tried to take Sulla's army away from him, but Sulla combined forces with his enemy in the east and came back and invaded Rome, this time killing many political enemies and setting himself up as a dictator for life. This was a formal position in Roman politics but was actually elected and temporary. A very dangerous precedent had been set and individual politicians and generals were learning how to curry favor with particular societal interests and even involve the military in civilian affairs. This would be a theme for the rest of Roman history. Surprisingly, after a few years, Sulla resigned as dictator and retired from public life.

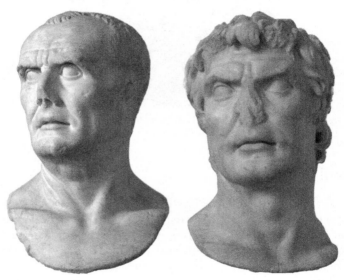

Figs. 128 (left) and 129 (right): The so-called busts of Marius and Sulla. (Glyptothek; ca. AD 10)

If you are not already confused, the period immediately following these issues only gets more complicated. This is where we begin to truly see the Republic begin to crumble. The next period was marked by a political alliance between Pompey and Crassus (the two generals who had successfully quelled the Third Servile War) and Julius Caesar. Today, we call this alliance the First Triumvirate. Not necessarily natural allies, the three men found enough common cause to support each others' ambitions. Caesar became *consul* in 59 BC and began instituting reforms to distribute state land to the poor (again playing on popular sentiment), dividing up conquered land to Pompey's troops after some of his military conquests, and helping Crassus secure some political and economic wins as well.

Caesar himself was positioning himself for a governorship in Gaul (modern France), which would help build his wealth and legacy. Caesar spent nearly 10 years fighting the Gauls, which he detailed in *The Gallic Wars*, which you will read a section of below, and eventually secured the entire province for Rome. He even brought his army into Germany and into Britain (the first ever to do so) to tease later Roman conquest there. Crassus ended up taking an army into Parthia and getting annihilated, which upset the balance of power between Caesar and Pompey.

The senate and Pompey were growing concerned by how powerful Caesar was becoming and attempted to strip him of command. In 49 BC, they offered him an ultimatum to lay down his command and return to Rome or be labeled an enemy of the state. They made Pompey a dictator and chief adversary to Caesar. On January 10, 49 BC, Caesar crossed the Rubicon, the legal boundary of Italy, thus declaring war, and marched into Rome unopposed by his adversaries who fled to the eastern Mediterranean. Caesar eventually defeated Pompey's army and Pompey fled to Egypt where he was murdered on Caesar's behalf.

Caesar thus secured military control and got to work coalescing governmental power by holding various positions, some alternating and some concurrent, including a permanent tribunate so he would have veto power and be personally protected from attack (good luck with that). He flooded the senate with supporters. As Caesar prepared for war and took it upon himself to appoint all Rome's magistrates, he was assassinated by a group of senators, among them his old friend Marcus Junius Brutus, the descendant of Lucius Junius Brutus who helped expel Tarquin the Proud, the last king of Rome. Caesar is not considered the first emperor, but the power he obtained laid the groundwork for what was to come. The Republic was squarely on its deathbed.

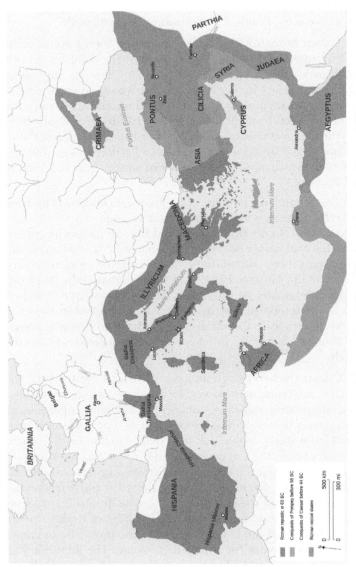

Fig. 130: Map of the Roman Republic at the time of Caesar (1st Century BC)

At this moment, a so-called Second Triumvirate came to prominence, composed of Caesar's closest allies, Mark Antony (Caesar's general), Marcus Lepidus (Caesar's ally), and Octavian (Caesar's adopted son). As a group, they held Caesar's powers and were able to avenge Caesar's death, killing the assassins and defeating their armies. The triumvirs divided up Rome's territories between them but their trust in each other was tenuous. Octavian ended up defeating Lepidus and sending him into exile. Antony married one of Caesar's former lovers, Cleopatra, the queen of Ptolemaic Egypt, whose wealth could help him consolidate power. Octavian and Antony squared off, and Octavian eventually proved victorious in the Battle of Actium in 31 BC.

Fig. 131: Marble bust of Cleopatra VII
(Altes Museum, Berlin; ca. 40 - 30 BC)

To say he became a powerful figure at Rome would be an understatement: eventually in 27 BC, returning to Rome, he was called *princeps*, (Latin for the "first citizen") and *Augustus* (Latin for the "Revered One"), to indicate his primacy. He added these to his title of imperator: he was now an emperor.

*Fig. 132: Marble statue known as the "Prima Porta" Augustus
(Vatican Museums; early 1st century AD)*

The Roman Empire: Reign of Augustus and the Julio-Claudians

Augustus went on to be one of the most effective statesmen of all time. He nominally left the Republic in place, allowing for the continued existence of the senate, the various magistracies, and other governing bodies, but he held ultimate power by controlling the military and by making sure that the Roman nobility who served in government answered to him. He created a standing army of about 170,000 troops, who could be used to hold or obtain territory and prevent rebellion. His reign saw a significant expansion of the empire in terms of territory like central Europe, northern Spain and Portugal, Turkey and others including Egypt, which technically belonged to the emperor privately and which acted as a key source of grain and thus a cash cow for all other investments. Augustus' reign started what is called the *Pax Romana*, the "Roman Peace," which constituted about 200 years of Roman history (through the death of Marcus Aurelius), which was prosperous and relatively peaceful, at least internally, despite wars of expansion and defense. When we think of empire, and all that it entails, we should not ignore the violent and oppressive path the Romans took to create and maintain peace, but it was effective in perpetuating a system for many centuries hence.

Augustus and his bureaucracy were masters at public relations but also found the time, talent and resources to build the empire. His accomplishments, called the *Res Gestae Divi Augusti* (*The Deeds of the Divine Augustus*) were inscribed on the front of his mausoleum in Rome. His titles abounded; his busts were sent throughout the empire. Investment in infrastructure showed the value of empire to its citizens, and so his administration built aqueducts, roads, temples, altars, arches, baths, and other public works that demonstrated the power and ability of the empire and its emperor. It is said that Augustus' last words were, "I found Rome a city of brick and leave it a city of marble." Augustus instituted services in Rome itself, like a brigade that would fight fires and keep the peace. He created the Praetorian Guard which was a personal bodyguard for the emperor that became a powerful force in its own right, eventually bullying the government and overthrowing and installing new emperors.

Augustus also took control over succession to make sure his legacy would live on, and offered up a number of candidates to succeed him from among his family. He outlived most of them, and so he ended up passing on his reign to his step-son (his wife's son from a previous marriage), Tiberius, whom Augustus adopted, which was a wide-spread practice. Augustus died in August of 14 AD, probably of natural causes and there was a peaceful transfer of power to Tiberius at the age of 55.

Tiberius had never wanted to rule. He had tried to retire on the island of Rhodes in 6 BC, and was reclusive and aloof, especially after the deaths of his adopted son Germanicus and his son Drusus, both potential heirs. He never got along well with the senate and had offended the nobility by not accepting all the honors they had tried to bestow on him. This tendency to withdraw, even physically, from rule became an issue in particular because he allowed his head of the Praetorian Guard, Sejanus, rule in his stead. But Tiberius eventually caught Sejanus in a coup plot and ordered his execution. Even after that, Tiberius was hesitant to rule and did not make much of an effort to prop up a successor by giving out titles and responsibilities. He even went so far as to leave Rome entirely for the last ten years of his rule, spending his time in his luxurious villa on the island of Capri. Despite all this, perhaps because he simply left the empire machine running without too many costly expenditures, Tiberius created a massive budgetary windfall that would soon be spent by his successor. He died at the age of 78 in 37 AD.

By the time he died, Germanicus' son, Caligula, had won enough support to be made the next emperor. Tiberius' will had anointed him a co-emperor so Caligula negated the will as his first act. Caligula was technically the first Julio-Claudian, a term that refers to the combination of the Julian family and the Claudian family as they intermarried and adopted each other during this period. Caligula's real name was Gaius Julius Caesar Augustus Germanicus. We call him "Caligula" today because it translates as "Little Boots," a nickname he earned

*Fig. 133: Bust of the emperor Caligula, who sports a beard as a
sign of mourning for the death of his sister Drusilla
(Louvre Museum; AD 39-40)*

as a child wandering around the military camps wearing, well, little boots. You can see why historians use clarifying shortcuts.

According to the ancient sources, the first few months of Caligula's reign were normal enough, but then things took a darker turn and we now know Caligula as a crazed autocrat. Indeed, his biggest preoccupation seemed to be the building of a big palace for himself, though he also turned the apparatus of the state toward construction to benefit (or at least placate) the public. At the same time, Caligula did not have the same nominal respect for the Republican institutions as his predecessors and worked to build his own individual power, even making a point to state publicly that he could make his favorite horse, Incitatus, a *consul*. He also had a penchant for walking around dressed like a god. These and other stories may or may not be true as the contemporary sources for Caligula's reign are lost and the historians we do have were writing later and enjoyed scandal and fanciful tales.

Caligula was assassinated in AD 41 by some Praetorian guardsmen and some senators. The Praetorian Guard quickly proclaimed Claudius, Caligula's uncle (and whom they found hiding in a closet), as the new emperor. Claudius had likely survived political purges because he was partially deaf and walked with a limp. Perhaps the Praetorians thought he could be controlled. But he turned out to be a competent administrator, getting the imperial coffers back in order after Caligula's lavish spending, and yet was still able to continue the imperial program of building roads, aqueducts, canals and especially a port at Ostia to be able to store grain, all of which would help with economic development and imperial reach. It was also under his reign that the Romans finally conquered Britain, about 100 years after Caesar first brought troops there. Claudius was interested in literature, history, and law, and he was tutored for a time by Livy. Claudius was married four times, which was at least one too many. He was said to have been cheated on by one wife, abused by another, and poisoned to death by his last wife, Agrippina who was intent on ensuring that her own son gained the throne instead of Claudius' intended successor. This is how we get the emperor Nero.

Fig. 134: Bust of the emperor Nero (and his neckbeard)
(Capitoline Museums; 1st century AD)

Nero was the fifth and final Julio-Claudian emperor, coming to power in AD 54 and ruling until AD AD. Once again, contemporary historical sources for Nero's reign and life are lost and we must rely on later writers who may be once or twice removed from these original sources. Nero's early reign was seen as successful, probably because it was run by bureaucrats and advisors, or perhaps because he was kept in check by his mother, Agrippina. He killed her in AD 59 and his reign seems to go downhill from there. This period includes a massive fire in Rome and rumors swirled that Nero had ordered it so he could clear space for a big palace. Nero is also famous in modern times because he is mentioned by the historian Tacitus as having tortured and executed Christians. Nero's reign came to an end as the result of revolts by governors of various provinces. During this episode, Nero was abandoned by all of his supporters. He couldn't even find someone to help him escape, couldn't find the courage to kill himself, and in the end asked a servant to do it. He was only 30 years old. His death would mark the beginning of the Year of Four Emperors, a brief period of civil war with competing generals, with control over armies, coming to power and then quickly losing it to a competitor. We will pick the story up from there in the next chapter.

Roman Military

The military is what powered Rome's rise, facilitated its expansion, and allowed it to maintain its hold over the Mediterranean basin and beyond for centuries. As we head into a reading by one of the Roman army's most famous commanders, Julius Caesar, it might be helpful to know a little about how it functioned. The composition, recruitment, structure and control of the military of course changed dramatically over the course of Roman history. Over time, the army became more professional, with soldiers being paid a salary and turning their 20 plus years in the military into a full career. The Romans were known for their uniformity and organization. Training focused on taking orders, alignment and teamwork, rather than on individual action or bravery. Units would move in specific formations to beat enemies by staying in "closed ranks" and minimizing weaknesses.

The biggest unit of the military was the legion, which generally had about 5,2000-5,600 infantry and 300 cavalry or 200 auxiliary troops (non-citizen cavalry, archers, or specialists) during the empire. Each legion was broken up into ten cohorts and the cohorts into six centuries and then each century was divided into ten squads. This allowed for large scale organization as well as micro movements. Legions would be strategically placed throughout the empire to fight wars of expansion and to defend existing territory. Legions posted around the empire allowed the Romans to spread not just their military might but also their socio-cultural dominance throughout their territories.

Each legion had a standard, a post with the statue of an eagle, and if this was lost in battle it was a major disgrace. The Roman military, during times of expansion, created revenues for the state in the form of land, plunder, slaves, and goods, but was still incredibly expensive to maintain and we see during the civil wars that various leaders have to try to find ways to pay their armies and settle them on land. The Roman state also maintained a navy to ensure safe trade routes. Pirates were a big problem and Pompey, referenced above, was famous for clearing out some major pirate networks. The navy could also help transport and supply the army, as movement over water was faster than movement over land. Armies could become loyal to particular leaders - we certainly saw this with Caesar as he led his troops across the Rubicon River and into Rome - and we will see the military and its control be key to coups, revolts, and the ultimate division of the empire throughout the course of its history.

Caesar's *The Gallic Wars*

Julius Caesar is perhaps the most famous individual in all of Roman history. He is best known as a general and politician, operating in the middle of the 1st century BC, and his military accomplishments - in Gaul, across the Mediterranean, and beyond - are still famous today. Politically, he was, and still is, a profoundly divisive character, with some viewing him as a champion of the common people, while others see him as an aspiring despot and dictator. Regardless of your perspective on his character, his political moves played a pivotal role in the collapse of the entire Roman Republic and eventually led to his own downfall at the hands of his friend Brutus and the other Roman senators.

It might not be surprising that ancient Roman historians found Caesar a fascinating character to write about, and Plutarch, Suetonius, Appian, and Cassius Dio all write about him at length (as did Livy but that section is lost). What might be more unusual, to those learning about Caesar for the first time, is that we actually have his own autobiographical writings as well. They cover both his exploits in Gaul (*Commentarii de Bello Gallico* / *The Gallic Wars*) and his subsequent battles against the senatorial opposition (*Commentarii de Bello Civili* / *The Civil Wars*). This would be like having the personal writings of Alexander the Great or Charlemagne or Genghis Khan, a personal set of memoirs from one of the world's greatest conquerors.

Fig. 135: Marble Bust of Julius Caesar
(Vatican Museums; 1st century BC)

235

However, don't think about Caesar's writings as some sort of personal journal of thoughts and feelings and emotions. Instead, these texts were meticulously curated and meant to be shared publicly. These are more like an influencer's social media posts - thoughtfully planned, heavily edited, and meant to show their subject in the best light possible - than they are candid photos of an unsuspecting subject. On the one hand, these are the best sources you could possibly imagine for some of the late Roman Republic's most important events, and yet it is often difficult to separate out fact from fiction, not so much because Caesar was creating stories out of thin air, but rather because he wasn't above a little embellishment. His estimates regarding Gallic populations and army sizes, for example, seem a little outlandish. In his early battle against the Helvetii, he claims there were over 250,000 Helvetians and more than 100,000 of their allies. Modern historians think that this was likely unrealistic, and even ancient authors reduced the numbers downwards a bit, with Plutarch suggesting a total of 300,000 and Orosius, writing centuries after Caesar, estimates only about half that, at 157,000.

Gaius Julius Caesar was born in Rome in 100 BC. As his name suggests, he was part of the Julii clan, an ancient and respectable family whose roots go back to the earliest days of Rome. His specific branch of that family, the Caesars, weren't quite as famous. His father, for example, dabbled in politics and served as a provincial governor, but he never attained the consulship, the highest office of the Roman Republic. His aunt Julia, however, was married to Gaius Marius, and Caesar grew up a staunch supporter of Marius and the *populares* faction in Rome.

Caesar's rise to power began long before he set foot in Gaul. When he was in his twenties, he trained as an orator and lawyer, and he won his first military accolades while serving in Bithynia (modern day Turkey). Around this time he was captured by pirates and famously chastised them because they didn't ask for enough money to ransom him. During the 60s BC, Caesar began to climb the *cursus honorum*, the traditional political ladder of the Roman elite, and he was elected *pontifex maximus*, the highest priest in Rome, during this time as well. These accomplishments, however, came at a high cost, quite literally. Caesar went into massive amounts of debt, both to win his elections (sometimes through bribery) and to operate in office once he got there. In his position as *aedile*, for example, he borrowed vast sums to put on a set of festivals with a whopping 320 gladiatorial battles, over ten times the amount that would normally be on display.

Fig. 136: Denarius showing Caesar, the first living Roman to have his face on a coin (44 BC)

In 59 BC, Caesar reached the consulship, the highest office of the Roman Republic. Although there were always two *consuls* at any given time, Caesar so belittled his consular colleague that Romans joked it was the consulship of Julius and Caesar. In this role, Caesar worked to pay back his supporters, trying to secure land for Pompey's veterans and pass favorable tax laws for his financial backer Crassus. The traditional senatorial aristocracy was already wary of his rising popularity, and they tried to assign him to the most dull of all proconsular appointments - the forests and trails of Italy. Caesar used his connections to have this appointment overturned, however, and was instead made *proconsul* in Cisalpine Gaul (i.e., Gaul on the Italian side of the Alps) and Illyricum (i.e., the Balkans).

Caesar never thought there was much glory to be had in simply serving as *proconsul*, essentially a governor of lands already under Roman control. So once he arrived in Cisalpine

Gaul, Caesar began looking to expand. Technically, he was only allowed control of an army within his assigned provinces, but Caesar decided that Gallic movements on the far side of the Alps were pushing into Roman territory and this gave him the perfect excuse to lead his army into new lands. And so the Gallic wars - and Caesar's text - begins.

Fig. 137: Title page of a 1783 printing of Caesar's The Gallic Wars

Caesar's *Commentarii de Bello Gallico* (*The Gallic Wars*) is divided into seven books, each one covering one year of the campaign. A final eighth book was penned by one of Caesar's officers, Aulus Hirtius, after Caesar's death. Book 1 focuses on the year 58 BC and the origin of the war. The Helvetii tribe were purportedly planning to migrate into a Roman province, giving Caesar the pretext to move his army into Gaul on the far side of the Alps, defeating both the Helvetii and the German mercenaries led by Ariovistus. The following year, as recounted in Book 2, Caesar moves his troops north to battle the Belgae, known as particularly ferocious warriors. Book 3 recounts his campaign against the Veneti, a strong naval state in northwestern Gaul. Caesar was particularly upset that the Veneti had killed his messengers, and as a result executed the Veneti leaders and sold the rest of the population into slavery. Book 4 recounts one of Caesar's most impressive engineering feats, his crossing of the Rhine River, becoming the first Roman general to invade Germany. He doesn't stay long, however, and soon

crosses the English channel as the first Roman general to invade
Britain. Book 5 details Caesar's second, and far more massive,
naval invasion of Britain. Caesar is victorious but again does
not stay long and soon returns to the continent. In Book 6,
Caesar moves his troops back into the interior of Gaul, leading
up to the decisive battle.

That decisive battle - the Siege of Alesia - took place in 52
BC and is described in detail in Book 7 of Caesar's text. Over
the course of the previous six years, Caesar has been successful,
in large part, because of his ability to divide and conquer the
many diverse Gallic tribes. The revolt of the Aedui has given
the Gauls new hope, however, and now the Gauls are discussing a multi-state coalition against the Romans.

It is in this context that we pick up with Caesar's description of the Gallic wars.

Words of the Ancients
Julius Caesar's *The Gallic Wars*
Book 7.63-90

[63] When word of the Aedui revolt got out, the war grew
bigger. The Gauls sent messengers in every direction, and they
leveraged all their power and influence and wealth to drum up
even more rebels. Moreover, they took the hostages they had
from Caesar's army and executed them, to terrify any of the
Gallic tribes that might be against putting up a fight. The Aedui
then sent to Vercingetorix [of the Arverni tribe] and asked him
to come and explain his plans for the war against the Romans.
Once he agreed to do so, the Aedui insisted that they serve as
the leaders of the collective forces, and when this caused an
argument, a council of all the Gallic tribes was called. They
came in massive numbers, from every corner of Gaul, and all
gathered at Bibracte. There, they put the issue of leadership to
a vote, and every single soldier voted for Vercingetorix to be
their commander-in-chief. There were a few tribes that didn't
make the council: the Remi, the Lingones, and the Treviri. The
first two had already flipped and allied themselves with Rome,

while the last was in the farthest reaches of Gaul and under attack by the Germans (which is actually why they never entered the war on either side). The Aedui were furious that they lost the vote and that command of the combined armies was given to Vercingetorix instead of themselves. This change of luck, combined with the loss of Caesar's good graces, greatly upset the Aedui. But they had already started the revolt, and they didn't dare break away from the rest of the Gallic coalition. The promising young Aedui leaders, Eporedorix and Viridomarus, both agreed to serve under Vercingetorix.

VERCINGETORIX LEADS THE GAULS

[64] Vercingetorix demanded hostages from each of the tribes [to ensure allegiance], and he set a day for all the Gallic cavalry - 15,000 in number - to quickly come together. He told the council that he didn't need any more infantry or foot soldiers, since he didn't intend on fighting a pitched battle against the Romans. But since they had lots of horsemen, it would be easy to prevent the Romans from gathering corn and foraging for food. There was only one catch - the Gauls would need to destroy their own crops, agricultural buildings, and food supplies in order to force the Romans to forage. For only through destroying their own food and property could they gain their land and freedom forevermore. After making these plans, Vercingetorix required the Aedui and the Segusiavi (both neighbors of "The Province")[1] to provide 10,000 infantry and another 800 cavalry. He placed the brother of Eporedorix in charge of these troops, and then ordered them to attack the Allobroges. Then on the other side, he sent the Gabali tribe and the closest divisions of the Arverni tribe against the Helvii[2] and similarly send the Ruteni and Cadurci tribes to wreak havoc in

---

1 "The Province" is a nickname that the Romans use for their province of *Gallia Narbonensis* in southern Gaul (modern day France). The nickname has lasted more than 2,000 years - we still call the region "Provence" today.

2 Not to be confused with the Helvetii, one of Caesar's enemies at the beginning of the Gallic wars (and the namesake of the font Helvetica). The Helvii, at this point, were allies to the Romans.

the land of the Volcae Arecomici. At the same time he was laying siege to the Allobroges, he was also sending secret messengers to them, hoping that they were still bitter about the recent Roman conquest and occupation. Vercingetorix promised their chiefs huge sums of money if they were to flip, and even swore that the Allobroges would rule the entire Province in the end.

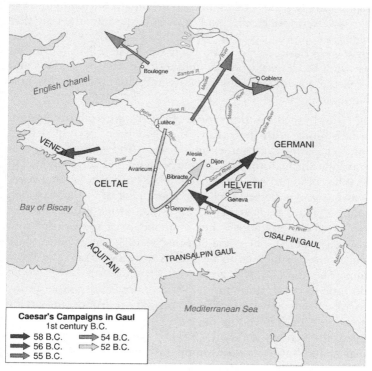

Fig. 138: Map of Caesar's campaigns in Gaul (58 - 50 BC)

[65] The only defense against the coalition of Gallic forces were 22 cohorts, which had been assembled from the whole province by Lucius Caesar, the lieutenant, and they were now ready to oppose the enemy in every location. The Helvii joined the battle against their fellow Gauls on their own volition, but they have been defeated, and their leader Gaius Valerius Donotaurus has been slain alongside several others. Thus, they've

241

been forced to retreat within their walls. The Allobroges, on the other hand, have placed defensive garrisons all along the Rhine River and have been defending it vigilantly. Caesar saw that the Gauls had more cavalry and that communication had been cut of from his allies in Italy and in the Province (i.e., Gallia Narbonensis), and so he sent across the Rhine into Germany - to the tribes he defeated on his previous campaign there - to ask for more cavalry and infantry (especially the type that fights among the cavalry). When the German cavalry arrived, they were riding horses completely unusable in battle, so Caesar took the horses from his military *tribunes* and soldiers and even the equestrians and veterans and gave them to his new German allies.

[66] In the meantime, the enemy's troops from the Arverni tribe - along with the cavalry that had been assembled from all over Gaul - were gathering together. And while Caesar was traveling through the land of the Sequani and the Lingones so that he could provide better help to the Province, Vercingetorix was bringing together a massive contingent of Gallic warriors, and he placed them in three camps, about ten miles from the Romans. He summoned the commanders of the cavalry to a council, and there he explained that victory was at hand, since the Romans appeared to be fleeing from Gaul into the Province. This, he said, was great for the time being, but it would do little to bring peace and freedom to the Gauls in the future, for the Romans would certainly raise more troops and attack again, rather than ending the war. Therefore, Vercingetorix argued, the Gauls should attack while the Romans were on the march and burdened with supplies. If the Roman infantry had to slow down to help the cavalry, then they wouldn't be able to finish their march, and if they dropped their supplies and ran for safety (as he thought they would), then the Romans would lose both their goods and their dignity. As for the Roman cavalry, there's no doubt that they will stay in tight formation, for none of them would dare to advance in front of the pack. And to ensure the Gauls fought with great courage, Vercingetorix promised to parade all his troops in front of the camp to strike fear into the heart of the Romans. At this, the Gallic cavalry

shouted with one voice:

> *"Let us swear a sacred oath, that anyone who does not ride through the enemy's army at least twice should never find shelter or hospitality in any house - for them or for their wives or children or parents!"*

Fig. 139: Statue of Vercingetorix commemorating his victory at Gergovia (Clermont-Ferrand, France; 1903)

[67] The Gauls roared with applause, and all of them swore the oath. The next day, the Gallic cavalry was divided into three groups, with two of them marching out in front of our flanks, and the third blocking our march forward. When this happened, Caesar also divided the Roman cavalry into three groups and ordered them to attack the enemy. The battle started everywhere all at once, and the main Roman force stopped and brought their baggage inside the formation. If any of the Romans were hard pressed, he ordered the rest of the troops to advance, swing around, and form a battle line in that spot. This helped stymie the enemy attacks and boost the Ro-

man morale, since the troops knew they would be supported. Eventually, the Germans on the right flank took control of the hilltop and pushed the enemy back from their original position, all the way to the river where Vercingetorix was stationed with his infantry, and they even killed a few. This caused the rest of the Gauls - fearing that they might be surrounded - to flee. When that happened, it became a full-fledged slaughter. In the process, three of the high-ranking Aedui leaders were captured and brought to Caesar. They were Cotus, the commander of the cavalry (who argued with Convictolitavis[3] at the last election), Cavarillus, who commanded the infantry after the revolt of Litaviccus,[4] and Eporedorix, the leader of the Aedui when they fought the Sequani before Caesar arrived.

Caesar's Circumvallation of Alesia

[68] After all his cavalry were routed, Vercingetorix reorganized his troops in the same order he had previously, and he immediately started to march to Alesia, a hilltop town of the Mandubii tribe. And he ordered the supplies to be brought out of the camp and to closely follow them. Caesar, on the other hand, had brought his supplies to the nearest hill, and he placed two legions there to guard them. Then, he went in pursuit of Vercingetorix's forces, slaying about 3,000 of the ones who lagged at the rear, and the next day he made camp at Alesia. Upon scouting the situation, he realized the Gauls were in a panic, since their cavalry - the group they had placed their highest hopes in - had just been routed. So Caesar urged his soldiers to begin the undertaking of building a circumvallation (i.e., a circular fortification wall) around Alesia.

[69] The town itself sat high on top of a hill, a very lofty position indeed, so it didn't seem likely to be taken except

---

3   Originally, the Aedui were allies of the Romans against the Gauls. But Convictolitavis convinced them to abandon the Romans and support Vercingetorix instead.

4   Litaviccus was a Gallic general during the Siege of Gergovia. Again, originally an ally of Caesar, Litaviccus convinced his troops to betray the Romans and flip to Vercingetorix.

through siege warfare. The hill was surrounded by rivers on two sides, and a plain about three miles in length lay in front of it. On all the other sides, the town was surrounded by hills, a fair distance away and about the same height as the town itself. The Gallic forces were assembled below the wall on the eastern side of the hill, filling the whole space in between the town and the Roman defenses, and they had created a ditch and stone wall about 6 feet high. The perimeter of the circumvallation that the Romans were starting was 11 miles long. Along the length of the Roman wall, 23 watch towers were constructed, and these were manned by a small group of soldiers during the day (in case the Gauls should try to break through) and staffed by an even larger number of troops at night.

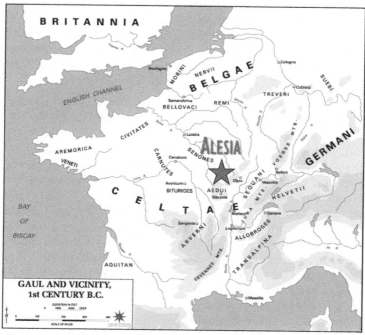

Fig. 140: Map of Gaul showing Alesia (1st century BC)

[70] Once the circumvallation wall was under construction, a cavalry battle broke out in the plain in between the town and the wall, and it was fought by both sides with a fiery

intensity. Caesar sent in the German allies to help his troops when they were hard pressed, and he brought the legions out in front of the camp, just in case the Gauls suddenly tried an infantry attack. The sight of the legions boosted the spirits of the Roman troops, and the enemy was put to flight. But the huge numbers of Gauls, combined with the narrowness of the gates of their city walls, slowed their retreat, and the German allies were in hot pursuit all the way to their fortifications. This led to a great slaughter, with some of the Gauls abandoning their horses and trying to cross the ditch and climb the walls by hand. Then, Caesar commanded the legions, which he had drawn up in front of the camp, to advance a little. This caused the Gauls to panic even more, thinking that the Romans were about to start an infantry attack against them. They shouted their call to arms, while some of the Gauls fled for the safety of their town. Vercingetorix then ordered the gates to be shut to ensure they didn't completely desert their camp. And only after capturing lots of horses and slaughtering many more did the Germans retreat.

[71] Vercingetorix then adopted a new strategy, sending away all his cavalry in the middle of the night, before the Roman circumvallation wall could be completed. On their way out, he told them each to go to their hometown and tell their people that they needed to send reinforcements, anyone and everyone who was old enough to fight. Then Vercingetorix recounted his own achievements, pleading with his troops not to let himself - who had done so much for the freedom of all the Gauls - be captured and tortured by the enemy. For if he were to fall, 80,000 of his best men were doomed to perish with him. And he let them know that, according to his calculations, they had barely enough corn for 30 more days, but they might be able to hold out a bit longer if they ration it wisely. Then he silently dismissed his cavalry during the second watch of the night, and they went through a gap where our wall had not yet been completed. Afterwards, Vercingetorix ordered that all the corn in the town be brought to him, and that the cattle be distributed among the men (the Mandubii had gathered quite a lot from the surrounding countryside). Then he measured out the

corn and divided it into meager rations, little by little. Finally, Vercingetorix called all of his troops that had been camped in the field to come back inside the town, and there they would wait for the Gallic reinforcements before continuing the war.

CAESAR'S NEW FORTIFICATIONS

[72] Upon learning all these from some Gallic deserters and captives, Caesar started a new system of fortifications. He dug a trench 20 feet wide, with vertical sides so that the base of the trench was just as wide as the top of it. The rest of his fortifications were set back about 400 feet from this trench. Since the Roman circumvallation wall was so long that it couldn't be continuously staffed with troops at each point, Caesar thought this trench would help prevent nighttime infantry attacks as well as shield his people from arrow attacks while they kept building during the day. Behind this, he dug two more trenches, each 15 feet wide and the same amount deep. And he filled the innermost trench, which was about the same level as the plane, with water from the nearby river. Behind these trenches, Caesar built a ramp and defensive wall 12 feet high. To this wall, he added parapets and battlements, and he placed giant stakes that looked like stags' antlers where the two joined, in order to prevent the enemy from scaling the walls. And finally he surrounded the entire structure with turrets, each one placed 80 feet from the next.[5]

[73] Since it was necessary to gather timber for the fortifications and food for the troops - both of which were quite some distance from camp, our forces were often stretched quite thin. And the Gauls would occasionally take advantage of this by sending out masses of troops from several gates to try to attack our siege works. Because of this, Caesar thought he should make further additions to the fortifications so that it could be staffed by just a small number of soldiers. So he had his

---

5   A parapet is a small wall that often sits upon the larger fortification wall and is meant to protect and conceal troops. A battlement refers to the gaps in the parapet where soldiers could appear to shoot arrows and attack the enemy. A turret is a small tower built on top of a larger fortification.

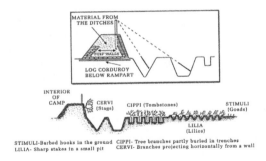

Fig. 141: Diagram of Caesar's defenses at Alesia

people cut down tree trunks as well as thick branches, strip the bark off of them, and sharpen their ends into a point. Then he had them dig a trench, 5 feet deep, and anchor the trees in the trench, with their roots spreading out underground so they couldn't be easily pulled up, and only the sharp branches of the trees stuck out above the ground. There were five rows of these, interspersed and intersecting with one another, and anyone who tried to make their way through was very likely to impale themselves. The soldiers called these "tombstones."[6] In front of these, they dug diagonal rows[7] of pits, 3 feet deep and narrow at the bottom. Into these pits they fastened stakes - the width of a man's leg, sharpened at the top, and hardened by fire - and these stuck out only about four inches from the ground. To make sure they stayed in place, the pits were filled and packed with one foot of clay, but then the rest of the pit was filled with leaves and twigs to hide the trap. There were 8 rows of these, each 3 feet apart, and the soldiers called these "lilies" because of their resemblance to the flower. Then in front of these, were another set of stakes, this time a foot long with an iron hook attached, and these were set firmly in the

---

6   The Latin term here is *cippi*, which means both boundary stone and tombstone. This is likely a bit of play on words by the soldiers - this was a boundary between the Roman camp and the Gauls, but also a place where many Gauls were likely to die.

7   The Latin term here is *quincunx*, which is also the shape of the Roman infantry formation. These are rows that are offset with one another so that the gaps in row one are filled by row two. It looks like a repeating pattern of the number "5" on a die.

ground. These scattered across the ground at various intervals, and the soldiers called these "spurs."

[74] After finishing this set of defensive works, Caesar constructed parallel fortifications of exactly the same kind facing outwards in the opposite direction.[8] He tried to follow flat, favorable contours of the land as best he could, and when complete, the outer circuit was 14 miles long. Caesar did this in order to prevent his soldiers from being surrounded and attacked by an outside force, no matter how large it might be. And so they wouldn't have to leave the fortified confines of the camp, he ordered his men to collect thirty days of corn and rations.

Fig. 142: Recreation of Caesar's defenses at Alesia

GALLIC REINFORCEMENTS

[75] While all this was happening at Alesia, the Gauls called for a council of their leaders, and they decided to go against Vercingetorix's idea of gathering all men who were old enough to bear arms. Instead, they decided that each state should provide a set number of men to help support the Gallic

---

8   This second set of defensive structures is known as the contravallation because it's meant to keep people out rather than hem people in.

cause. This was done because they were worried that with such a massive force, they wouldn't be able to keep order among the troops, nor tell them apart, nor feed them all. They asked for 35,000 men from the Aedui and their dependents (the Segusiavi, Ambivareti, Aulerci Brannovices, and the Blannovii) and the same number from the Arverni and the groups they ruled (the Eleuteti, Cadurci, Gabali, and Vallavii). They required 12,000 men each from the Senones, Sequani, Bituriges, Santones, Ruteni, and the Carnutes. They demanded 10,000 from the Bellovaci and just as many from the Lemovices. From the Pictones, Turoni, Parisii and Helvii, they asked for 8,000 each, and they sought 5,000 each from the Seussiones, Ambiani, Mediomatrici, Petrocorii, Nervii, Morni, and Nitobriges, and an equal amount from the Aulerci Cenomani. There were 4,000 men requested of the Atrebates; 3,000 each from the Bellocassi, Lexovii, and Aulerci Eburovices; and 2,000 each from the Rauraci and Boii. A total of 30,000 troops were requisitioned from all the states that border the Atlantic Ocean, which they call the Armoricae in their own language (and which include the Curiosolites, Redones, Ambibarii, Caletes, Osismi, Lemovices, Veneti, and Unelli). Of all these groups, only the Bellovaci did not meet their quota of troops, since they declared they would fight their own war against the Romans and they didn't take orders from anyone. But when Commius asked them personally, they sent along 2,000 troops out of respect for their relationship with him.

[76] As previously mentioned, Caesar had allied with Commius much earlier and made use of his valuable services years during his invasion of Britain. As a result of his faithful service, Caesar ensured that Commius' tribe was exempt from taxation, and he personally gave him control of the land of the Morini. But the Gauls have such a strong spirit when it comes to maintaining their freedom and preserving their heroic reputation, that neither lavish gifts nor private friendship made a lasting impact on them. Now, they completely devoted themselves in heart and mind to the war at hand, and in doing so, they gathered 8,000 cavalry and about 240,000 infantry soldiers. They gathered in the land of the Aedui and were counted

and organized there, with officers appointed for each of the contingents. Supreme command was entrusted to the leading generals: Commius of the Atrebates, Viridomarus and Eporedorix of the Aedui, and Vercassivellaunus of the Arverni, who was a cousin of Vercingetorix. They had men from each of the states assigned to them to form an advisory council for how to conduct the war. And so they all marched to Alesia, full of spirit and bursting with confidence. Not a single one of them could imagine that the Romans could withstand the sight of such a massive force of troops - especially since they were surrounded in the front and the rear. For the besieged Gauls in the town would come out to attack the Romans' inner walls, while at the same time this enormous force of cavalry and infantry would show up at their outer walls.

[77] But when the day on which they expected the Gallic reinforcements to arrive had passed, the besieged Gauls inside Alesia called together a council. For they were out of food and had no idea what was happening with the Aedui, and they needed to discuss what to do about it. Several plans were proposed - some suggested they surrender, while others advocated an attack while they still had the strength. Among these was Critognatus' scheme, and his speech is worth hearing if only for its incredibly vile cruelty. He was from the most noble family of all the Arverni, and from this position of power he spoke.

> *"I'm not even going to acknowledge those who suggest surrender, disgracing us by making us slaves. These people shouldn't even be considered Gauls, nor should they be allowed to stand and speak here in the council. No, my business is with those of you who want to attack, in whom ancient memories of our Gallic courage still remain.*

> *Not being able to endure hardship and hunger for even a little bit isn't courage - it's cowardice! It's easier to find men who are willing to die recklessly in battle than it is to find those who can calmly endure the suffering of the siege. And I'd be in favor of this plan if we had nothing else to lose other than our own lives.*

> *But let us look to the rest of Gaul, who we have asked to come to our aid. What kind of effect will it have on our brothers and friends, if, when they arrive, they see a heap of 80,000 dead*

Gauls? How will they react if they're forced to fight over our corpses? So if not for your own good, do it for them. Don't rob them of your support, for they have left the safety of their homes and thrown themselves into danger to help you. Set aside this craziness, carelessness, and cowardice, which will doom all of Gaul to everlasting slavery.

Do you doubt the faithfulness and courage of your countrymen just because they didn't arrive on the exact right day? Do you think the Romans are out there building their defensive walls just for the fun of it? If you can't be assured that our comrades are on their way through messages from your friends - I know all roads are blockaded - then look at what the Romans are doing, and take that as evidence that our reinforcements grow close. They're out there working on their ditches and walls and towers 24-hours a day!

So what am I suggesting we do? The same thing our ancestors did decades ago in the war against the Cimbri and Teutones - a war which wasn't nearly as important as this one. When they were driven back inside their towns and forced to suffer similar hardships, they stayed alive by eating those who weren't able to bear arms in battle. They didn't surrender to the enemy!

And even if we didn't have such a gruesome example to go on, I'd say we should be proud to create it today, so that our acts of liberty might live on forevermore. How in the world was that war worse than this one? The Cimbri, after devastating Gaul and destroying our people, left our land to go conquer others. They left us our land, laws, life, and liberty!

But what other motives could the Romans have - having become so jealous of us - than a desire to permanently settle down in our lands, and subject our noble and powerful people to perpetual slavery? For they've done this in every war they've ever fought!

But even if you don't know what Rome's done in far off nations, just look to our Gallic neighbors to the south, who have been reduced to a mere province. They've been stripped of their rights, lost their laws, and been pressed under the fasces[9] into eternal slavery."

---

9   The Roman *fasces* were bundles of sticks with an axe through the center. Roman *consuls* and *praetors* would have a series of attendants carry the *fasces* in front of them as a sign of their power or *imperium*. In more recent history, these *fasces* have served as the basis for our term "fascism," which implies a far-right authoritarian government with a dictatorial leader.

[78] After everyone's ideas had been heard, they decided that those who weren't fit for battle, either because of their age or health, should leave the town. Moreover, they decided that they should do everything in their power not to have to resort to Critognatus' plan [of eating the weak], but if their Gallic reinforcements were even further delayed, they all agreed they would rather follow through with that than surrender to the Romans. Then the Mandubii, who let the Gauls into their town (i.e., Alesia) were sent away with their wives and children. When they reached the Roman camp, they surrendered and begged the Romans for food, saying they'd happily serve them as slaves. But Caesar just posted more guards along the rampart[10] and turned them away.

THE BATTLE OF ALESIA

[79] While this debate was going on, Commius and the rest of the generals, who were entrusted with ultimate command, arrived at Alesia with all their troops, and they made camp on a hill outside the city, no more than a mile from our own fortifications. The next day their cavalry rode out and filled the entire plain, which, as I mentioned earlier, was 3-miles long. Then they placed their infantry behind them on higher ground. The town of Alesia had a bird's-eye view of the entire plain, and the troops within rejoiced and congratulated each other at the site of the Gallic reinforcements. And so the soldiers poured out of the town and set up a camp outside its walls, and they built small bridges over the nearest trench, filled it in with soil, and prepared for an assault and the chaos of war.

[80] Caesar positioned his army on both sides of the fortifications so that everyone knew their responsibility, and then he ordered the cavalry to ride out and start the battle. They had a commanding view from the camp since it included several ridges and hilltops, and the troops were jittery and restless as they waited for the fight. The Gauls had positioned archers and skirmishers among their cavalry to help out in case they needed to

---

10 A rampart is an earthen, ramp-like embankment that serves as part of a fortification

retreat and to bolster their defense against our cavalry's charge, and a few of our soldiers were unexpectedly wounded by these troops and had to leave the battle. When the Gauls were confident they were winning the battle and saw our troops beaten back by their sheer numbers, all of them everywhere - the ones inside the circumvallation walls as well as the reinforcements outside - shouted and screamed to bolster the morale of their comrades. As the battle raged for all to see, no action - brave or cowardly - could be hidden, and both sides were spurred on by their desire for glory and their fear for failure. And so the battle went from noon to dusk, without either side gaining a decisive edge. Then our German allies gathered their horsemen and charged a contingent of the enemy, soundly routing them, and when that group of Gauls turned to flee, the Germans surrounded their archers and hacked them to death. The same was happening elsewhere too, and our men had pushed the enemy all the way back to their own camp, so they had no chance of rallying their troops. And those Gauls who had come out of Alesia turned around and trudged back into the town, discouraged and on the verge of despair.

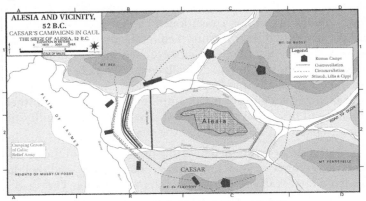

Fig. 143: Map of the Siege of Alesia (52 BC)

[81] Over the course of the next day, the Gauls [outside our walls] made a huge number of bridges and ladders and grappling hooks, and then they snuck out in the middle of the night and crept towards our fortifications. Suddenly, they raised a booming war cry so that their comrades in the town

could hear that they were making their move. The Gauls threw down bridges over our trenches, and they were knocking our men off the rampart with their slings and arrows and stones. They were really conducting a proper assault. While they were doing this, Vercingetorix heard their show, and he blew his war trumpet and led his troops outside the walls of Alesia. Just like before, our troops returned to their assigned positions and began harassing the Gauls with slings and cannonballs and bullets and sharp stakes that they had fixed into the walls.[11] Since it was pitch black outside, no one could see, and many were wounded on both sides, and our artillery fired several stones into the fray. Then, Marc Antony and Gaius Trebonius, the lieutenants who were in charge of this part of the wall called up troops from the more remote parts of the fortifications and had them help out the Romans soldiers wherever they were hard pressed.

[82] The Gauls did more damage when they fought far away from our fortifications, simply because of their numbers. But as they got closer, they were unaware of our traps and were snagged on our spurs, or impaled in our pits, or taken down with the large bolts fired from the ramparts and turrets. And so many were dying all over the place. Many of our own men were wounded, but our wall was never breached, and as the new day dawned, the Gauls became nervous that we might surround them on one of their flanks, and so they regrouped with the rest of their force. Meanwhile, Vercingetorix's forces inside the walls were bringing out the supplies and tools they'd prepared and they began filling in our trenches. But they took too long, and the outside force was already retreating before the inside force ever got close to our walls. And thus, they returned to the town unsuccessful in their mission.

[83] By now the Gauls had been defeated twice, with numerous casualties each time, and so they met to discuss what

---

11 The "cannonballs" were 1 to 2 pound stones that would have been launched with a machine. No gunpowder was involved, and these stones were not large enough to break down walls, but they were useful for impeding an enemy's assault. The "bullets" would have been small stones that were used in slings.

to do. They summoned men from the local area who were familiar with the landscape, and they learned from them about the position of our upper camp. There was a hill on the north side that couldn't be included in our fortifications since it was just too big around, and so our men built their camp below it on its steep slopes, putting them at quite the disadvantage. It was Gaius Antistius Reginus and Gaius Caninius Rebilus, both lieutenants, who commanded this camp with two legions. The Gallic leaders learned about this location from their scouts, and they secretly decided what needed to be done. They chose 60,000 men from the most courageous tribes and planned for an attack around noon. To lead this, they appointed Vercassivellaunus of the Arverni, a relative of Vercingetorix. He left camp with his troops during the first watch of the previous night and was just about done with the march by daybreak.[12] They hid behind the large hill, and he told them to rest up after the long night's march. Just before noon he quickly assembled his troops and marched them against our camp (the one mentioned above), and at the same time the cavalry rode towards the defenses in the plain, and the rest of their forces presented themselves in front of their own base.

[84] When Vercingetorix saw his countrymen from the citadel of Alesia, he marched out of the town gates, and his army brought bridges and grappling hooks, poles, and ladders, and everything necessary to make an assault on the walls. Fighting broke out everywhere all at once, and both sides tried every conceivable strategy. The Gauls gathered wherever the walls seemed to be the weakest, and the Roman army was stretched so thin that putting up a good fight was difficult. And the Gallic troops back behind the fighting boomed war cries that frightened our troops: truly what you can't see is often the scariest thing of all. And each Roman knew that their own personal safety depended on everyone else holding up against the assault.

[85] Caesar found a vantage point so he could see every-

---

12 The Roman military divided the night into four watches, with each one lasting 3 hours. Since he left during the first watch, Vercassivellaunus would have started his march shortly after the sun went down.

thing that was going on in each part of the battle, and he sent help to where it was needed most. Both sides felt that this was the critical moment to make their strongest push. The Gauls knew they were done for if they couldn't break through walls, and the Romans knew victory was at hand if they could just hold out. The fiercest fighting took place near the camp on the slopes of the hill, where, as we mentioned earlier, Vercassivellaunus had been sent. The steep slope was a huge disadvantage. Some of the Gauls rained down bolts and arrows upon us, while others approached in a *testudo* formation,[13] and fresh troops were continuously replacing the exhausted and wounded. The Gauls made a dirt ramp up against the fortifications, both giving them a way into the fort and covering up the traps we laid in the ground. Our soldiers had lost their strength and their weapons.

[86] When Caesar saw what was happening there, he sent Labienus with six cohorts to relieve the soldiers who were under attack. If they weren't able to defend the fort, Caesar said, he should gather the cohorts and fight their way out, but only do that if it was absolutely necessary. Then Caesar went around to the other troops, shouting encouragement not to collapse under the pressure. He urged them that everything that had worked so hard for in every other battle came down to this very day, this very hour. Meanwhile, the Gauls on the inside of the fortifications couldn't make any progress on flat ground because of the size of the defensive structures, and so they started to scale some of the more precipitous parts with the ladders and hooks that they had brought with them. They slew the defenders in the turrets with a cloud of bolts and arrows, filled in the trenches and pits with soil, and tore down the ramparts and parapets with their grappling-hooks.

[87] Caesar sent young Brutus forward with six cohorts and then sent Gaius Fabius with seven more. And finally, as the

---

13 *Testudo* is the Latin world for "tortoise." The *testudo* military formation indicated a tightly-packed group of soldiers, with some holding their shields out front and others holding their shields above their heads, both in an overlapping manner. This would create a defensive shell that looked something like a tortoise as they approached the enemy.

fighting got even tougher, he himself led a fresh set of troops into battle to help out the others. Once the battle picked back up and the enemy was pushed back, Caesar quickly marched to where he'd sent Labienus, and he took along 4 cohorts from the nearest fort and brought part of the cavalry along with him as well. And then he led them outside the trenches to try to attack the enemy from the rear. Meanwhile, Labienus, when he realized that neither the ramparts nor the ditches would stave off the enemy, gathered 40 cohorts (which just happened to be at a nearby post), and sent word to Caesar about what he was about to do. Caesar then rushed in to join the action.

Fig. 144: Ancient Roman marble statue known as "The Dying Gaul" (Capitoline Museums; Roman copy of a Hellenistic original from the 3rd century BC)

[88] They could all see Caesar coming because of the color of his cloak,[14] as well as his cavalry and cohorts, which were easy to see on the lower slopes from the fort and upper hillside. Then the enemy entered the battle, and both sides shouted their war cries, and these were echoed by yells across the ramparts throughout the entire set of fortifications. Our troops threw down their spears and started fighting with their swords. Then the Gauls noticed our cavalry behind them as our cohorts ap-

---

14 Caesar wore a red cloak known as a *paludamentum* in battle. During the Republic, this was a common garment for military commanders, but during the reign of Augustus it was restricted to the emperor himself.

proached in front; they tried to flee the battle but ran into our cavalry, and there was a tremendous slaughter. Sedulius, the leader of the Lemovices was slain, and Vergasillaunus of the Arverni was taken prisoner. In all, Caesar captured 74 military standards, and out of the vast hordes of the enemy, only a few returned safely to their camp. When the men in the town saw their comrades slaughtered and retreat, they brought their troops back inside the town walls. When they heard about what happened to their countrymen, the Gauls in the main reinforcement camp fled immediately, and if our soldiers weren't so exhausted from all the fighting, all of the enemy's troops could have been destroyed. Just after midnight, our cavalry was sent out to chase them down, and many of those in the rear were taken prisoner or cut to pieces. The rest escaped and fled in different directions back to their home states.

Vercingetorix Surrenders

[89] The next day Vercingetorix convened a council and said to the group that he hadn't undertaken this war for his own personal gain, but rather for the freedom of all the Gauls. And so, since Fortune had sealed their fate, he gave himself to the Gauls to try to appease the Romans - either by putting him to death or by handing him over alive. They sent messengers to Caesar to get his take on the matter, and he ordered the Gauls to give up their weapons and hand over their leaders. Caesar sat in front of his camp's defenses as the Gallic leaders were brought before him. Vercingetorix surrendered, and Gauls threw down their weapons. Then Caesar gave one Gallic prisoner to each of his soldiers as a spoil of war, although he withheld those from the Aedui and Arverni, in case he needed them to gain leverage over those states.

[90] After all this had been settled, Caesar marched into the land of the Aedui and took power there. The Arverni sent ambassadors to him there, promising to do as he wished, and Caesar demanded a vast number of hostages from them. He then sent his own legions to camp for the winter, and he gave back around 20,000 prisoners to the Aedui and the Arverni.

Fig. 145: The Surrender of Vercingetorix by Lionel Royer
(Musée Crozatier 1899)

Next he sent Titus Labienus into the land of the Sequani with two legions and cavalry, and ordered Marcus Sempronius Rutilus to go along with him. And he sent his lieutenant, Gaius Fabius, along with Lucius Minucius Basilus and two legions into the land of the Remi to help prevent attacks from their neighbors, the Bellovaci. He sent Gaius Antistius Reginus into the land of the Ambivareti, Titus Sextius into the land of the Bituriges, and Gaius Caninius Rebilus into the land of the Ruteni, all with one legion each. Then he placed Quintus Tullius Cicero and Publius Sulpicius in the land of the Aedui at Cabillonum and Matisco near the Arar River to safeguard the corn supply. Caesar himself chose to winter at Bibracte, and when messengers from his campaign told news of it in Rome, the senate decreed a 20-day festival in our honor.

The Rest of the Story

The story of the siege of Alesia that you've just read comes near the end of Caesar's *The Gallic Wars*. By this point, Caesar had ascended to Rome's highest political position (the consulship), led armies into Gaul, Germany, and Britain, killed a million men, and enslaved a million more. Caesar's story, however, was only getting started. His legate, a man named Aulus Hirtius, added an eighth book to Caesar's *The Gallic Wars* after his death. This focused on the Gallic uprisings of 51 and 50 BC, before Caesar marched his army into Italy. After Alesia, the Gauls realized there was little chance of defeating Caesar in a large pitched battle, so they attempted a series of smaller, simultaneous uprisings throughout the land. It didn't work, and Caesar led his troops home having brought a new province under Roman control.

Caesar continued to chronicle his battles and accomplishments in the years to come. His *Commentarii de Bello Civili*, what we call *The Civil Wars*, details the beginning of Caesar's clash with the senatorial aristocracy across three books. The first of these books details the senatorial attacks on Caesar and the dissolution of his friendship with Pompey. He makes a point of saying he did everything in his power to mend that relation but, alas, had no success. Book 2 centers on the wars of his generals, with Gaius Trebonius laying siege to Massilia (modern Marseille, France) and Gaius Scribonius Curio doing battle against the governor of Africa and the Numidian King Juba. Book 3 then takes the reader into Caesar's showdown battle with Pompey at the site of Pharsalus (located in northern Greece). After being crushed on the battlefield, Pompey fled to Egypt where he was promptly executed. Caesar followed only to find Pompey had already been killed. Caesar did, however, find a very alive political leader - Cleopatra VII, the last rule of the Ptolemaic dynasty in Egypt.

Caesar ended his autobiography with this encounter, but noted that a description of his future conquests would come in subsequent volumes. These focused on his wars in Egypt, Africa, and Spain, and were most likely penned by his officers. We'll pick up Caesar's story after hearing Plutarch's account of his war in Gaul.

Plutarch's *Life of Caesar*

Plutarch was a Greco-Roman author living around 100 AD (ca. 46 AD - after 119). He was Greek because he was born in the town of Chaeronea in central Greece and writing in Greek, and Roman because he was living at the peak of the Roman Empire. He lived most of his life in Greece, and in addition to writing, Plutarch served as priest and, perhaps, a political magistrate. His priesthood is particularly interesting: he served the cult of Apollo at Delphi, site of the famous Oracle, and thus acts as an important source for the way that ancient Greeks would have consulted the Oracle to receive her divinely inspired prophecies. There is no doubt, however, that Plutarch is most famous for his writings. During his life, Plutarch penned a variety of texts: the *Moralia*, which was a collection of essays and speeches, the *Lives of the Roman Emperors*, which detailed the lives of the early Roman emperors from Augustus to Vitellius, and the *Parallel Lives*, which gave biographical accounts of Classical history's most famous individuals.

Fig. 146: Engraving of Plutarch by Leonard Gaultier
(National Gallery of Art, Washington, D.C.; 1561 - 1641)

It was the last of these, the *Parallel Lives*, that Plutarch is most famous for, and this is the collection of texts from which we get our excerpt about Julius Caesar. In this series of biographies, Plutarch pairs up one Greek with one Roman who had a similar set of actions, fate, or impact over the course of their lives. It begins with a few mythical examples, with the Athenian hero Theseus being placed next to the Roman founder Romulus, and next we get the Spartan leader Lycurgus paired with the second king of Rome, Numa Pompilius. After this, Plutarch moves into more historical examples. So, for example, Pericles gets matched with Fabius Maximus, Pyrrhus gets paired with Marius, and the Roman leader Julius Caesar is paired with the Greek leader Alexander the Great. There were a total of 48 individual biographies 24 pairs), although scholars have suggested that there may have been a few more that are no longer preserved, and many of the ones we do have are fragmentary.

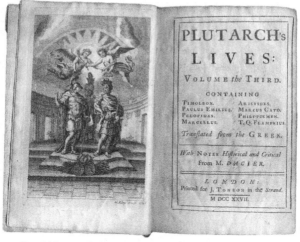

Fig. 147: An edition of Plutarch's Parallel Lives from 1727

One of the things that makes these biographies so intriguing is that Plutarch seems more interested in using short stories and anecdotes to illustrate each individual's character or spirit - the overall vibe of each person - rather than simply list their political or military accomplishments. So, as we'll see in this excerpt from his *Life of Julius Caesar*, Plutarch spends quite a bit of time telling stories about random soldiers in Caesar's army, just to give the reader a sense for how inspiring of a leader Julius Caesar was. His main goal, then, was not so much a perfect accounting of each individual's deeds, but rather to show how the lives of famous ancient Greeks and Romans could set examples - good or bad - that might give people in Plutarch's own time a model to emulate or avoid.

That's not to say that Plutarch's writings aren't useful for historians. Because he covered such a long time period with the various "great men" he wrote about, Plutarch actually serves as one of our most important historical sources for much of Greco-Roman antiquity. His *Life of Pyrrhus* - the man who lends his name to the term Pyrrhic Victory - is, in fact, our best source for what was happening in Greece and Italy during the period from around 300 to 264 BC. On a smaller scale, Plutarch leaves clues that help fill in the historical picture with fine-grained details. In his *Life of Caesar*, for example, Plutarch tells a story about how Caesar used to dictate his memoirs from horseback as he rode through Gaul, so that he wouldn't have to waste time doing it once they were camped. That sort of small detail helped scholars settle a debate about whether Caesar actually wrote his *Commentaries* himself, or whether he dictated them to a scribe.

Plutarch's *Life of Caesar* begins with Caesar's childhood, in the aftermath of the conflict between Marius and Sulla. Caesar's aunt Julia was married to Marius, leader of the *populares* faction in Rome. As a result, Caesar was seen as a threat to Sulla (Marius' political adversary) from the very beginning, enough that he had to flee Rome in his early years. So as a young man, Caesar sailed eastward across the Mediterranean, to start making his name as a soldier. From the very beginning he stood out from the crowd, being awarded the civic crown for saving a fellow soldier's life in battle.

After Sulla died, Caesar returned to Rome and started to train as an orator and lawyer. This took him east once again, but this time he was captured by pirates. Plutarch's story about this episode perfectly captures Caesar's spirit. As he's locked up, Caesar continues his oratory training, composing speeches in the hull of a ship. He mocks his pirate captors, chastising them for only setting his ransom at 20 talents (ca. 1400 lbs) of silver, claiming that he was worth at least 50 talents (ca. 3400 lbs). He promised the pirates that upon his release, the first thing he was going to do was come back, capture them, and kill them - and it turns out that's exactly what he did. Overall, this story epitomizes what Plutarch is trying to do: it doesn't mention any of Caesar's political machinations or military glory, but it perfectly shows Caesar's calm in the face of danger, his lofty opinion of himself, and his ability to follow through on his promises.

From there, Plutarch describes Caesar's climb along the political ladder. His successes again seem to know no bounds. He is elected *quaestor*, *aedile*, and praetor, and along the way bribes his way to be elected *pontifex maximus* - the chief priest of the Roman state - as well. Caesar went into massive amounts of debt, both to win the elections and to perform his duties once he was in office. Plutarch tells a short story that during his time as *aedile*, the elected position in charge of festivals and games, Caesar put on a show with 320 pairs of gladiators, over ten times what was normally expected.

Caesar was eventually shipped off to Spain as a *propraetor* (a provincial governor), and his battles there were largely to raise money and repay his creditors. Upon his return to Rome, Caesar solidified his allegiances with Pompey - Rome's most famous general - and Crassus - Rome's richest of the rich, and he leveraged these alliances to be elected *consul* in 59 BC. As *consul*, he worked to repay Pompey and Crassus for their support, trying to get land for Pompey's veterans and pass tax policy favorable to Crassus' vast amounts of wealth.

During his time as *consul*, Caesar was perceived as an increasingly formidable threat by the traditional senatorial aristocracy. Plutarch says that he so shamed his fellow *consul*, Bibulus, that he shut himself up in his house for most of his term. The senate tried to limit Caesar's power as his time in office drew to a close, awarding him the measly "forests and tracks of Italy" as area to serve as *proconsul* (also a provincial

The First Triumvirate: Pompey, Caesar, and Crassus

Fig. 148 (left): Bust of Pompey
(National Archaeological Museum of Venice; 1st centuy BC)

Fig. 149 (center): Bust of Caesar
(Vatican Museums; 1st century BC)

Fig. 150 (right): Bust of Crassus
(Louvre Museum; 1st century BC)

governor). Caesar used his connections to have this overturned, however, and was soon given a 5-year appointment to serve as *proconsul* with *imperium* in the provinces of Cisalpine Gaul (the Italian side of the Alps) and Illyricum (modern Croatia).

As you read Plutarch's description, you'll notice some (but not complete) overlap with Caesar's own account of the Gallic wars. Consider what's the same, what's different, and why that may be the case. These similarities and differences could be in terms of the content that's included or omitted or in terms of the style of the writing itself.

We'll let Plutarch take it from there.

Words of the Ancients
Plutarch's *Life of Caesar*
The Wars in Gaul (15.1-27.10)

[15] So far we've covered Caesar's life before the Gallic wars, but now he seemed born anew, entering a new life and

a new land. His time in Gaul, and his many conquests during his subjugation of it, showed that he was every bit as good of a soldier and general as any leader who has ever appeared at the head of an army. If we compare him to Fabius or Metellus or Scipio - or even men closer to his own time like Sulla, Marius, Lucullus, or even Pompey himself (whose fame and glory in war reached all the way to the heavens), we'll see that Caesar's achievements surpassed them all. One of them he surpassed because of the difficulty of the terrain he was fighting in; another he surpassed because of the amount of land he conquered. Still another he bested in the number and strength of the troops he defeated. He was more impressive than another one in his ability to make Roman allies out of such savage and treacherous barbarians. He was better than yet another in the mercy and clemency to those he defeated, and surpassed another in gifts he gave to his own soldiers. And he surpassed them all in the number of battles he fought and the number of enemies he killed. For even though he fought in Gaul for less than 10 years, he laid siege to more than 800 towns, conquered 300 tribes, and fought battles against a grand total of more than 3,000,000 men. In total, he killed 1,000,000 and took another 1,000,000 as prisoners.

CAESAR'S INSPIRING LEADERSHIP

[16] He was so good at leading and inspiring his soldiers, that those troops - who were just ordinary men on any other military expedition - were nearly invincible when it came to any battle where Caesar's glory was at stake, courageously throwing themselves into all kinds of danger. Take, for example, Acilius. In a naval battle at Massilia, he had his right hand cut off with a sword. But he clung to his shield with his left hand, bashing the enemy in the face with it, until he had routed the entire crew and taken control of the ship. Or look at Cassius Scaeva. When he was in a battle near Dyrrhachium, he had one of his eyes shot out with an arrow, had his shoulder struck with a spear, had another spear lodged in his leg, and on top of all that, he had 130 darts and arrows sticking out of his shield. So he shouted at the enemy as though he were going to surren-

der. But when two of them came up to meet him, he sliced the shoulder off of one guy and cracked the other guy in the face, making him run away. Then his friends ran up to help him, and he made his escape. Another time, in Britain, many of Caesar's senior centurions got themselves stuck in marshy waters and were under serious attack. Then a common soldier, with Caesar looking on, dashed into the middle of the fight, and after beating back the enemy through a series of incredibly daring deeds, rescued the centurions. After this, he went back into the muddy water, partially swimming and partially wading through it, and in doing so, he lost his shield. Caesar and his officers saw all this and went to meet the soldier with cries of joy and applause. But when the soldier emerged from the water, he threw himself at Caesar's feet, begging forgiveness for losing his shield in the process. There was another instance where Scipio captured one of Caesar's ships in Africa, and Granius Petro, a newly elected *quaestor*, was on it. Scipio took all the other passengers as war prizes, but decided to let the *quaestor* keep his life. Granius, however, responded that Caesar's troops were accustomed to granting - rather than receiving - mercy, and he killed himself with his own sword.

[17] It was Caesar himself who created this dedication to honor and glory in his men. First of all, he spared no expense when it came to distributing the spoils of war and military honors. He didn't keep all this wealth for himself to live some luxurious life, but rather pooled it all into a public fund as a reward for courageous deeds. And he wouldn't take any more of this than he gave to his most deserving soldiers. Second of all, Caesar threw himself into all sorts of danger and never avoided any of the hard work. Now the fact that he liked danger didn't surprise his troops, for they knew that he loved glory more than anything. But the fact that he worked so hard amazed them, for Caesar was a scrawny guy, with soft white skin, and he had a mental condition that made him susceptible to epileptic seizures, which started up when he was in Corduba.[15]

But he didn't use this weakness as an excuse to live a leisurely life; instead, he used war as the best medicine for his

---

15 Modern Cordoba, a town in the Andalusia region of Spain.

Fig. 151: Sculpture of Roman legions in Gaul
(Gallo-Roman Museum, Lyon; 1st to 3rd centuries AD)

shortcomings. Through his endless marches, his meager meals, his camping out in the elements, and his continuous physical exercise, he built his body to deal with his disease and to repel all attacks. He usually slept in his carts or litters,[16] so that he was on the move even when he was resting. During the day, he was taken to forts and camps, with one slave sitting next to him, writing down everything he was saying, and another soldier behind him at the ready with his sword drawn.

He moved so quickly that once he left Rome, he made it to the Rhone river in only eight days. Caesar had been an excellent horseback rider since he was a child, and he would often sit

---

16 A litter is a bed or small compartment that was carried on the shoulders of people.

on the horse with his hands tied behind his back, and then have it gallop full speed ahead. And during the war with Gaul, he was so good that he was able to dictate letters while on horseback – and not only that, he could give directions to two scribes at once (or even more, as Oppius claims). It's generally thought that Caesar was the first to communicate with his friends using a secret code, if either the urgency of the situation or the vastness of the city itself left no time for an in-person meeting about important matters.

And you can see how little he cared about the fanciness of his food in the following story. When he was having dinner with Valerius Leo in Mediolanum,[17] he had a dish with asparagus in front of him, but instead of olive oil, perfume had mistakenly been poured on it. Caesar ate the dish without making the slightest fuss, and then he yelled at his friends for saying something was wrong with it. "It was fine," he said, "to simply not eat what you don't like. But to criticize someone's lack of refinement, shows a lack of refinement in oneself." There was another time that a storm caused him to take refuge in the cottage of a poor man. There was only a single room, and it could barely house a single person. So Caesar told his companions that honors should be reserved for the strongest men, but necessities should be reserved for the weakest. So he had Oppius, who was sick at the time, sleep in the single room, while Caesar himself and the rest of his crew slept in a shed.

CAESAR ENTERS GAUL

Caesar first went to war in Gaul against the Helvetii and the Tigurini. After burning 12 of their own towns, and 400 of their own villages, they were going to march through the part of Gaul that had already been turned into a Roman province, just like the Cimbri and Teutones had done before.[18] This new

---

17 Modern Milan, a major city in northern Italy.

18 The Cimbri and Teutones were tribes from northern Germany and Scandinavia that migrated into Roman territories around 100 BC. They dealt the Romans a massive defeat at the Battle of Arausio in 105 BC, killing more than 100,000 Roman troops and auxiliaries.

group of Gauls were just as courageous as their predecessors, and just as numerous as well: there were a total of 300,000 of them, and 190,000 of those were able to fight. Caesar didn't personally go to war with the Tigurini, but instead ordered Labienus to do so, and he routed them near the Arar River.

The Helvetii, on the other hand, surprised Caesar when they unexpectedly attacked him as he was marching his army to an allied town. But he was able to retreat to what he thought was an advantageous position, and there he gathered his troops and had his horse brought to him. Then he said, "I'll use this horse to chase down the enemy after we win, but for now let's attack," and so he led his infantry against them on foot. It was a long and difficult battle, but eventually he was able to make the main part of their army retreat. The hardest part, however, was taking their wagons and tents, for in these places the Gallic women and children defended themselves, fighting alongside the men. In the end they were hacked to pieces, but this resistance caused the battle to last until nearly midnight. This victory was glorious in and of itself, but then Caesar did something even more impressive. He gathered up about 100,000 of the Helvetii who fled the battle, and he forced them to reoccupy the land they just left, making them reinhabit the cities they'd just burnt to the ground. For Caesar feared that if these places were left uninhabited, the Germans might come through and take it for themselves.

His second war in the region was actually defending the Gauls against the Germans. Caesar himself had previously made Ariovistus king of the Germans, and they were once an ally of Rome. But they were terrible neighbors to those under Roman rule, and he thought it likely that once the opportunity presented itself, the Germans would break this alliance, march into Gaul, and try to take it over.

Caesar, however, found his own officers afraid, especially the young aristocratic ones, who only came along to use the campaign to improve their wealth and status. So he called them all together and told them to leave, to not risk fighting if they were going to act like cowards instead of men - he'd attack the Germans with only the 10th Legion. And although he didn't expect these Germans to be any less tough than the Cimbri, they weren't going to find him a general any less impressive than Marius himself.[19] When they heard this, the 10th Legion sent Caesar a messenger to thank him for the compliment, and the soldiers in all the other legions complained about their officers' cowardice. This made everyone all the more eager to fight, and the entire army followed him into battle, marching for days on end, and camping only about 200 25 miles from the enemy.

When he saw the Roman army approaching, Ariovistus' confidence vanished. He never expected the Romans would actually attack the Germans, since he didn't think they'd even be able to put up a viable defense against a German attack.[20] Moreover, he could see that his troops' morale sank when they saw the Roman army. They became even more discouraged when they heard the prophecies of their priestesses, who tell the future by reading the rapids in the rivers and interpreting the flow and noises of the streams, for they advised not to engage in battle until the new moon rose in the sky.

When Caesar got word of this and saw that the German still hadn't moved, he thought it prudent to attack while they were afraid, rather than sit around and wait. So he approached the hilltop forts where the Germans camped, and he mocked and antagonized them so badly that they finally, furiously rushed down the slopes to fight. But Caesar decisively routed them, and he then gave chase for 50 miles as they retreated – all the way to the Rhine River[21] – and that whole area was covered with the weapons and armor and bloodstained bodies. When Ariovistus finally tried to cross back over the Rhine, it was with

---

19 After their defeat at Arausio, the Romans called upon Marius to lead the war against the Cimbri and Teutones. He was elected *consul* for an unprecedented fifth consecutive term and soundly defeated them. This reconfirmed his status as one of Rome's greatest generals ever.

20 In the ancient world, attacking was usually more dangerous than defending, since the defenders could make use of fortifications and choose advantageous terrain.

21 The Rhine River was the border between Germany and Gaul, and today it still stands as a border between Germany and France.

Fig. 152: Etching of Ariovistus surrendering to Caesar (British Museum; 1808)

only a small army, for it is said that 80,000 were killed on that day.

After this, Caesar sent his troops to their winter camps in the land of the Sequani. He was headed to Rome to handle his business, and along the way he passed through the part of Gaul which contained the Po River (since it's the Rubicon River that separates Cisalpine Gaul from Italy). While he was there, he stayed for a while and used the time to make friends with the locals. People were constantly coming to Caesar, and they always found their requests granted, for he never let them go without a promise and a kind word (and the hope for even better things down the road). And this whole time, Pompey never got wise to the fact that Caesar was using Roman weapons and a Roman army to achieve his conquests, while at the same time using the wealth from those conquests to personally win the love of the Roman people.

However, when Caesar heard that the Belgae, who were the fiercest fighters in all of Gaul and took up a third of the country, were revolting with tens of thousands of armed men, he immediately marched back to Gaul. He caught up with the Belgae as they were laying waste to Rome's Gallic allies, and he quickly defeated the largest contingent of them. For even though they had massive numbers, they didn't put up much of a defense, and the Roman infantry could cross the rivers and marshes by walking on the bodies of the dead.

Out of all the groups that revolted, the tribes living near the Atlantic Ocean surrendered to Rome without fighting, so Caesar instead took his army to attack the Nervii, the most vicious and belligerent tribe in the Gaul's most violent region. The Nervii lived in a land covered with thick, unending forests, and they hid their women and children and belongings deep in the woods, out of harm's way. Then they launched a surprise attack with 60,000 troops against Caesar, before he was ready and while they were still constructing their defenses. Soon they overtook the Roman cavalry, and then they surrounded the 12th and the 7th Legions, killing all the officers. If it wasn't for Caesar himself taking up a shield and pushing his way through his own men to the front of the fighting, and if it wasn't for the 10th Legion rushing down the hill and breaking through the enemy lines to rescue him when they saw he was in danger, then it's likely that not a single Roman would have survived. But when they saw Caesar's heroic effort, they fought – as the saying goes – with inhuman strength. Even with this, however, they couldn't force the Nervii to turn and flee, so they hacked them to death where they stood defending themselves. Out of the 60,000 to start the battle, not more than 500 survived it, and out of their 400 senators, only 3 made it through alive.

Caesar Returns to Rome

When the Roman Senate heard about this, they decreed 15 days of festivals and sacrifices to the gods, a longer time than had ever been approved for any other victory. For they felt that the simultaneous revolt of so many different tribes posed an enormous danger, and the people's love for Caesar gave an extra shine to his victories.

After everything in Gaul calmed down, Caesar returned once again to handle his affairs in Rome, this time spending the winter near the Po River. Anyone running for office went to him for help, and he gave them money to bribe the people and buy their votes. Then, when they won the election, they did whatever they could to give Caesar even more power. Even the most powerful men in Rome came up to see Caesar in Lucca: Pompey and Crassus, Appius, the governor of Sardinia, and Nepos, the *proconsul* of Hispania (Spain). There were so many important men there, in one place and at one time, that there were 120 lictors and over 200 senators.

After discussing the matter, it was decided that Pompey and Crassus should be *consuls* again the next year, that Caesar should get new funding, and that he should also get another 5-year term as *proconsul*. It seemed a little absurd to anyone with a brain that all those politicians who received money from Caesar to win their elections would then turn around and award him even more money, like he was broke. It wasn't like they persuaded the senators to do this, though; it was more like they forced it. Cato wasn't there since he'd been sent away to Cyprus for the winter, but Favonius, who acted a lot like Cato, was present. And when he decided it wouldn't do any good to put up a fight in the senate, he ran out into the streets shouting about these absurdities and raging against Caesar. Nobody paid him any attention though, some of them ignoring him out of respect for Pompey and Crassus, but most of them doing so to please Caesar, for all their hopes depended on him.

THE FIRST ROMAN GENERAL IN GERMANY AND BRITAIN

[22] When Caesar returned to his troops in Gaul, he found the whole region embroiled in a massive war. For two of the mightiest German tribes - the Usipes and the Tenteritae - had just crossed the Rhine into Gaul. Caesar described the battle fought against those groups in his *Commentarii de Bello Gal-*

lico (*The Gallic Wars*). He said that the Germans had sent ambassadors to broker a truce with the Romans, and during these negotiations, they launched a surprise attack, routing Caesar's 5,000 infantry and 800 cavalry since they'd been taken off guard. Then the Germans sent another group of diplomats to trick him again, but this time he took the envoys captive and marched his army against the barbarians, since he thought faithfully negotiating with people who would break their oath was a fool's errand. Tanusius said that the Roman senate decreed festivals and sacrifices in honor of his victory, but Cato said that Caesar should be handed over to the Germans, which would help expunge Rome's guilt for having attacked the Germans while still under a truce by handing over the person directly responsible for it, placing the curse on the individual instead of the state.

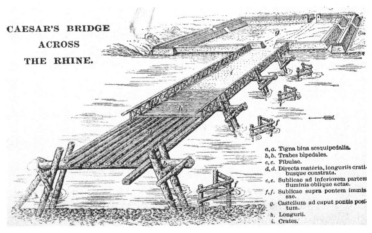

Fig. 153: Caesar was the first Roman general to enter Germany in 55 BC

Out of all those who crossed the Rhine into Gaul, 400,000 of them were hacked to pieces, and the few that escaped took shelter with the Sugambri, one of the Germanic states. Caesar used this as an excuse to lodge a formal complaint against the Sugambri, but really he wanted to be the first Roman to lead an army across the Rhine into Germany. So he began building a bridge across the river even though it was very wide. And at this particular place, it was nearly flooded with rough and turbulent waters , and the trunks and branches from nearby trees kept getting swept downstream and destroying the support beams for his bridge. But Caesar dealt with this by sinking massive wooden stakes into the river upstream of the bridge in order to catch the debris as it was swept downwards. And with the river tamed, Caesar finished construction of the bridge in just 10 days, a feat nearly beyond belief.

[23] He then marched his army across the river, but no one dared to put up a fight against him. Even the Suevi, the most warlike of all the Germans, fled with their belongings deep into the forest. So Caesar laid waste to the country, setting it ablaze, and he stopped by his faithful Roman allies to boost their morale. Then he went back to Gaul after spending 18 days in Germany.

But it was Caesar's invasion of Britain that stood as the most impressive testament to his courage. For he was the first to sail a navy into the Atlantic Ocean and the first to bring an army to lay siege to the island - an island whose geographical extent was still a matter of great debate among our historians, with many of them not believing it was a real place at all. So you might say that Caesar brought the Roman Empire beyond the edges of the known world. He crossed into Britain twice from the shores of Gaul across the channel, and in the battles he fought there, he hurt the enemy more than he helped himself. For the local populations were so dirt poor that there wasn't anything worth plundering. When Caesar couldn't finish his conquest of the island the way he wanted, he decided to take a few hostages from the local king and demand a tribute. Then he left the island.

When he got back to Gaul, Caesar received some letters that were about to be sent to him in Britain. These told him of the death of his daughter [Julia], who died giving birth to Pompey's child. Her death took an emotional toll, both on Caesar and on Pompey, especially considering the child died just a few days later. Their friends were just as heartbroken because they thought that this also spelled doom for their

Fig. 154: Caesar was the first Roman general to lead his men into Britannia in 55 and 54 BC

alliance, which had been barely keeping the Republic in peace.[22] Despite opposition from the tribunes, the Roman people took Julia's body and carried it into the Field of Mars. There, they performed her funerary rites and laid her to rest.

THE SIEGE OF ALESIA

[24] By this time, Caesar had so many troops that he had to place them in winter camps all over the place, while he himself headed back to Italy (as he normally did). Then another massive revolt broke out all across Gaul, and they started attacking Roman forts and trying to take over their camps. The largest and strongest of the Gallic tribes was led by Ambiorix. They completely annihilated Titurius and Cotta and their

---

22 Caesar and Pompey had been friends and allies years earlier, and together with Crassus they formed the informal alliance known as the First Triumvirate. Pompey was renowned as one of Rome's greatest military leaders, and Caesar was the new up-and-comer. Their relationship began to fray, however, during Caesar's time in Gaul, and the death of Caesar's daughter (who was Pompey's wife) furthered the disintegration of their friendship. When Caesar marched on Rome years later, he would also be marching against Pompey.

troops while also surrounding Cicero[23] and his legion and laying siege to them with 60,000 men. Cicero and his men just
barely avoided having their camp taken by storm, and all of
them ended up wounded as they defended their camp beyond
what was humanly possible.

When Caesar heard about what was going on, he immediately turned around and took 7,000 men to rescue Cicero from
the siege. But the Gauls heard he was coming, and they went to
cut his approach, utterly confident that they would overwhelm
his measly number of troops. Caesar helped feed the Gallic arrogance by continuously avoiding battle, that is, until he found
the perfect place for a small number of men to fight against
massive numbers. There he built a fortified camp, and instead
of allowing his soldiers to fight, he had them build the ramparts
and walls of the fort even higher than normal, like they were
terrified of the Gallic attack. The Gauls were overly cocky, and
instead of a concerted siege, they sent out unorganized groups
to attack. That's when Caesar unleashed his troops upon them,
forcing them to flee and killing many in the process.

[25] Caesar's success helped calm the many revolts that
were happening throughout Gaul, and during the winter, he
traveled far and wide to make sure they knew he was keeping
an eye on the rebels. Three new legions arrived from Italy to
replace the men he'd lost; two of those were sent by Pompey
and under his command, while the third was newly raised in
the region of Cisalpine Gaul, near the Po River. But the seeds
of war, which had been planted by the most vicious leaders in
Gaul, soon sprouted into the largest and deadliest conflict in
all the land. The Gallic forces grew strong with massive numbers of young men from all over the region ready to take up
arms, and they amassed their wealth and resources from their
well-fortified cities and from their remote towns, both of which
were difficult to invade. Moreover, the weather made it nearly
impossible for Caesar to put down the revolts. During the winter the rivers froze over, the forests were covered with snow,

---

23 This Quintus Tullius Cicero, the brother of the Roman orator and politician Marcus Tullius Cicero, who is usually who we refer to as ther
"Cicero."

the plains had been flooded, and their paths were obscured, either by snow drifts or swampy marshes, which made moving through the landscape almost hopeless. Therefore, many of tribes were engaged in revolt,, but the leaders of the revolt were the Arverni and the Carnutes, and the commander-in-chief of the Gallic forces was Vercingetorix, whose father had been put to death by the Gauls for trying to become a tyrant.

[26] After dividing up the Gallic forces and appointing officers for the troops, Vercingetorix continued recruiting soldiers from all over Gaul, all the way up to the Arar River. And when he learned that Caesar had enemies in Rome as well, he called all of Gaul to join the war. If he had done this just a bit later, when Caesar was embroiled in his civil war, Italy would have been in just as much trouble as they were with the Cimbri a half century earlier. But as it turned out, Caesar was perhaps the most blessed man ever when it came to waging war, and he was particularly good in the most crucial moments. So when he heard about the revolt, he returned along the same path he had just come, and he marched his army so fast, through such difficult conditions, that the barbarians thought they were up against a truly invincible force. It would have been credible if a single messenger could make it such a long way in such a short time, but Caesar's entire army had covered that whole distance, and they immediately started laying waste to the countryside, besieging their forts, conquering their cities, and granting clemency to those who surrendered. Then the Aedui entered the war against him. Up until this point, they'd been allied with the Romans, and had been loudly praised for doing so, but their flip to the Gallic rebels really sank the morale of Caesar's troops. So Caesar left this region, marching through the land of the Lingones all the way to the realm of the Sequani, who were friendly with Rome, standing as a buffer between Italy and Gaul. When he was there, however, the enemy pounced, surrounding his army with tens of thousands of troops. Caesar was eager to fight a decisive battle, and after a long time and countless slaughter, he defeated the Gallic forces. It does look like he struggled at first, however, since the Arverni display a short-sword in their temple that they claim once belonged to

Caesar. But upon his victory, Caesar saw this display himself, and it made him smile. His friends and advisors suggested that he take it down, but Caesar wouldn't allow it because it was now sacred.

[27] Most of the Gauls who escaped this battle took shelter with their king in the hilltop town of Alesia. And while Caesar was laying siege to this city, which most people thought was impregnable because of its mighty walls and myriad defenders, a threat came from the outside that was almost too great to put into words. For the strongest warriors from all the Gallic tribes had come together and marched to Alesia, about 300,000 troops in all. And the number of Gallic soldiers inside the city was around 170,0000. Caesar was caught between two mighty forces, both ready to lay siege to the Roman camp, so he ordered the construction of two walls for their protection, one facing the city and the other facing the outside reinforcements. For he felt that the Romans were doomed if the two groups united .[24]

The unparalleled danger that Caesar faced at Alesia brought him great fame and glory, since it provided more chances for brave and heroic deeds than any of his previous battles. But what's even more impressive is that he was able to battle and conquer tens of thousands of Gauls outside the city, without those inside the town even knowing they were there - and it goes beyond that, for the Roman troops fighting on the city-side of the wall didn't even know these reinforcements had arrived. They didn't even learn about the outside victory until they heard the cries of the men and women inside Alesia, as they witnessed the Roman army carrying heaps of shields decorated with gold and silver, armor stained with blood, drinking cups and Gallic-style tents into their own camp. That's how quickly this unbelievably massive force vanished from sight - like a ghost or a dream - and most of them lay dead on the battlefield. Then, after giving Caesar serious problems, the Gauls who were inside Alesia surrendered. The Gallic leader of the entire war, put on his best armor, clothed his horse, and rode

---

24 See Fig. 140 (page 245) for the location of Alesia and Fig. 143 (page 254) for the plan of the siege of Alesia.

through the city gates. He rode in a circle around Caesar, who just sat there, before leaping off his horse, throwing his armor to the ground, and kneeling at Caesar's feet. There, he sat motionless, until he was thrown in chains to be imprisoned until Caesar's triumph.[25]

Fig. 155: Colossal statue of Vercingetorix (Alesia, France; 1865)

---

25 The leader referenced is of course Vercingetorix. Compare the account of the Battle of Alesia in the last two paragraphs with Caesar's own account in the last section of our book.

The Rest of the Story

Plutarch continues to tell Caesar's story all the way through his assassination, and even a little bit beyond. When Caesar finished in Gaul, he was left with a dilemma. Many of the senators wanted to throw him in jail (or worse) for overextending his power: he was supposed to stay in Cisalpine Gaul, but he ended up leading his army all over Transalpine Gaul, Germany, and Britain. While he was in office as proconsul, he was immune from prosecution, but his term was running out, and in order to get a new appointment, he had to return to Rome. But Caesar wasn't allowed to march his army into Italy - the previous civil wars of Marius and Sulla had halted that practice - and if he arrived without his army, he was likely to be imprisoned before that reappointment could ever come to fruition.

So on the night of January 10, 49 BC, Caesar made his decision, illegally leading his army across the Rubicon River into Italy and marching on Rome. As Plutarch recalls, his words were *alea iacta est* ("The die is cast."); there was no turning back now. The senate expected that the towns in between the Alps and Rome would put up some resistance to this intruder illegally leading his army into Italy. But as Plutarch emphasizes, Caesar was so magnanimous with his gifts and words and promises, that he was welcome wherever he went.

Back in Rome, Pompey was in a bind because his legions - the only possible resistance to Caesar's own army - were still stuck in Spain. So as Caesar neared the walls of the city, Pompey fled, first to the south of Italy and then across the Adriatic Sea into Greece. Caesar pursued his former friend, turned enemy, and the decisive battle was found at the site of Pharsalus in 48 BC. As happened so many times in Gaul, Caesar was outnumbered, about 2 to 1 when compared with Pompey's forces. But he laid his trap, with his best infantry hiding in the brush, and when Pompey's cavalry reached the perfect spot, Caesar's forces leapt from their hiding spot and surrounded the cavalry, chopping them down and turning the tide in Caesar's favor.

Pompey fled the battle, sailing to Egypt for safety, but he was killed promptly upon his arrival, as the young king Ptolemy XIII tried to curry favor with Caesar. When Caesar arrived in hot pursuit, however, he allied with Ptolemy's sister, and enemy, Cleopatra VII - *the* Cleopatra. For a year Caesar helped Cleopatra defeat her brother in their war over control of Egypt, and during this time she bore Caesar his only son, Caesarion.

But Caesar was never one to stay in one place long, and soon after the unrest in Egypt was calmed, he went north and east into Pontus, where he defeated Pharnaces, the son of mighty Mithridates, at the Battle of Zela. As Plutarch records, it was in the aftermath of this victory that Caesar penned the words *veni, vidi, vici* ("I came; I saw; I conquered."). Then Caesar set off for North Africa, to chase down the rest of the senators who opposed him. Again, he was successful, both at Thapsus and at Utica, where Caesar's long standing senatorial opponent Cato the Younger met his end. And finally Caesar sailed for Spain, where he defeated the sons of Pompey, the supposed last of his opponents, at the Battle of Munda in 45 BC.

It was only after all this - a full 10 years in Gaul and 5 more years fighting all around the Mediterranean - that Caesar returned to Rome. As Plutarch tells the tale, he was a far more effective general than politician. It is true that Caesar made some genuinely good reforms, instituting the solar Julian calendar, founding new colonies, and expanding Roman citizenship. But he frequently appeared to desire absolute power. He made himself dictator for 10 years; he often refused to rise for the senate; he would wear purple robes; and he even had his general Marc Antony attempt to crown him in the Roman forum. Only the tepid response from the crowd - and the cheers once the crown was denied by Caesar - kept him from accepting the symbol of a king.

As Caesar was preparing to lead a new expedition to Parthia in the early part of 44 BC, many of the senators decided this absolute power could not be tolerated. To preserve the Republic, Caesar had to die. And so on the Ides (15th) of March, 44 BC, they launched a surpise attack upon Caesar as he read an announcement in the senate house attached to the Theater of Pompey. More than 60 senators were involved in the conspiracy, and Caesar was stabbed 23 times, including by his friend

Marcus Junius Brutus, whose ancestor help drive the last king out of Rome 500 years earlier. Caesar lay bloody and dying at the base of a statue of Pompey.

Plutarch's *Life of Caesar* continues a little further, however. He talks of the love for Caesar by the common people, especially in the aftermath of his death. And he concludes with the downfall of the senatorial conspirators - especially Brutus and Cassius - at the Battle of Philippi two years after Caesar's assassination.

CHAPTER VI

Decline and Fall

C ompared to the chaos of the Late Roman Republic, the early Roman Empire was actually quite stable and resilient. By the time Augustus died, after 41 years as emperor of Rome, there were few people still alive who remembered what life was like when Rome was still a Republic. And those that could remember probably recalled the rampant fighting and bloodshed more than the thrill of participatory government. Most people view Augustus as a particularly adept leader, the perfect person to lead the Roman people out of civil war and into a new form of imperial rule. His ability to superficially restore the Republic, praise the senate, enact moral legislation, stabilize the economy, and create propaganda to justify his - and the Roman Empire's - place at the top of the world was better than anyone could have ever hoped for.

The *Pax Romana*

What was even more surprising, however, was how well the entire system held up to a series of totally insane emperors. After Augustus died in AD 14, we got Tiberius, who became so paranoid that he retired to the island of Capri halfway through his reign and never again stepped foot in Rome. Then we had Caligula, who tried to make his horse (Incitatus) a senator. He was killed by his own Praetorian Guard, who then found Claudius hiding in a closet, expecting to be killed himself. Instead, the Praetorian Guard made him the new emperor. He would have rather been a historian than the emperor, and actually wrote a dozen books on everything from Carthage to the Latin alphabet. Notoriously unlucky in love, Claudius' first wife cheated on him publicly, his second wife abused him, and his third wife both cheated on him and killed him. That led to Nero becoming emperor. Nero spent much of his time singing, wishing he were a Greek actor. He famously "fiddled" while Rome burned, and then built a golden mansion on the ashes, leading many to believe that he set the fire himself to get himself a nice new plot of land in the middle of the city. Unsurprisingly, Nero was also killed by his own Praetorian Guard.

And so, after one good emperor (Augustus), Rome had four consecutive crackpots as emperors (Tiberius, Caligula, Claudius, and Nero). The amazing thing is that this doesn't seem to have negatively affected the empire much, if at all. During the Republic, Rome had some of the greatest leaders the ancient world had ever seen - Marius, Sulla, Pompey, and Caesar - and yet they spent as much time fighting each other as they did expanding Roman power. Now, in the early Roman Empire, this series of completely inept leaders seems to have had essentially no negative effect on the functioning of the empire as a whole.

Explaining Imperial Success

How is that the case? Well, it turns out that the social, political and economic structures underlying the Roman Empire were incredibly solid. In fact, all that was needed was for Roman leaders to stop using Roman armies to fight other Romans, and if that happened, then everything went just fine. There are several reasons why this worked so well. Part of it was due to the success of the Roman army. The Roman army was notoriously well organized and disciplined, and this helped deter both invasion and rebellion. Moreover, by the middle of the 1st century AD, Rome had already dealt with most large scale enemies on the borders of their empire. External enemies were now rather small in scale and posed little threat to the mighty Roman legions.

Another part of Rome's success was their ability to govern with a light touch. They governed their entire empire with only about 5,000 officers, magistrates, and administrators. Compare that with the more than 2,000,000 bureaucrats in America today, and you get the sense that this was a government that just barely sat on top of political and social structures that were already in place locally. In fact, that's more or less exactly what they did. When they expanded into new places, they would leave the local leaders in charge, try to co-opt them into the Roman cause, and then let the local leader slowly bring his people around to the Roman way of doing things. Additionally, Rome didn't care if local populations kept their own traditions. If they ate their own unique foods or worshiped their own unique gods, that was all fine by Rome. Sometimes, as with the case of Mithras or Magna Mater, Rome would even incorporate those provincial gods into the greater pantheon of Roman deities. Just make sure to worship the emperor and pay your taxes, and the rest was pretty much up to you.

Fig. 156: Marble sculpture of Mithras killing the bull
(Archaeological and Ethnological Museum of Córdoba; 2nd c. AD)

289

Fig. 157: Map of the Roman Empire at its greatest extent under the emperor Trajan (AD 117)

Low taxes, in fact, were another reason the Roman Empire remained successful for so long. With such a light bureaucracy, Rome could afford to not extract too much from its citizens, and most scholars estimate they would have only been taxed at about 5 to 10% (compared with 10 to 37% in America today). Although no one loves paying taxes, it did have several other benefits for the empire. First, it allowed for some of the most incredible infrastructure the ancient world ever produced. Aqueducts ran dozens of miles to bring clean water into densely populated cities. Roads allowed for efficient transportation throughout Italy and beyond. Amazingly, many of these structures still stand today - you can walk along the ancient Via Appia as it departs south out of Rome, and you can drink water from the Aqua Virgo, which still feeds Trevi Fountain today. Second, Roman taxes promoted the use of a common currency. This meant you could use the same coins to buy grain in Egypt, wine in Gaul, or olives in Spain. Taken together, the economic system of the early Roman Empire operated like a well-oiled machine.

The acceptance of imperial rule, light bureaucracy, cultural open-mindedness, low taxes, impressive infrastructure, and powerful army all led to a period of prosperity and peace that we call the *Pax Romana* ("Roman Peace"). After the death of Nero, Rome went on to have more than a century of relatively effective (and sane) emperors, many of whom imbued Rome with some of its most impressive monuments. Nero's successor Vespasian, for example, started construction on the Colosseum, and his son and successor Titus finished it a decade later. Domitian, the last of the Flavian dynasty, built a stadium in the Campus Martius, and the outline of it can still be seen in Rome's historic Piazza Navona. Trajan, the second of the "five good emperors," erected his triumphal column to commemorate his victories in Dacia. The Pantheon, which had the world's largest dome for a thousand years, was rebuilt by Hadrian and still stands almost perfectly preserved today. And Marcus Aurelius created a lasting legacy by composing his philosophical *Meditations*.

Fig. 158: Bronze equestrian statue of Marcus Aurelius from the Capitoline Hill in Rome (Capitoline Museums; AD 161-180)

The Decline and Fall of the Roman Empire

Throughout the first two centuries AD, the borders of the Rome Empire fluctuated a little, growing a bit here, shrinking a bit there. But for the most part, the Empire hummed along relatively peacefully for those within its borders. With the death of Marcus Aurelius, however, the cracks in the Roman Empire would start to show. His son and successor Commodus, it turned out, was not the thoughtful philosopher and temperate ruler that his father was. Instead, he was a lunatic megalomaniac. He renamed the city of Rome after himself, calling it the "Colony of Commodus," and he loved fighting in the arena as a gladiator. After about a decade of rule, a group of conspirators tried to poison Commodus, but that didn't work, so they brought in a gladiator to strangle him to death.

It had been quite some time since an emperor met an untimely demise as a result of profoundly unnatural causes. However, Commodus' death was the perfect lead up to the 3rd century AD, often known as the 3rd Century Crisis. During this period, there were well over 30 emperors, meaning their average reign lasted less than three years. This isn't because they had some unfortunate health problems; rather, it's the result of rampant political instability and frequent assassinations.

Following Commodus, Septimus Severus established his own Severan dynasty and was notable for being the first emperor from Africa. He ruled for nearly twenty years, but upon his death, the rest of the dynasty fell into shambles. In 211 AD, the co-emperor Geta was murdered in his mother's arms on the orders of his brother, and co-emperor, Caracalla. Caracalla, then the sole emperor, was murdered by a member of his guard while he was peeing on the side of the road. Marcrinus became emperor for a single year and then was executed by his own troops who installed Elagabalus as emperor. Elagabalus lasted all of four years before he was murdered, along with his mother, by the Praetorian Guard. Severus Alexander took over, but he too was murdered (also with his mother) by his own troops. That's five out of six emperors assassinated - all from just one dynasty!

*Fig. 159: Marble statue of Commodus dressed as Hercules
(Capitoline Museums; AD 180 - 192)*

The rest of the 3rd century AD gets even worse, if that's possible. We get six different emperors in 238 AD, all of whom die violently (see Herodian's text below). Sometimes the Praetorian Guard killed the emperor they were supposed to be protecting, sometimes the emperors died in the midst of civil war, sometimes they'd commit suicide after losing in their civil wars, and sometimes their own soldiers would kill them after losing in their civil wars. If they ever took time off from fighting each other to fight an external enemy, the emperors could die that way too. In 244, Gordian II was killed while fighting the Persians, and in 251 Decius was killed in battle against the Goths.

The highest honor - at least in terms of ridiculous imperial deaths - goes to Valerian. In the year 260, Valerian was captured and tortured by the Persians, with the Persian king using him as his personal footstool. Then he was executed by having molten gold poured down his throat. Finally, he was stuffed, taxidermy fashion, and his corpse was put on display in the Persian court. Honorable mention goes to Carus, who may have been struck by lightning in 283, and Carinus, who was killed by a magistrate whose wife the emperor had seduced in 285.

Political instability was a major cause of the decline and fall of the Roman Empire, but it certainly wasn't the only one. A confounding factor that led to Roman decline was the migration of barbarian tribes. It began with the Huns, led by Attila, pushing west from Asia. While they did indeed bump up against the eastern part of the Roman Empire, their bigger impact was starting a chain reaction that pushed other barbarian tribes - the Goths, Visigoths, and Vandals - into Roman territory. In 410, the city of Rome was sacked for the first time in 800 years, and then it happened again in 455 and 476.

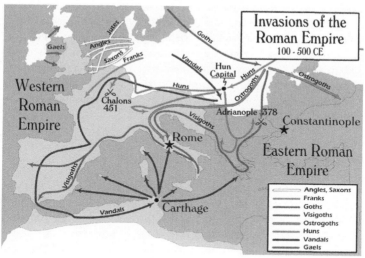

Fig. 160: Map of the "barbarian" invasions by the Angles, Saxons, Jutes, Franks, Goths, Visigoths, Ostrogoths, Huns, and Vandals (AD 100 - 500)

Part of the reason these barbarian invasions were successful was that the army had changed over the centuries. As the

295

empire continued to expand, soldiers from the core had less of an interest in serving a thousand miles from their homes, families, and friends. As a result, the army increasingly relied on local auxiliaries and mercenaries. This happened to such a great extent that the Roman word for barbarian, *barbarus*, came to refer to Roman soldiers as well. These soldiers had little allegiance to Rome, so if the tides of war started turning the other way, it wasn't uncommon for them to flip sides.

This mercenary approach was also incredibly expensive and led to severe economic problems. Growth into marginal lands brought in a relatively small amount of tax revenue but dramatically increased the area that needed to be defended. To account for this, Roman Emperors simply debased the currency; that is, they reduced the amount of silver in the coins. People caught on quickly, however, and this led to rampant inflation. As expansion ground to a halt, the supply of slaves also dried up. For centuries, Rome had been reliant on slave labor, but the source of that labor was driven almost exclusively by winning wars and expanding territory. Without this influx of labor, the whole system began to deteriorate. Finally, as barbarians made headway into formerly Roman lands, long distance trade networks broke down. This had detrimental effects on regional specialization and forced many areas to turn inwards, becoming less interconnected and more self-sufficient than they had been in the past.

In this Sign, You Will Conquer

Despite these structural problems, the Roman Empire pushed on, even if it was a little less glamorous than it had previously been. By the end of the 3rd century AD, the Roman emperor Diocletian had devised a completely new political structure, known as the Tetrarchy, which divided the empire and instituted forced retirement and planned succession for the emperors. This worked for all of one generation before claimants to the throne decided they no longer wanted to share authority. To his credit, Diocletian did indeed retire to Split, Croatia where you can still see his palace today.

Fig. 161: Fragments of a colossal statue of the emperor Constantine (Capitoline Museums; early 4th century AD)

In 312 AD, one of those rulers, Constantine, made his way down from Eboracum (modern York, England) to the outskirts of Rome. There, he met his cousin and co-ruler, Maxentius, and prepared to go to war against him. Constantine, apparently, had no interest in sharing power. The night before the battle, Constantine had a dream, seeing the *chi-rho* symbol of Christ in the sky and hearing the words, *in hoc signo vinces* ("in this sign, you will conquer"). The following morning he had his soldiers paint the symbol on their shields and breastplates. That day, Constantine's army routed that of Maxentius, and Constantine became sole ruler of the western part of the empire.

By the end of his rule, Constantine had defeated his eastern counterparts as well, reuniting the empire under a single imperial authority. He had also moved the capital eastward, from Rome to Constantinople (modern Istanbul, Turkey). It was under the reign of Constantine that Christianity became formally allowed (although not mandated) within the Roman Empire, and it is said that Constantine himself converted to Christianity on his deathbed.

The End of the Roman Empire?

Many scholars suggest that this cultural, religious, and political shift - from a polytheistic empire centered on Rome in the western Mediterranean to a monotheistic empire centered on Constantinople in the eastern Mediterranean - was a major turning point in the downfall of the Roman Empire. During the course of the 4th century AD, Christianity was made the official religion of the Empire. And by the end of the century, the empire was divided for good between East and West. The western Roman Empire, centered on Rome, was crumbling, and the sack of the city by the Ostrogoths in AD 476 saw the last Roman emperor, Romulus Augustulus deposed.

The eastern Roman Empire, however, continued to flourish under the leadership of its new Christian emperors. Today, we often call this the "Byzantine" Empire, but that is a title created by modern historians. Even though most of the people in the east spoke Greek, they called themselves Romans, and they called their state the Roman Empire. This Christianity-based eastern Roman Empire lasted over 1,000 years, before eventually falling to Sultan Mehmet II and the Ottomans in 1453. Upon that conquest, however, the sultan also took the title of "Kayser i-Rum" (which translates as Caesar of Rome), thus proclaiming himself to be the heir of the Roman Empire nearly 1,500 years after Augustus.

By this time, however, a new Roman Empire had begun in the west. The Holy Roman Empire was founded by Charlemagne on Christmas Day in AD 800. It too would last for over 1,000 years, often playing the role of adversary to the Catholic pope in Rome. It was not until 1806 that Napoleon Bonaparte officially disbanded the Holy Roman Empire for good.

At this point, the Ottoman ruler, centered in Turkey, still held the title of "Caesar of Rome." But Ottoman power was waning, and by the end of the century it had become known as the "sick man of Europe." In the aftermath of World War I, the Ottoman Empire, and their "Caesar of Rome" was brought to a close. Greek speaking people in Turkey, descendants of the Byzantine Empire of centuries before, are still often called the

Fig. 162: Gold bust of Charlemagne, crowned Holy Roman Emperor on Christmas Day in AD 800 (Aachen Cathedral Treasury; 14th century)

"Rum" or the "Rumlar," which translates as the Romans. So in some small way, the Roman Empire still lives on today.

Herodian's *History of the Empire from the Death of Marcus Aurelius*

It is perhaps fitting that we know so little about an author detailing one of the most chaotic periods of Roman history. We do know that the author of the *History of the Empire from the Death of Marcus Aurelius*, was a man by the name of Herodian. Although living in the Roman Empire, he wrote in Greek, and his history covers the political turmoil in Rome from AD 180 to 238.

We can gain a few clues about the life of Herodian from snippets of his history. He twice mentions, for example, that he's writing about events that happened during his lifetime (1.1.3, 2.15.7). If that's the case, then we know he must have been born before 180 and died after 238. In all likelihood, he was probably born sometime around 170, which would have made him about 10 years old when his history starts. And he probably died sometime in the mid-240s, after the death of Gordian III, since his take on the last emperor he covers isn't particularly flattering, and it's unlikely that he would have published it while Gordian III was still emperor.

We're also not totally sure where Herodian is from. We can feel confident he's not from Italy or from anywhere near the Alps, since he says that "the Alps are bigger than anything in our part of the world (2.11.8)." Moreover, his history is written in Greek instead of Latin, suggesting that he was likely from the eastern part of the Roman Empire. Herodian also seems to spend extra time detailing Italian and Roman cultural practices in a way that might suggest they were unfamiliar to his home audience. Sometimes he's referred to as Herodian of Antioch, which would place him in modern-day Syria, but other scholars have argued he's from Alexandria because he goes into great detail when discussing Caracalla's massacre of Alexandria's population.

Herodian's day job is also a mystery. Some scholars believe he was in politics, eventually becoming a senator, because of his familiarity with senatorial procedure. Others claim he might have been a freedman, ie. a former slave. Still other historians suggest that Herodian may have been a scribe or assistant to one of the emperors, which would have given him the ability to travel throughout the empire and gain access to important documents he could use to create his history.

Regardless of the exact answers to these questions, the reason we remember Herodian today is because of his *History of the Empire from the Death of Marcus Aurelius*, one of our best sources for Roman history between the years of AD 180 and 238. Other historians, both ancient and modern, give him credit for being relatively unbiased in his assessment of a wide variety of emperors during a particularly tumultuous period of Roman history. Furthermore, his ability to weave together chronological events with the personal stories of various emperors led to the creation of a narrative that is as engaging as it is informative.

The *History of the Empire from the Death of Marcus Aurelius* is divided into eight books. Book 1 covers Marcus Aurelius' son and successor, Commodus, ending with his assassination in AD 192. Book 2 focuses on the year 193, also known as the "Year of the Five Emperors" for its rapid turnover in imperial leadership. Book 3 centers on the reign of Septimius Severus, from 193 to 211, and Book 4 focuses on the rule of his son, Caracalla, from 211 to 217. This is where things really start to go off the rails, as Caracalla kills his own brother, Geta, in order to have sole control of the Roman Empire. Book 5 covers the reign of Elagabalus (218 to 222), who elevated Elagabal, also known as Sol Invictus or the "Invincible Sun" to the top of the Roman pantheon of gods, forcing Roman government officials to do the same. He was killed by his own imperial guard after just 4 years on the throne, and his body was thrown in the Tiber River. Book 6 highlights the last of the Severan emperors, Severus Alexander, who also was assassinated by his own troops.

Fig. 163: Marble bust of Marcus Aurelius
(Louvre Museum; ca. AD 161-69)

The death of Severus Alexander plunged Rome into what's known as the Third Century Crisis, a fifty year period of political instability, outside invasion, and financial collapse. Book 7 of Herodian's *History* covers the early part of this crisis from 235 to 238. The last year, 238, is also known as the "Year of the Six Emperors." After the death of Severus Alexander, his general Maximinus Thrax (i.e., the Thracian) ascended to the emperorship. Maximinus had made his name as a soldier out in the provinces, but people in Rome generally hated him, and he, in turn, didn't care much for them either. While Maximinus was still laying claim to the throne, a small coup in North Africa led to the local elites asking the governor Gordian to proclaim himself emperor. Gordian I was nearly 80 years old at the time, but he agreed and named his son, Gordian II, co-emperor, hoping to ensure a smooth transition.

The transition was sooner - and less smooth - than he likely expected. After only a couple weeks as "emperors," Gordians I and II were under siege by the neighboring governor, a guy by the name of Capelianus. He led his army against the two Gordians, winning the battle against them at the site of Carthage. Gordian II was killed in the fighting, and Gordian I hanged himself in the aftermath. Maximinus, way up in the northern provinces, decided to use this opportunity to march on Rome, where the Senate and people of Rome had declared him an enemy of the state, despite the fact that he was the only living emperor.

It is within this context that we pick up with Herodian's story.

Words of the Ancients

Herodian's *History of the Roman Empire from the Death of Marcus Aurelius*

Year of the Six Emperors (7.10.1 - 8.8.8)

FEBRUARY-MARCH AD 238: PUPIENUS AND BALBINUS BECOME EMPERORS

[7.10.1] So that's what was going on in Africa. When news of Gordian II's death reached Rome, the people - and especially the Senate - were in complete shock. They'd placed all their hopes in Gordian II, and now he was dead. Moreover, they knew that Maximinus [a general and emperor who rivaled Gordian II and the Senate] already hated them and was in no mood for mercy. Now that his anger was justified, Maximinus was going to rage against them as though they were true enemies.

[7.10.2] The Senate decided to call a meeting to figure out what to do. Since the die had been cast, they voted to declare war on Maximinus. They chose two men from the Senate to be joint emperors, with the idea that splitting up the emperorship might help ensure that all power wasn't consolidated in the hands of a single crazy dictator. Instead of meeting in the Senate house, however, they met at the Temple of Jupiter Optimus Maximus, the god that the Romans worship on the Capitoline Hill.

Fig. 164: Denarius (silver coin) of the emperor Maximinus Thrax (AD 235-36)

[7.10.3] They holed up alone in the temple, almost like they wanted Jupiter to see what was happening; maybe he could join the meeting and lead the group. Then the Senate chose two of the most honorable and respectable men and voted them in as emperors. Some of the other Senators received votes as well, but once all the votes had been counted, Pupienus and Balbinus were elected emperors by a clear majority.

[7.10.4] Pupienus seemed like a great choice: he'd held a variety of military positions, he was prefect in Rome, and he ran things diligently, earning himself a good reputation for being compassionate, smart, and even-keeled. Balbinus, his co-emperor, had been *consul* twice before and had also served as a governor out in the provinces. He never had any complaints against him, but he was much more straightforward and direct.

[7.10.5] After they were elected, Pupienus and Balbinus were proclaimed emperors, and the Senate gave them all the imperial honors. But while all this was happening up on the Capitoline Hill, the Roman people heard about the death of Gordian II, either from his friends or relatives or just rumors swirling around. And the people grabbed rocks and clubs, and a huge mob filled the streets and started moving up towards the Capitoline. For they didn't like what the Senate was doing, and they especially disliked Pupienus.

[7.10.6] This was because, when he was prefect, Pupienus was way too strict in the eyes of the people, and he was especially harsh in how he treated criminals and the lawless mobs. So fearing that Pupienus was about to get ultimate power, the people took to the streets shouting that both of these new emperors should be killed. The Senate, they said, should name someone else from Gordian II's family as the new emperor; they should keep it within the family.

[7.10.7] So Balbinus and Pupienus gathered an entourage of young knights and old soldiers who had retired in Rome, and the group tried to push its way up the Capitoline. The angry mob, however, was still armed with clubs and rocks, and they wouldn't let them pass. Then someone came up with a plan to trick the masses. For at the time, there was a child in

Fig. 165 (left): Bust of the emperor Pupienus
(Capitoline Museums; AD 238)

Fig. 166 (right): Bust of the emperor Balbinus
(Hermitage Museum; AD 238)

Rome who was the son of Gordian's daughter, and he had his grandfather's name (i.e., Gordian).

[7.10.8] The two new emperors ordered a couple of their entourage to go get the kid and bring him up to the Capitoline. When they found him playing at home, they hoisted him up on their shoulders and started marching him through the crowd up to the Capitoline. They were showing him off to the people as they went, calling him Gordian and saying he was the son of the previous emperor. And the masses cheered as he was carried through the crowd, and they scattered leaves along the path in his honor.

[7.10.9] The Senate then made him "Caesar" since he wasn't old enough to be an "Augustus." This pleased the crowd, and they allowed Pupienus, Balbinus, and their entourage to head up to the palace.

MARCH AD 238: FIGHTING IN THE STREETS OF ROME

[7.11.1] While all this was happening, two reckless senators in Rome made a huge mistake. At that time, many people in Rome would often come to the Senate house to figure out what was going on.

[7.11.2] When they learned about this, two soldiers from Maximinus' Praetorian Guard[1] showed up at the door of the Senate house (they'd been discharged from Maximinus' army because of their old age, and thus were living in Rome). These two were unarmed and dressed like regular people, and they stood around waiting to hear what was happening inside, just like the rest of the crowd.

[7.11.3] While most of the people were standing around outside, a couple of the Praetorian soldiers pushed their way past the statue of Victory and went into the Senate chambers so they could better hear what was going on. Then Gallicanus, a senator of Carthaginian descent and one who'd recently been *consul*, along with Maecenas, another senator of Praetorian rank, attacked the soldiers. While the soldiers stood around with their hands in their pockets, the two senators stabbed them in the heart with daggers they had hidden under their robes.

[7.11.4] As it turned out, all the senators had daggers (some hidden, some carried openly) as a result of the recent riots in the city. They said it was for their own protection, just in case the enemy had any treacherous plans. In reality, however, these soldiers were killed before they ever had a chance to defend themselves, since the attack was totally unexpected and unprovoked. And the dead bodies of those two soldiers lay slumped in the shadow of the statue of Victory.

[7.11.5] When the other Praetorian soldiers saw what happened, they were horrified by the death of their comrades. They were also terrified by the size of the mob, especially be-

---

1   The Praetorian Guard was the personal bodyguard of the emperor. As you'll see, the weren't always as protective of him as that should have been. In fact, sometimes they were the emperor's biggest threat.

cause they were unarmed, so they turned and quickly ran away. Gallicanus came running out of the Senate house after them, clutching his dagger in his blood-soaked hand, and he shouted at the crowd to kill the friends and allies of Maximinus, for they were the enemies of the Senate and people of Rome.

[7.11.6] The mob bought this hook, line, and sinker, and they shouted their applause at Gallicanus. Then they raced after the Praetorian soldiers, throwing stones as they ran. The soldiers were outnumbered and most were wounded as well, so they fled the mob and ran back into the Praetorian camp. There, they locked the gates, grabbed their weapons, and posted sentries along the walls. And thus, through his careless crime, Gallicanus brought civil war and slaughter to the city of Rome.

[7.11.7] He continued urging the mob, now telling them to break into the armory where they kept the ceremonial armor (the ones used for triumphal processions, not actual battle), urging each man to grab whatever they needed to protect themselves. Then he went over to the gladiatorial schools, freeing the fighters and having them bring their own weapons. And finally he went around to the common houses and shops and gathered up all the spears and swords and axes that he could muster.

[7.11.8] Those in the crowd acted crazy, almost like zombies, and they grabbed whatever tools they could and made weapons out of them. Then they marched on the Praetorian camp, attacking its walls as though they were actually besieging a city. The soldiers inside the camp had far more training and fighting experience, and they used their shields and walls for protection, striking at their attackers from a distance with arrows and spears. Soon they had driven the mob back from the camp's walls.

[7.11.9] As the sun set, the horde of attackers decided to go home. After all, most of them were just regular people and many of the gladiators were injured. They retreated in a haphazard, random sort of way, no one really thinking that the Praetorian soldiers would dare chase after such a large group. But gave chase they did. The Praetorians rushed out of their gates, cutting down the gladiators and slaughtering most of the mob, which was in utter chaos. Then the Praetorians returned to the safety of their camp and stayed inside its walls.

Spring AD 238: Praetorians Set Fire to Rome

[7.12.1] This disaster just made the masses and the Senate in Rome even angrier. They appointed generals and drafted troops from all over Italy, and these young soldiers armed themselves with anything that might be considered a weapon. Pupienus led most of these troops out to attack Maximinus, but a few stayed behind to protect the city.

[7.12.2] Everyday Pupienus and his troops attacked the Praetorian camp, but they didn't make the slightest dent because the soldiers inside were able to mount a tough defense from their fortified, higher position. And the attackers were often hurt in the fighting, and they suffered heavy casualties. Balbinus was back in Rome while this was going on, and he issued a proclamation - really more of a plea - to stop the fighting, and that any soldiers who laid down their weapons would be pardoned.

[7.12.3] But neither side - the attacking mob nor the defending Praetorians - listened to him. The crowds in Rome thought it was embarrassing to fail against such a small group of men, and the Praetorian soldiers were furious to be attacked like they were some group of barbarians. As the attacks against the fortified camp continued to fail, however, the generals decided it would be a better strategy to dam up all the streams that flowed into the Praetorian camp, cutting off their water supply and forcing the soldiers to surrender.

[7.12.4] So the attackers dug channels to divert the streams and dammed up the streambeds that went under the camp walls. When the Praetorians got wind of this, however, they panicked and rushed out to attack. It was a quick fight, and the mob fled once again, as the Praetorians chased them throughout the city of Rome.

[7.12.5] Since they weren't any match for the Praetorians

in hand-to-hand combat, the crowds rushed into their houses and climbed up to the roofs, where they hurled down stones and pots and tiles onto the heads of the soldiers. This ended up injuring quite a few of the soldiers, who were scared to chase after them because they didn't know the layouts of the houses and most of them were locked up anyway. They did start setting houses on fire, though, especially the ones with wooden balconies, and there were quite a few of those in the city.

[7.12.6] Because so many of the houses were made out of wood, the fire quickly spread, and a sweeping wave of flame spread across the city. Even the rich lost their massive villas, incredibly valuable properties both because of the income they generated and their elaborate decor. In a flash they went from rich to poor.

[7.12.7] Hordes of people died in the fire since the flames blocked their doors and prevented an escape. Afterwards, the houses of the rich were looted, as the lowlifes and gangsters joined the soldiers in looting their ruined properties. In all, the area destroyed by this fire was larger than the full size of any other city in the empire.

[7.8.12] While all this was happening in Rome, Maximinus had finished marching his army to the borders of Italy. There, he made the appropriate sacrifices at the boundary stones, and then ordered his army to advance, marching in battle formation with their weapons at the ready.

[7.12.9] Up to this point, we've covered the revolt in Africa, the civil war in Rome, and Maximinus' march into Italy. What happened next will be covered in the following book.

SPRING AD 238: MAXIMINUS MARCHES ON ROME

[8.1.1] Maximinus' march into Italy after the death of Gordian II was discussed in the previous book, along with the revolt in Africa and the clash between the Roman mobs and the Praetorian camp. Now, as Maximinus waited on the borders of Italy, he sent out scouts to determine whether any traps lay ahead, whether any soldiers were hiding in the canyons or brush or forests ahead.

[8.1.2] Maximinus then led his troops down from the mountains into the flat land below. There he organized them in a large rectangle, so big that it took up most of the plain. In the center of the troops he put his supplies and wagons, and then Maximinus himself took command of the rear and marched ahead with his army.

[8.1.3] A battalion of armed cavalry went forward on each flank, the African spearmen on one side and the Eastern archers on the other. The emperor also had a lot of German auxiliaries, and he put these at the very front to absorb the enemy's initial attack. They were known for being particularly vicious during their opening charge, and even if it didn't turn out well, it wasn't a big deal to lose the German troops.

[8.1.4] After Maximinus' soldiers made their way into Italy, still marching in a tight, orderly formation, the first Italian city they came to was Hema, at least that's what it was called by the locals.[2] Hema's located on a high plateau at the base of the Alps, and Maximinus' scouts returned to let him know that the city had been abandoned. All its citizens had left *en masse*, but not before they set their houses and shops and temples on fire. Not only that, they took all their possessions, food, and animals, so there was nothing left to eat for Maximinus' troops.

[8.1.5] The fact that the Italians had fled Hema put a smile on Maximinus' face, since he imagined that citizens in towns throughout Italy would flee when they saw his army approaching. His army, however, wasn't so happy to find themselves starving right from the start since all the food had been taken away. So after they spent the night in Hema, some of the troops sleeping in the destroyed houses in the city, others sleeping out in the fields, they pressed on the very next morning to the Alps. The Alps are massive mountains, a natural defensive barricade protecting Italy. They tower high above the clouds, and they stretch on for ages, from the Tyrrhenian Sea in the west to the

---

2   Modern Ljubljana, Slovenia, located a little northeast of Venice, Italy.

Ionian Sea in the east.[3]

[8.1.6] These mountains are covered with thick, endless forests, and the passes through them are tight, with towering cliffs and jagged rocks on either side. Mortal men actually built these passes, the result of countless hours of labor by the ancient Italians. Maximinus' army marched slowly and anxiously through the Alps, expecting enemy forces occupying the peaks and blocking the passes. And in that region, they were right to be worried.

March AD 238: The Siege of Aquileia

[8.2.1] But they met no resistance as they crossed the Alps, and as they marched down the slopes back to the flat lands, their confidence grew and they sang songs and offered thanks. Making it through the treacherous Alps without any problems led Maximinus to further believe that everything was going to turn out perfectly. The Italians hadn't launched an ambush nor had they rained down arrows from the lofty peaks, making the most of their advantageous position.

[8.2.2] As the army marched through the fields, Maximinus' scouts reported that Aquileia, the greatest city in that region of Italy, had barricaded its gates. His Pannonian legions[4] that had gone on ahead were already viciously laying siege to its fortifications, but despite their frequent attacks, they weren't making the slightest dent in the defenses. All this time the Aquileians were raining down arrows and spears and rocks upon their heads, and so the Pannonian legions eventually quit and retreated. Maximinus was furious that his generals fought so weakly and gave up so easily, so he had the rest of his army rush forward to continue the siege, expecting to easily capture the city.

---

3   The Tyrrhenian Sea is the name for the part of the Mediterranean that sits on the west coast of Italy. The Ionian Sea is the name for the part of the Mediterranean in between southern Italy and Greece.

4   Pannonia was a Roman province that corresponds to western Hungary and eastern Austria. Maximinus' legions from Pannonia went out ahead of the rest of his troops to lay siege to Aquileia.

Fig. 167: Map of Italy with the location of Aquileia

[8.2.3] Before all this went down, Aquileia was already a vast city with lots of people. It's located along the Adriatic Sea, and with the provinces of Illyricum[5] lying just to the east of it, Aquileia served as the border town and point of entry into Italy. It was strategically located, and products from the interior of Europe could be transported to Aquileia, loaded on boats, and then shipped out across the Mediterranean. The reverse happened too. Goods from across the Mediterranean would arrive at Aquileia, get loaded onto smaller riverboats or wagons, and then be transported into the inland and upland regions

---

5   Originally Illyricum was its own province, but as Rome expanded, it split into multiple provinces. Pannonia was to the north and Dalmatia was to the south, occupying much of modern day Croatia.

that were generally too cold to produce many of the imported products. The region was particularly good at producing wine, so they shipped a lot of this abroad to areas that didn't grow grapes.

[8.2.4] The permanent population of Aquileia was massive, both with locals but also with foreigners and traders. At this particular time, the city had even more people than usual, since everyone from the surrounding countryside had holed up within the walls of the city. They'd hoped that the sheer size of the town - and its fortification walls - would help protect them. But these walls were ancient and crumbling in many places. Since it had become part of the Roman Empire, the cities in Italy didn't really need walls or weapons anymore. They had traded war for everlasting peace, and for a role in the Roman government.

[8.2.5] The siege, however, forced the people of Aquileia to repair their walls and build new defensive walls and towers. They constructed a rampart to fortify the city as quickly as they could, and then they closed and blockaded the gates, with everyone staying inside 24-hours a day, as they fought off their attackers. And they named two former senators - Crispinus and Meniphilus - generals of the Aquileians.

[8.2.6] These two generals planned out every detail. They carefully predicted exactly what they would need and had all kinds of food and supplies brought into the city so they could hold out against a long siege. They were able to get lots of water from the numerous wells within the city walls, and there was also a river that flowed down below the city walls, serving both as a defensive moat and as a great source of water.

MARCH-APRIL AD 238: MAXIMINUS NEGOTIATES WITH THE AQUILEIANS

[8.3.1] That was how the city prepared for war. When Maximinus heard that the Aquileians had barricaded the city, he thought it would be a good idea to negotiate with them from outside the walls and try to convince them to open the gates.

One of the men in Maximinus' army was from Aquileia, after all, and his wife and children and family were all still inside the town.

[8.3.2] So Maximinus sent this guy, along with a couple of centurions, out in front of the walls, thinking he'd easily win over his fellow citizens. The messenger told the people of Aquileia that Maximinus was also their emperor, so they should put down their weapons, open their gates, and switch from killing people to offering sacrifices. He also reminded them that their hometown was in danger of being burnt to a crisp, but they themselves had the power to save their city and their people because Maximinus was merciful and would not hold a grudge. It was others in Italy - not the Aquileians - who needed to be punished.

[8.3.3] The messenger yelled this from down below the walls so that everyone could hear. Most of the city's people were up on the wall, and only the guards on active duty were away at their posts. So everyone listened quietly to what he had to say.

[8.3.4] Crispinus, the general, was scared that the towns-people might actually believe the messenger's lies, desire peace, and open up the gates. So he ran up and down the city walls yelling at them to hold strong and put up a fight. He urged them not to fail in their duty to the Senate and people of Rome, but rather to write their names in the history books as the saviors of Italy. And he told them not to put any faith in the promises of a liar, hypocrite, and despot. Why let yourself fall prey to a few nice words that will certainly lead to our downfall? Put up a fight and let Fortune determine the outcome!

[8.3.5] The general went on to say that there were many times throughout history where a small group of underdogs were able to upset a larger, stronger army. So don't be scared of the size of the attacking horde. Crispinus urged them on, "People who fight someone else's battle know that the spoils of war won't be theirs, and so they're going to fight with less heart and less spirit. They know that they share the risks, but the rewards will go to someone else!"

[8.3.6] Crispinus went on, "But those of you who fight for the motherland, for your own hard-earned property are going to be blessed by the gods. You're not praying to steal someone else's property, just asking to keep what is rightfully yours! Our zeal on the battlefield doesn't stem from following orders of some high up general, but rather comes from within. We know that everything we gain belongs to us and us alone!"

[8.3.7] Crispinus was an honorable leader, quite good at Latin oratory, and had governed his people justly. So his speech had its intended effect, convincing the Aquileians to hold strong in defense. He sent the messenger back to Maximinus to deliver the bad news. Part of the reason Crispinus continued the fight is that the augurs[6] in the city said that the signs favored the townsfolk, and Italians place a lot of weight in divining the will of the gods.

[8.3.8] The oracles also indicated that their local god, Belis,[7] would bring them victory. Worshiping this god was especially popular in the region, and they associated him with Apollo. Sometimes, Maximinus' soldiers claimed, they could see the god's image in the sky fighting alongside the Aquileians.

[8.3.9] I have no idea whether this actually happened. Whether the god really was seen by the attacking army. Or whether it was all made up to appear less embarrassing that such a large army could be defeated by a town full of regular people. At least then, they'd been beaten by divine gods rather than mortal men. But the fact that this is so incredibly weird makes me think it just might be true.

April AD 238: The Siege of Aquileia Fails

[8.4.1] When Maximinus' messengers returned to him and gave him the bad news, he flew into a rage, and started marching his army at a breakneck pace towards Aquileia. But about

---

6   Augurs were like prophets, they sought to understand the will of the gods, often through natural phenomena such as the flight of birds, the pattern of lightning, or the form of a sheep's liver.

7   Belis is a version of the Celtic god Belenus, who was a healing god, and thus became associated with the Greco-Roman god Apollo.

16 miles from the town, he ran into a really wide and deep river.

[8.4.2] The warming springtime temperatures melted the snow up in the mountains that had accumulated all winter, and this created a massive flood rushing down the mountain slopes. Maximinus' army couldn't cross the river because the Aquileans had destroyed the bridge, which had been an enormous construction, with nicely squared stones and tapered support piers, built long ago by the Roman emperors of old. So because there was no longer a bridge and they didn't have any boats, Maximinus' army had to stop and figure out what to do.

[8.4.3] Some of the German troops thought that these roaring rivers of Italy might be like their slow-swirling rivers back in Germany (so slow, in fact, that they'd often freeze over in winter). So a few Germans rode their horses into the river, and even though they'd been trained to swim, they were swept away and drowned.

[8.4.4] So Maximinus had his army dig a defensive ditch around the camp and then stopped for a few days to figure out how to cross the river. There wasn't much wood in the area, and they didn't have enough boats to tie together to form a bridge across the river. A few of Maximinus' engineers, however, pointed out all the empty wooden barrels that were strewn across the fields, which the locals would use to store and transport wine. These were hollow just like a boat, and if they were tied together and fastened to the shore, then they wouldn't be swept downstream. So they did just that: tied them together, anchored them to the shore, laid planks on top, and then covered the whole thing with soil to even it out. And thus they had a relatively flat and steady bridge to cross.

[8.4.5] Once they finished the bridge, Maximinus' army crossed over and marched on Aquileia. And as they approached, they found all the houses and farms on the outskirts of town completely abandoned. The soldiers then took to chopping down the trees and grapevines in the area, burning the debris, and ravaging the crops which had already started sprouting up. Since the trees were planted in perfect rows and the vines elegantly wove through them, the whole place felt almost magical. You could even say it glowed. But Maximinus' troops cut everything down to the very roots and then marched on to Aquileia.

[8.4.6] By this point, however, the army was tired and worn down, so it seemed like a bad idea to immediately attack. The troops spread out all around the town, making sure to stay out of range of arrows. Then they grouped together into cohorts, with each digging into their assigned spot. But after their one day of rest and relaxation, they laid siege to the city every day from then on. Their attack held nothing back; they brought out every type of siege engine known to mankind, fought with every ounce of energy in their body, and tried every trick in the book.

[8.4.7] Everyday Maximinus' soldiers were launching attack after attack, and they had the whole city hemmed in, as if it were caught in a fisherman's net, but the citizens of Aquileia put up a hell of a fight, and they fought with an enthusiasm unknown to mankind. Everything inside the city was shut down - shops, temples, houses - and the whole population was defending the city, even the women and children. Moreover, they had the advantage of holding the high point and having the defensive fortifications. Everyone aged 8 to 80 fought to defend the city, and because of all this, they were able to ward off the attacking army.

[8.4.8] Maxminus' troops destroyed all the buildings in the suburbs and countryside, everything outside the walls, and they built siege engines with the wood they procured. They tried everything they could to break down some part of the wall so that their army might pour into the city, sack the town, and leave the place in smoldering ruins. There was no way Maximinus could have a respectable march on Rome if couldn't even capture the first Italian city to put up a fight.

[8.4.9] Maximinus and his son (and his heir to the throne) rode up and down the battlelines, encouraging their troops and promising the spoils of war should they succeed. The Aquileian townsfolk, however, were hurling down rocks on the attackers' heads. And not only that, they were creating a mixture of olive oil and tar, lighting it on fire, and then pouring it on the besiegers through hollowed-out jars. The walls were lit ablaze and it was like it was raining fire on the invaders.

[8.4.10] The flaming mixture seeped through the cracks and crevices of the soldiers' armor and got all over their bodies. The troops tore off their breastplates and the rest of their armor too, since the metal began to burn their skin. The leather and wooden parts of their armor, of course, burst into flames. So Maximinus' soldiers were stripping right there on the battlefield, throwing away their armor, which the Aquileians took as spoils of war, even though they got them through a clever strategy rather than courageous combat. Many of the attackers suffered horrific injuries, losing eyeballs or hands, getting scorched faces, and really sustaining serious wounds wherever they weren't fully protected. Then the Aquileians did the same to the siege engines. They created torches that were sharpened like spears, and they covered those in the same oil and tar mixture. Then they lit them ablaze and hurled them down to stick in the siege machines. As they were made of wood, these also quickly caught fire and burst into flames.

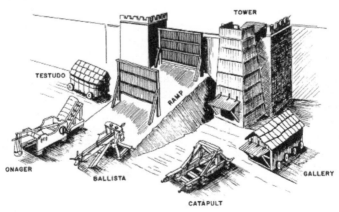

Fig. 168: Roman siegecraft and defensive works. We don't know what equipment Maximuns' army had, but it doesn't seem to have been very effective.

April-May AD 238: Maximinus Loses His Troops

[8.5.1] So in the early days of the war, the sides were more or less even. But as it stretched on, Maximinus' troops got depressed as their hopes for an easy victory faded. They grew more and more despondent, for they had expected to win in their first assault on the city, but now the Aquileians weren't just putting up a good defense, they were actually pushing them back.

[8.5.2] The opposite was true for the Aquileans. They became increasingly confident as the war went on, fighting with even more skill and courage than they started with. Soon they started mocking the attackers, and they cursed Maximinus and his son, launching insults at them as they rode through their lines. And the longer this went on, the angrier the emperor got, because he couldn't do the least bit about it.

[8.5.3] Because he couldn't take out his frustration on the Aquileians, Maximinus went ballistic and raged at most of his lieutenants for the timid and half-assed siege they were conducting. As a result, his own troops turned on him, and their hatred for him grew each day. While all this was going on, the Aquileians had plenty of supplies to withstand the siege. They had done a great job anticipating their needs, storing up plenty of food and water for both their people and livestock. The attackers, however, were in the exact opposite situation. They lacked almost everything they needed because they chopped down all the fruit-bearing trees and laid waste to the countryside.

[8.5.4] Although a few of the troops in Maximinus' army built shelters, most of them were just living outside with no protection from the sun or the rain. And with the lack of food, many of them starved to death. They couldn't get any food shipped in, because the Romans had closed off all the roads with walls and small gates.

[8.5.5] The Senate had also sent out a few of its former *consuls* to gather some hand-picked soldiers and blockade all the harbors and beaches to prevent anyone sailing in or out.

They didn't want Maximinus to have any idea what was going on in Rome, hence barricading the roads and blockading the harbors so that no one could get through. As a result, the army that started the siege itself became besieged, since it couldn't take Aquileia nor could it leave and march on Rome. The boats and carts had all been hidden away, so the troops were stuck walking everywhere.

[8.5.6] They started spreading over-the-top rumors that the entire Roman Empire had taken up arms to fight against Maximinus: all of Italy, Dalmatia, Pannonia, and even the barbarian groups in the east and south had united in their hatred of this one man. This depressed Maximinus' troops even more, for they were missing almost everything they needed and barely had enough water to get by.

[8.5.7] A nearby river was their only source of water, and that was polluted with blood and corpses. The Aquileians tossed everyone who died - from battle or disease - into the river, since they couldn't bury people within the city walls.[8]

May AD 238: Maximinus Killed by His Soldiers

[8.5.8] Maximinus' army had no idea what to do, so they became more hopeless by the day. One day, Maximinus was lounging around in his tent during a break in the fighting, while most of the soldiers had gone back to their posts. Then, all of a sudden, the soldiers who were normally camped outside of Rome near the Alban Hills (where their wives and children had stayed behind), decided that the best thing to do was kill Maximinus and put a stop to this endless siege. They were sick and tired of laying waste to Italy on behalf of an emperor who was a terrible tyrant.

[8.5.9] So the soldiers steeled themselves, and around noon they walked over to Maximinus' tent. The Praetorian Guard was also in on the plot, and when their co-conspirators showed up, they tore the image of Maximinus from the imperial stan-

---

8   It was a common Roman practice to always bury the dead outside of the city walls. This was a cultural practice, but it clearly had a hygienic function as well.

dards. The emperor came out with his son to talk with them, but the soldiers were in no mood for chit chat, and they promptly killed both of them. They handed over the dead bodies to some of the soldiers who wanted to stomp on them and chop them up and left the rest for the vultures and dogs. They sent the heads of Maximinus and his son to Rome. That was the price Maximinus and his son paid for being a tyrant of an emperor.

MAY AD 238: MAXIMINUS' TROOPS SURRENDER

[8.6.1] When the soldiers heard what happened, they were shocked. And it wasn't like all of them were happy about it. The troops from Pannonia and from Thrace were thoroughly pissed off, since they were the ones who helped Maximinus win the emperorship in the first place. But since the deed had been done, they put up with it. Even though they didn't like what happened, they really didn't have any other choice except to fake a smile and act pleased with the situation.

[8.6.2] So the attacking troops laid down their weapons and peacefully went up to the walls of Aquileia to tell them that they'd killed Maximinus. Because of this, they expected a warm welcome and for the gates to be thrown open. But the generals inside the town didn't open the gates right away. Instead, they brought out statues of Pupienus and Balbinus (and little Gordian III). Since the Aquileians were strong supporters of these emperors who had been installed by the Senate and people of Rome, they thought it was a good idea for Maximinus' troops to publicly acknowledge their right to rule by shouting their approval.

[8.6.3] The Aquileians told their former attackers that Gordian I and Gordian II had both gone to meet Jupiter up in heaven. Then they set up an impromptu market on the city ways, selling all sorts of stuff: lots of food and drinks and clothing, basically everything you could find to eat and drink in a thriving city.

[8.6.4] When the soldiers outside the walls saw all this, they were stunned. It dawned on them that the townsfolk of Aquileia had everything they needed to survive the longest of sieges, while they themselves had almost nothing. There was no doubt they would have died before capturing a city that was so well supplied. So the army stayed outside the city as the soldiers bought everything they wanted from the vendors on the walls. As they talked about what was going on, the two groups came to embrace peace and friendship, even though the city still looked like it was under siege with soldiers surrounding the city walls.

[8.6.5] That's what was happening at Aquileia. The horsemen who were carrying the heads of Maximinus and his son were riding at a breakneck pace towards Rome. All along the way, city gates were thrown wide open to welcome these messengers, and the townsfolk waved laurel branches at their arrival. They made their way through the marshy lowlands between Altinum and Ravenna, and when they got to Ravenna they found the emperor Pupienus hand-picking soldiers from Rome and Italy.

[8.6.6] When he was governor of Germany, Pupienus ruled in a kind and caring manner, and so now the Germans sent him lots of auxiliary troops since they liked him so much. But while Pupienus was preparing to go to war against Maximinus, the messengers arrived with the heads of Maximinus and his son, and they told him the war had already been won. Not only that, they said that the attacking army was now on the side of the Romans and that they swore allegiance to the emperors elected by the Senate.

[8.6.7] After he heard the unexpected good news, Pupienus ordered a series of sacrifices, and everyone rejoiced that they'd won without striking a single blow. Then, once he determined that the omens looked good, he sent the messengers on to Rome to announce their victory and deliver the heads of Maximinus and his son. When the horsemen arrived, they stuck the heads on spears and carried them throughout the city so everyone could see what happened to their enemies. Words can't capture the celebration that took place that day.

[8.6.8] Everyone ran out of their house, and all the men, no matter how old, bolted for the altars and temples to make

Fig. 169: Roman coin with Pupienus on one side and clasped hands (representing the emperor and the senate) on the reverse (AD 238)

sacrifices like they were possessed by the gods. The people cheered and hugged each other, gathering in the Circus Maximus like there was an official festival going on. Balbinus sacrificed a hundred oxen, and all the senators and magistrates rejoiced, feeling like they escaped an ax dangling over their necks. Then, messengers were sent with laurel branches to the provinces to announce the good news.

LATE SPRING AD 238: PUPIENUS ARRIVES IN AQUILEIA

[8.7.1] While the festivities were going on back in Rome, Pupienus left Ravenna and headed up to Aquileia, crossing the marshy lowlands of the Po River. These wetlands empty into the sea through seven different streams, and so the locals call this marshy area the "Seven Seas" in their own tongue.

[8.7.2] The Aquileians wasted no time throwing open the games and cheering Pupienus as he entered the city. Cities throughout Italy then chose their most notable citizens to send to him as heralds. They arrived wearing white togas and wielding laurel branches, and each of them brought gifts including statues of their gods and golden crowns. The heralds shouted in applause as Pupienus rode through the city and they threw leaves along his route. Then the former attacking soldiers went up to him, carrying their own laurel branches as a sign of peace, not necessarily because they loved the guy, but rather because it was important to act respectful in the presence of the emperor.

[8.7.3] In reality, most of those soldiers were pretty upset that the man they made emperor (Maximinus) had been killed, and now they had to deal with these new emperors (Pupienus and Balbinus) chosen by the Senate and people of Rome. Pupienus spent his first two days in the city making the appropriate sacrifices, and then on the third day he rode out of town into the countryside. He assembled the whole army there and built a platform so he could speak to the crowd. Pupienus began:

[8.7.4] "Now you know from personal experience how smart you were to change your minds, to start supporting the will of the Roman people! As you can see, you're now at peace instead of at war. Your gods are now protecting you, and you're keeping the soldier's oath, one of the most sacred in all the Roman world. From now on, enjoy the good life! Everything you want is yours, because you swore allegiance to the Senate and people of Rome, and to us (i.e., Pupienus and Balbinus), your new emperors. We were chosen based on our families' status, our track record of leadership, and our political experience, having only gained this position after completing the traditional *cursus honorum*.[9]

[8.7.5] The Roman Empire doesn't belong to any one person. Since its earliest days, it has belonged to the Roman people, the core of the Empire's greatness. We the emperors, and you the army, have been given the honor of running that Empire. If we do a good job, and everyone acts honorably and has respect for their leaders, then all of you will live a glorious life, full of every wonderful thing you could imagine. There will be peace in the cities and provinces throughout the empire, with the citizens properly respecting their governors. You'll have the opportunity to live wherever you'd like, be with your own people, and not be shipped off to dwell in some far off land.

[8.7.6] If you're wondering how we're going to keep the

---

9   The *cursus honorum* or the "course of honors" was the traditional political ladder in ancient Rome. It went from *quaestor* (financial official) to *aedile* (public works and festivals official) to *praetor* (commander and official) to *consul* (commander-in-chief and top official).

barbarians at bay, just leave that to us. We two emperors (i.e., Pupienus and Balbinus) are sharing power equally, and we're running things in Rome jointly as well. So if there are any problems on the outskirts of the empire, one of us can ride out to handle the issue, while the other stays in Rome to rule from the capital. Don't worry about what you did here. We know that you were only obeying orders. And don't worry about what happened in Rome either, those people rebelled because they weren't being treated fairly. Let's put all of this behind us. Consider all charges dropped. Now let's swear a perpetual friendship between us, that we'll only have good will and good deeds for the rest of our days ."

[8.7.7] After finishing his speech, Pupienus promised all the soldiers lots of money. He only stayed in Aquileia a few more days, and then prepared to head back to Rome. As for the army, he sent them out into the provinces, each to their own local camps. Pupienus himself then headed for Rome with the Praetorian Guard, the guards of the palace, and Balbinus' troops.

[8.7.8] Pupienus also brought his German auxiliaries to Rome. He had no doubt about their loyalty since he governed Germany in such a kind and compassionate manner before ascending to the emperorship. As he approached the city, Balbinus came out to meet him on the outskirts of town, bringing the emperor-in-waiting, little Gordian III, along with him. And the people of Rome shouted their applause, as he rode through the city like he were on a triumphal procession.

May AD 238: Pupienus and Balbinus are Killed

[8.8.1] For a while, the two emperors governed together in an effective and efficient manner, and everyone inside and outside the imperial palace loved them for it. The people honored them, viewing them as true heroes of Rome, to be praised throughout the Empire. The Praetorian Guard, however, were secretly upset that the people of Rome took a shine to these two new emperors. They disliked that these emperors came from aristocratic families, and they hated even more that it was the Senate, not the Praetorians themselves, that had bestowed upon them the emperorship.

[8.8.2] The Praetorians were scared that, if they rebelled against the emperor, that Pupienus' German troops would put up a fight. Not only that, the Praetorians thought that Pupienus might be devising a trap to have them discharged from duty, and then replace them with his German troops, making them the new imperial guard. They thought back to Septimius Severus, who had the Praetorian Guard discharged after they killed the former emperor Pertinax.[10]

[8.8.3] Towards the end of the Capitoline Games, while everyone in Rome was busy watching the parades and gladiatorial games, the Praetorian Guard brought their secret anger out into the open. They didn't try to conceal their rage any longer, instead launching a wild attack. They stormed the imperial palace, looking for the two old emperors with only one thing on their minds.

[8.8.4] As it turned out, the two emperors didn't actually do a great job sharing the throne. It was unusual to try to divide imperial power, and now each of them wanted to rule alone. So they each tried to take the throne solely for themselves. On the one hand, Balbinus thought he was best suited to be emperor because his family was more prominent and he served as *consul* twice. On the other hand, Pupienus thought he was the right man for the job because he'd been Prefect of Rome and he had been praised for his leadership. Thus, both of the emperors wanted to rule alone, spurred on by their noble births, their aristocratic ancestry, and impressive families.

[8.8.5] This feud led to their demise. When Pupienus learned that the Praetorian Guard had stormed the palace and was on their way to kill them, he wanted to bring in the Ger-

---

10 The emperor Commodus - famed for his megalomania and desire to fight as a gladiator in the arena - was assassinated on December 31, AD 192. Pertinax took over as emperor, tried to reform the Praetorian Guard, but was instead killed by the Praetorian Guard after less than a year of rule. Septimius Severus was installed as emperor later that year, and although he deified Pertinax, he discharged the Praetorian Guard, filling the position with his own loyal troops.

man auxiliaries he had in Rome to help protect them. Balbinus, however, thought that this was a trap, knowing that the Germans were loyal to Pupienus. So he didn't let Pupienus summon his troops, since he believed they weren't coming to fight against the Praetorians, but rather to forcefully install Pupienus as the sole emperor.

[8.8.6] While the two emperors were arguing about this, the Praetorian Guard rushed into the palace. The palace guards had abandoned their posts, and the Praetorians took hold of the emperors, ripping off their robes (the regular ones they wore around the house). Then they dragged the emperors - now naked - out of the palace. There they abused them in every way possible. They mocked and insulted these two men who'd been proclaimed emperors by the Senate, and then they beat them mercilessly, tearing out their beards and eyebrows and generally beating them senseless. They didn't want to kill them in the palace and thought torturing them would force them to suffer a little longer. So they dragged the emperors through the streets of Rome to the Praetorian camp in the middle of the city.

[8.8.7] When the Germans heard what was going on, they grabbed their weapons and rushed to the rescue. But when the Praetorians heard that the Germans were coming, they immediately executed the emperors, leaving their bodies to rot in the streets. Then they grabbed little Gordian III and proclaimed him emperor, since there wasn't anyone else really suitable for the role. The Praetorians claimed they only killed the two men because they people didn't want them to rule anyway, and besides, Gordian III was actually related to the previous Gordian who the Romans actually chose as their emperor. So they kept Gordian III with them, headed into the Praetorian camp, shut the gates, and quietly stayed there a while. And when the Germans auxiliaries heard that Pupienus had been killed, they went back to camp; no use fighting for someone who's already dead .

[8.8.8] So this is how these two honorable emperors met their ghastly and unjust end, even though they were of noble birth and had been rightfully elected to the imperial throne. Thus, Gordian III, only 13 years old, became the new Roman

Fig. 170: Roman coin of the young emperor Gordian III (ca. AD 240)

emperor and the burden of the entire Roman Empire rested on his shoulders.

The Rest of the Story

Herodian's *History of the Empire from the Death of Marcus Aurelius* ends with the conclusion of Book 8, which is where the translation above wraps up. This was just the start, however, of the Third Century Crisis, which most historians date from 235 AD, when the last of the Severans was assassinated, to 284, when Diocletian rose to the throne and established the Tetrarchy.

This fifty year period is commonly seen as the real beginning of the end for the Roman Empire, although the structural factors that led to this decline started much earlier. Septimius Severus, for example, raised the pay for his soldiers and increased the size of the army, which on the surface seems like a good thing. To do this, however, he had to debase the currency, that is, reduce the amount of silver that each coin contained. This started a vicious cycle of inflation, since people now demanded even higher pay and higher prices, and this led to even further debasement of the coinage.

Political instability also goes back decades before the traditional start date. Every single emperor that Herodian covers, except for one, dies of unnatural causes. Commodus (193 AD) is poisoned and strangled. Pertinax is killed by the Praetorian Guard and the Senate orders that Didius Julius be executed. Septimius Severus does have a long and successful reign (193 to 211) and die of natural causes, but his successors, Caracalla and Geta, are both murdered. And the rest of the Severan dynasty - Macrinus, Elagabalus, and Severus Alexander - are all assassinated as well.

This chaos certainly did continue during the third century, however. There were 26 different emperors between 235 and 284, so the average reign was less than 2 years. Wars broke out both internally and externally. Generals used their armies for their own purposes, sometimes in support of Rome against the barbarian tribes, but sometimes against other Romans for their own political purposes. This instability led to further incursions by the barbarian tribes at the borders of the Roman empire.

Diocletian eventually brought a temporary end to the problems of the third century. He issued a pricing edict to stabilize costs and stem inflation, and he developed a new system of imperial rule and transition known as the Tetrarchy. Under this system, there would also be two senior emperors known as "Augusti" and two junior emperors known as "Caesars." After a given amount of time (20 years), the Augusti would retire, the Caesars would take their place, and new Caesars would be appointed. This only sort of worked. Diocletian did indeed retire. But the sharing of power was not to last. Within a few decades, Constantine had defeated all other claimants to the emperorship, moved the capital from Rome to Constantinople, and approved the practice of Christianity throughout the Roman Empire. The Roman Empire had not fallen, but it was fundamentally transformed.

Fig. 171: Diocletian's retirement palace (Split, Croatia, ca. AD 305)

Fig. 172: Porphyry statue of Diocletian and the Tetrarchs
(San Marco Cathedral, Venice; ca. AD 300)

CONCLUSION

The Classical Legacy

ongratulations on completing your journey through the wonderful worlds of ancient Greece and Rome! We hope that you found it intellectually fascinating and had some fun along the way. One of the main reasons we still study these cultures today is that they have made an indelible impact on American society. We are the product of a vast array of cultural influences, but those of ancient Greece and Rome played a particularly prominent role.

One need look no further than our government to understand how we are fundamentally indebted to the Classical past. The invention of Greek democracy was a turning point in the ancient world, giving all citizens a vote in nearly all matters of the state. It's hard to overstate how unusual this was at the time, when most empires were growing larger and consolidating more power in a single individual. Even though we call our American government a democracy today, however, it actually more closely resembles the Republicanism of ancient Rome. That is, we tend to vote directly (like the Greeks) on a pretty limited number of issues. Instead, we elect our representatives (like the Romans) to legislate on our behalf. Regardless of how ineffective that may seem at times, the principle of participatory government, where the citizens have a prominent say in the way their society runs, is one of the hallmarks of Greek, Roman, and American culture.

We also see the influence of ancient Greece and Rome in so many aspects of culture that make life interesting, fun, and, well, generally worth living. The Greeks more or less invented sports in the way that we think about them today - competitive athletic contests with winners, losers, spectators, and prizes. We wear significantly more clothes when we compete in sport in the modern world, but the fundamental principles are the same ones that were there at the very first ancient Olympics nearly 3,000 years ago. The Romans, of course, took this one step further, deciding that it'd be more fun to watch people compete if they were bashing each other with swords and shields upside the head. We might like to think that we've come a long way since then, but many of our most popular sports are still rooted in violence and have the potential for serious injury. The Romans also took spectating to another level. The Colosseum in Rome stands as the inspiration for many sports stadiums today, like the Colosseum in Los Angeles, the Coliseum in Oakland, or the Coliseum in Edmonton, not to mention all the other venues that borrowed from the architecture without borrowing the name.

Every time we sit down to watch TV, we are indebted to our Greek and Roman ancestors for their developments in the world of theater and drama. When the Greeks were putting on tragedies and comedies in honor of Dionysus, they likely had no idea that we'd be doing the same thing 2,500 years later, only now streaming them for the world to see. Moreover, many of those early plays have stood the test of time, and the themes expressed in plays like Euripides' *Medea*, Aeschylus' Oresteia trilogy, or Sophocles' Antigone still resonate with us today (and many ancient works have modern adaptations). If you ever want to experience something extremely cool, head over to Greece to catch one of these plays - still performed more than two millennia later - in the ancient Greek theater at Epidaurus; it's a transformative experience to watch one in the

Fig. 173: The Roman Colosseum (Rome; complete in AD 80)

Fig. 174: Yankee Stadium (New York; completed in 1923)

same place the ancients would have centuries ago.

Literature in the modern world is also intimately tied to our Greco-Roman ancestors. First, we have them (and the Sumerians and Egyptians) to thank for using writing to tell stories. Whether that's the epic of Gilgamesh, the *Poem of Pentaur*, or Homer's *Iliad*, these stories were meant both to entertain and to teach lessons. Those lessons have stayed relevant to us today, as we continue to question the impact of anger in our own lives or the characteristics of a true hero. In addition to these epics, the Greeks and Romans also expanded our sense of genres, composing lyric poetry, tragic and comedic plays, histories, and philosophical musings. So when you scroll through all the different categories on Netflix, make sure to give a quick thanks to the Greeks and Romans for diversifying the world of entertainment.

Fig. 175: The Birth of Venus by Sandro Botticelli
(Uffizi Gallery; 1485)

The artistic legacy of Greece and Rome has also stood the test of time. Walk through just about any art museum in the world, and you'll see the influence of the Greeks and Romans. Part of that is through the style of art itself. Classical art emphasized naturalism and realism, even if things were still a bit idealized. In creating sculptures like the Venus de Milo or the Apollo Belvedere or the Hercules Farnese, these ancient artists worked to express ideals of human beauty and bring them to life from solid stone. During the Renaissance - literally the re-birth of Classical culture - artists worked to incorporate ancient Greek and Roman myths into their own works, like Botticelli's *Birth of Venus* or Cellini's *Perseus with the Head of Medusa*. And you would be forgiven for thinking that Michelangelo's *David* was indeed a Classical rather than a Renaissance sculpture.

The Greco-Roman legacy impacts us in more practical ways as well. Things like long-lasting roads and efficient and effective water procurement systems can all be traced back to the roads and aqueducts of the ancient Roman world - many of which were so well built that they are still in use today. Stroll down the Via Appia or walk through the Parco Aquedotti (Aqueduct Park), both just outside the walls of Rome, and you'll get a sense for the scale of these building projects, which once stretched across the entire empire.

The Classical style of architecture has also been reused and reinterpreted through the ages. Wander through the downtowns of capital cities across the Americas and Europe, and you'll see elements that would have fit right in in the heart of Rome: columns, capitals, pediments, and decorative relief sculptures. Look at the Jefferson Memorial, for example, and compare it to the Pantheon in Rome, and you'll see just how much we rely on our Classical ancestors for architectural inspiration.

Part of what made this work in antiquity, and still allows for this type of construction today, are the technological advances that underlie these works. The invention of concrete by the Romans allowed for buildings to grow taller and larger than they ever had been before. And the use of sophisticated arches and vaulting systems allowed for enormous basilicas to securely hold up massive roofs. The dome on the Pantheon, for example, stood as the largest dome in the world until the Duomo in Florence was constructed 1,300 years later. And today, the Pantheon still has the largest unreinforced concrete dome in the world .

We also can thank the Greeks and Romans for major

Fig. 176: The Pantheon (Rome; AD 126)

Fig. 177: The Jefferson Memorial
(Washington, D.C.; 1943)

strides they made in the realm of medicine and health care. Sure, sometimes they told you to go pray to Asclepius and hope you get bitten by a snake to heal your illness, but the Greeks and Romans also started thinking about health and medicine in a far more sophisticated way. Doctor's today still use a variant of Hippocrates' oath, and some of his advice - like drink lots of water and get some sleep - is still a pretty good solution to many of our ailments. Other thinkers, like Aristotle and Galen, relied heavily on scientific observation and testing to better understand the natural world and the human body, and that method of inquiry stands as the cornerstone of science in the world today.

One might consider the languages and scripts of the Greeks and Romans as an influential technology as well. We saw that the development of an alphabetic script by the Greeks (or at least the adaptation of their script from the Phoenicians), allowed them to convey nearly the entire range of human sounds in writing. This led the earliest alphabetic Greek texts to be things like the *Iliad* and *Odyssey* rather than the admittedly dry Linear B accounting tablets of the Aegean Bronze Age. These developments allowed for a vastly diversified array of texts to be created, and we've seen how these different genres still exist in literature, drama, and entertainment today. In total, about 60% of the words in the English language are derived from either Greek or Latin origins.

The way that the Greeks and Romans thought about the world, and the heavens beyond, has also left its mark. Sure, most of us today don't worship Zeus the God of Thunder or Ares the God of War, but it's important to remember that Christianity emerged during the heart of the Roman Empire. St. Peter's Basilica, after all, is built on top of the Circus of Nero, where the apostle Peter was crucified upside down in AD 64. Constantine's acceptance of, and supposed conversion to, Christianity in the early 4th century AD gave Christianity the political support it needed to grow into one of the most popular religions in the world today .

Even if you don't subscribe to that, however, the way that Greek and Roman philosophers thought about the world has

Fig. 178: St. Peter's Basilica (Rome; completed in AD 1626)

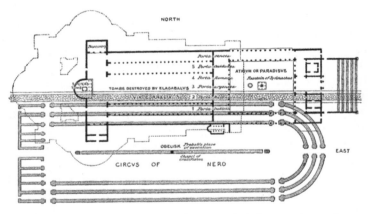

*Fig. 179: Plan of St. Peter's Basilica (est. AD 1626) superimposed
on a plan of the Circus of Nero (est. AD 65)*

made a major impact. The Ionian philosophers of the 6th century BC started asking questions about the way the world worked. A century later, Socrates and Plato would pose questions about what it meant to be a good person in the world. Stoics, ranging from the philosopher Zeno of Citium in the 4th century BC to the emperor Marcus Aurelius in the 2nd century AD, advocated for living a life of virtue in accordance with nature. We're still grappling with these same sorts of questions today in our attempt to figure out how to be good people and live happy lives.

And let's not forget one of the most important legacies of Greece and Rome - wine! The Greeks loved a good glass at their symposia, and the Romans drank, on average, about a liter of wine each day. There were even different vintages and varietals in the Roman world, and the finest ones cost ten or twenty times the cheapest. The Romans often mixed their wine with spices, sugars, and honey in a way that we would find, for the most part, rather disgusting, but the general idea - turning grapes into a delicious beverage - is something that we still do today.

Fig. 180: After fermentation, the Romans would store wine in amphoras, like these pictured as they would be stacked inside a ship

So now that you've made it through this book, pour yourself a nice glass of ancient Roman Falernian Red, and celebrate your accomplishment! As you do, we want you to reflect on one more thing. As influential as the Greeks and Romans have been in the development of modern American society, perhaps the most important takeaway from this journey is your ability to engage with the ancient texts themselves. In a world where we are bombarded with propagandistic messages everyday - what we should buy, who we should vote for, what we should eat and wear and watch - it's important to be able to think for yourself. Taking a deep dive into the words of the ancients allows you to practice these skills: identifying their purpose, their biases, and their rhetorical strategies for getting their ideas across. And if you can identify and understand those facets of ancient Greek and Roman writings, then you can do so in the modern world as well.

We hope you've enjoyed your journey and learned something useful from the ancients that you've met along the way. May this serve as a launching pad for an even deeper investigation into the lives, literature, and lessons of the ancient Greeks and Romans. Until then, hail and farewell!

APPENDIX

List of Figures

Fig. 1: Big Bang and Universal Exapansion
Date: 13.8 billion years ago
Attribution: NASA/WMAP Science Team
URL: https://en.wikipedia.org/wiki/File:CMB_Timeline300_no_WMAP.jpg
License: Public Domain

Fig. 2: Hadean Earth
Date: 4.5 billion years ago
Attribution: Tim Bertelink
URL: https://commons.wikimedia.org/wiki/File:Hadean.png
License: CC BY-SA 4.0

Fig. 3: Trilobite
Date: 500 million years ag
Attribution: Canva
Changes: Photo resized
License: Canva Pro License

Fig. 4: Homo sapiens skull
Location: Jebel Irhoud, Morocco
Date: 300,000 years ago
Attribution: Ryan Somma
URL: https://commons.wikimedia.org/wiki/File:Jebel_Irhoud_1._Homo_Spiens.jpg

Changes: Background removed, resized, color adjusted
License: CC BY-SA 2.0

Fig. 5: Replica of Upper Paleolithic cave paintings
Location: Chauvet, France
Date: ca. 30,000 years ago
Attribution: Claude Valette
URL:https://smarthistory.org/wp-content/uploads/2019/07/29_Panneau-DesChevauxVueGe%CC%81ne%C-C%81rale.jpg
License: CC BY-SA 4.0

Fig. 6: The positive feedback loop of the Neolithic Revolution
Date: ca. 10,000 BC
Attibution: Canva
Changes: Text added
License: Canva Pro License

Fig. 7: The Neolithic site of Çatalhöyük
Location: Çatalhöyük, Turkey
Date: ca. 7500-5700 BC
Attribution: Canva
License: Canva Pro License

Fig. 8: Reconstruction of the site of Çatalhöyük
Location: Çatalhöyük, Turkey
Date: ca. 7500-5700 BC
Attribution: Wolfgang Sauber
URL: https://commons.wiki-media.org/wiki/File:MUFT_-_Catal_H%C3%B6y%C3%BCk_Mod-ell.jpg
License: CC BY-SA 4.0

Fig. 9: Reconstruction of a house at Çatalhöyük
Location: Çatalhöyük, Turkey
Date: ca. 7500-5700 BC
Attribution: Elelicht
URL: https://commons.wikimedia.org/wiki/File:Catal_H%C3%BCy%C3%B-Ck_EL.JPG
License: CC BY-SA 3.0

Fig. 10: Bronze Age Empires
Attribution: Google 2023, TerraMet-rics
URL: https://www.google.com/maps
License: Fair Use

Fig. 11: Scorpion Macehead
Ancient Location: Hierakonpolis, Egypt
Modern Location: Ashmolean Museum
Date: ca. 3200-3000 BC
Attribution: Jon Bodworth
URL: https://commons.wikimedia.org/wiki/File:Scorpion_Macehead.jpg
Changes: Backround removed, resized, color adjusted
License: Free to use for any purpose

Fig. 12: Scorpion Macehead sketch
Attribution: Benutzer:Weneg
URL:https://commons.wikimedia.org/wiki/File:Skorpion_II.png
License: CC BY-SA 3.0 DE

Fig. 13: Archaeological ruins of the Ziggurat of Ur
Location: Ur, Iraq
Date: ca. 2050 BC
Attribution: Michael Lubinski
URL: https://commons.wikimedia.org/wiki/File:Ziggarut_of_Ur_-_M.Lubinski.jpg
License: CC BY-SA 2.0

Fig. 14: Digital reconstruction of the Ziggurat of Ur
Attribution: wikiwikiyarou
URL: https://en.wikipedia.org/wiki/Ziggurat_of_Ur
License: CC BY-SA 2.0

Fig. 15: The so-called Mask of Sargon
Location: Iraq Museum
Date: ca. 2300 BC
Attribution: Mallowan 1936
URL: https://commons.wikimedia.org/wiki/File:Sargon_of_Akkad_(1936).jpg
Changes: Background removed
License: Public Domain

Fig. 16: Hammurabi's Code
Ancient Location: Susa, Iran
Modern Location: Louvre Museum
Date: ca. 1800-1750 BC
Attribution: Mbzt
URL: https://commons.wikimedia.org/wiki/File:P1050763_Louvre_code_Hammurabi_face_rwk.JPG
Changes: Backround removed, cropped
License: CC BY 3.0

Fig. 17: Narmer Palette
Ancient Location: Hierakonpolis, Egypt
Modern Location: Egyptian Museum, Cairo
Date: ca. 3000 BC
Attribution: StudyBlue
URL: https://commons.wikimedia.org/wiki/File:Narmer_Palette.jpg
Changes: Backround removed, cropped
License: Public Domain

Fig. 18: The Pyramids of Giza
Location: Giza, Egypt
Date: ca. 2600-2500 BC
Attribution: Canva
Changes: Background removed
License: Canva Pro License

Fig. 19: Papyrus of Hunefer
Location: British Museum
Date: ca. 1275 BC
Attribution: British Museum
URL: https://commons.wikimedia.org/
wiki/File:The_judgement_of_the_dead_
in_the_presence_of_Osiris.jpg
License: Public Domain

Fig. 20: Mask of Tutankhamun
Ancient Location: Valley of the Kings,
Egypt
Modern Location: Egyptian Museum,
Cairo
Date: 1332-1323 BC
Attribution: Ronald Unger
URL: https://commons.wikimedia.org/
wiki/File:CairoEgMuseumTaaMask-
MostlyPhotographed.jpg
Changes: Background removed
License: CC BY-SA 3.0

Fig. 21: Temple of Karnak
Location: Karnak, Egypt
Date: ca. 1550-1069 BC
Attribution: Canva
License: Canva Pro License

Fig. 22: Ramesses defeating the Sea Peoples
Location: Medinet Habu, Egypt
Date: ca. 1200 BC
Attribution: Floam
URL: https://commons.wikimedia.
org/wiki/File:Medinet_Habu_Ram-
ses_III._Tempel_Nordostwand_Abze-
ichnung_01.jpg
License: Public Domain

Fig. 23: Map of Bronze Age Collapse
Date: ca. 12th century BC
Attribution: Lommes
URL: https://commons.wikimedia.org/
wiki/File:Bronze-age-collapse.svg
License: CC BY-SA 4.0

Fig. 24: Map of Egypt and Hatti
Date: ca. 1300 BC
Attribution: Enyavar
URL: https://commons.wikimedia.org/
wiki/File:Ancient_Near_East_1300BC.
svg
License: CC BY-SA 4.0

Fig. 25: Monumental statue of Ramesses II
Ancient Location: Ramesseum (Thebes,
Egypt)
Modern Location: British Museum
Date: 13th century BC
Attribution: Pbuergler
URL: https://commons.wikimedia.org/
wiki/File:Ramses_II_British_Museum.
jpg
Changes: Background removed
License: CC BY-SA 3.0

Fig. 26: Hittite Chariot Relief
Ancient Location: Carchemish
Modern Location: Museum of Anato-
lian Civilizations
Date: 9th to 8th century BC
Attribution: Dudva
URL: https://commons.wikimedia.org/
wiki/File:Orthostats_of_Long_Wall_
(Basalt,_Gaziantep,_900-700_BC).jpg
Changes: Background removed
License: CC BY-SA 4.0

Fig. 27: Drawing of relief of the Battle of Kadesh
Ancient Location: Ramesseum (Thebes,
Egypt)
Date: 13th century BC
Attribution: J. H. Breasted 1927
URL: https://commons.wikimedia.org/
wiki/File:Battle_scene_from_the_Great_
Kadesh_reliefs_of_Ramses_II_on_the_
Walls_of_the_Ramesseum.jpg
License: Public Domain

Fig. 28: Temple of Luxor
Location: Luxor, Egypt
Date: 13th century BC
Attribution: Canva
Changes: Background removed
License: Canva Pro License

Fig. 29: Papyrus Sallier III

Location: British Museum
Date: 13th century BC
Attribution: E. A. Wallis Budge 1923
URL: https://cplorg.contentdm.oclc.
org/digital/collection/p4014coll9/
id/5301/
License: Public Domain

Fig. 30: Relief of Ramesses attacking from chariot

Location: Abu Simbel, Egypt
Date: 13th century BC
Attribution: Dwkrider1
URL: https://commons.wikimedia.org/
wiki/File:2N9A6519-Pano.jpg
Changes: Cropped
License: CC BY-SA 4.0

Fig. 31: Relief of Ramesses smiting enemies

Location: Abu Simbel, Egypt
Date: 13th century BC
Attribution: Dwkrider1
URL: https://commons.wikimedia.org/
wiki/File:2N9A6519-Pano.jpg
Changes: Cropped
License: CC BY-SA 4.0

Fig. 32: Archival photo of Poem of Pentaur

Location: Temple of Karnak
Date: 13th century BC
Attribution: Antonio Beato (Royal
Trust Collection)
URL: https://www.rct.uk/collec-
tion/2581426/poem-of-pentaur
Changes: Cropped and straightened
License: Public Domain

Fig. 33: Archival photo of Poem of Pentaur

Location: Temple of Karnak
Date: 13th century BC
Attribution: Antonio Beato (Royal
Trust Collection)
URL: https://www.rct.uk/collec-
tion/2581425/exterior-wall-with-re-
liefs-and-columns-at-the-temple-com-
plex-of-karnak-egypt
Changes: Cropped and straightened
License: Public Domain

Fig. 34: Hittite treaty on bronze tablets

Location: Museum of Anatolian
Civilizations
Date: ca. 1235 BC
Attribution: Bjorn Christian Torrissen
URL: https://commons.wikimedia.org/
wiki/File:Hattusa_Bronze_Tablet_Cu-
neiform.JPG
Changes: Background removed
License: CC BY-SA 3.0

Fig. 35: Peace Treaty of Kadesh Hittite tablet

Location: Istanbul Archaeological
Museum
Date: 13th century BC
Attribution: Iocanus
URL: https://commons.wikimedia.org/
wiki/File:Treaty_of_Kadesh.jpg
Changes: Background removed,
recolored
License: CC BY 3.0

Fig. 36: Peace Treaty of Kadesh Egyptian relief

Location: Temple of Karnak
Date: 13th century BC
Attribution: Olaf Tausch
URL: https://commons.wikimedia.
org/wiki/File:Karnak_%C3%84gyp-
tisch-Hethitischer_Friedensvertrag_06.
jpg
Changes: Background removed
License: CC BY 3.0

Fig. 37: Map of Aegean Bronze Age

Attribution: Google 2023, TerraMet-
rics
URL: https://www.google.com/maps
License: Fair Use

Fig. 38: Palace of Knossos

Location: Knossos, Greece
Date: ca. 1900-1200 BC
Attribution: Canva
License: Canva Pro License

Fig. 39: Dolphin fresco
Location: Knossos, Greece
Date: ca. 1500 BC
Attribution: Canva
License: Canva Pro License

Fig. 40: Lion Gate of Mycenae
Location: Mycenae, Greece
Date: ca. 1550-1150 BC
Attribution: Canva
License: Canva Pro License

Fig. 41: Linear B Tablet (PY Ub 1318)
Location: National Archaeological Museum of Athens
Date: ca. 1450
Attribution: Sharon Mollerus
URL: https://commons.wikimedia.org/wiki/File:NAMA_Linear_B_tablet_of_Pylos.jpg
Changes: Background removed
License: CC BY 2.0

Fig. 42: Bronze Age "Marine" style amphora
Location: Heraklion Archaeological Museum
Date: ca. 1500 BC
Attribution: Wolfgang Sauber
URL: https://commons.wikimedia.org/wiki/File:AMI_-_Oktopusvase.jpg
Changes: Background removed
License: Public Domain

Fig. 43: Dark Age "Protogeometric" amphora
Location: British Museum
Date: ca. 975-950 BC
Attribution: Marie-Lan Nguyen
URL: https://commons.wikimedia.org/wiki/File:Protogeometric_amphora_BM_A1124.jpg
Changes: Background Removed
License: CC BY 2.5

Fig. 44: Map of Greek colonization
Atttribution: The British Library
URL: https://commons.wikimedia.org/wiki/File:71_of_%27A_History_of_Greece_for_High_Schools_and_Academies%27_(11251883206).jpg
Changes: Straightened
License: Public Domain

Fig. 45: Geometric Dipylon Krater
Location: Metropolitan Museum of Art
Date: ca. 750-735 BC
Attribution: Metropolitan Museum of Art
URL: https://images.metmuseum.org/CRDImages/gr/original/DT258.jpg
Changes: Background removed
License: Public Domain

Fig. 46: "Nestor's Cup"
Location: Archaeological Museum of Pithecusae
Date: ca. 725 BC
Attribution: Marcus Cyron
URL: https://commons.wikimedia.org/wiki/File:Nestorbecher_auf_Ischia.jpg
Changes: Background removed, cropped
License: CC BY-SA 4.0

Fig. 47: The Tyrannicides
Location: National Archaeological Museum of Naples
Date: Roman copy of a Greek original from the 5th century BC
Attribution: Miguel Hermoso Cuesta
URL: https://commons.wikimedia.org/wiki/File:Tiranicidas_04.JPG
Changes: Background removed
License: CC BY-SA 3.0

Fig. 48: Temple of Apollo at Corinth
Location: Corinth, Greece
Date: ca. 560 BC
Attribution: Berthold Werner
URL: https://commons.wikimedia.org/wiki/File:Korinth_BW_2017-10-10_10-55-28.jpg
Changes: Background removed
License: CC BY SA 3.0

Fig. 49: Plan of a Greek temple
Attribution: B. Jankuloski and Napoleon Vier
URL: https://commons.wikimedia.org/wiki/File:Greek_temples.svg
Changes: Text added
License: CC BY-SA 4.0

Fig. 50: Panathenaic prize amphora
Location: Metropolitan Museum of Art
Date: ca. 530 BC
Attribution: Metropolitan Museum of Art
URL: https://www.metmuseum.org/art/collection/search/248902
Changes: Background removed
License: Public Domain

Fig. 51: Old Kingdom statue of striding figure
Location: Metropolitan Museum of Art
Date: ca. 2500 BC
Attribution: Metropolitan Museum of Art
URL: https://www.metmuseum.org/art/collection/search/543903
Changes: Background removed
License: Public Domain

Fig. 52: Kroisos Kouros
Location: Anavyssos, Greece
Date: ca. 530 BC
Attribution: Jebulon
URL: https://commons.wikimedia.org/wiki/File:Kouros_NAMA_3851_Athens_Greece.jpg
Changes: Background removed
License: Public Domain

Fig. 53: Attic black-figure vase of Ajax and Achilles
Location: Vatican Museums
Date: ca. 550-530 BC
Attribution: xennex
URL: https://commons.wikimedia.org/wiki/File:Kouros_NAMA_3851_Athens_Greece.jpg
Changes: Background removed
License: Public Domain

Fig. 54: Boar's tusk helmet
Location: National Archaeological Museum of Athens
Date: 14th century BC
Attribution: Jebulon
URL: https://commons.wikimedia.org/wiki/File:Boars%27s_tusk_helmet_NAMA6568_Athens_Greece1.jpg
Changes: Background removed
License: Public Domain

Fig. 55: Statue of Homer playing the lyre
Location: Louvre Museum
Date: 1812
Artist: Philippe-Laurent Roland
Attribution: Urban
URL: https://commons.wikimedia.org/wiki/File:Homer_by_Philippe-Laurent_Roland_(Louvre_2004_134_cor).jpg
Changes: Background removed
License: CC BY-SA 3.0

Fig. 56: The Judgment of Paris
Location: Virginia Museum of Fine Arts
Date: 1808
Artist and Attribution: François-Xavier Fabre
URL: https://commons.wikimedia.org/wiki/File:Fran%C3%A7ois-Xavier_Fabre_-_The_Judgment_of_Paris.jpg
License: Public Domain

Fig. 57: Apulian red-figure krater depicting Chryses and Agamemnon
Location: Louvre Museum
Date: ca. 360-350 BC
Attribution: Jastrow
URL: https://commons.wikimedia.org/wiki/File:Chryses_Agamemnon_Louvre_K1.jpg
License: Public Domain

Fig. 58: Ivory statue of Apollo
Location: Stoa of Attalus Museum
Date: 3rd century BC
Attribution: Giovanni dall'Orto
URL: https://commons.wikimedia.
org/wiki/File:3248_-_Athens_-_
Sto%C3%A0_of_Attalus_Museum_-_
Ivory_Apollo_-_Photo_by_Giovan-
ni_Dall%27Orto,_Nov_9_2009.jpg
Changes: Background removed
License: Attribution necessary

Fig. 59: Mosaic of Achilles and Agamemnon
Location: National Archaeological
Museum of Naples
Date: 1st century AD
Attribution: Askelladd
URL: https://commons.wikimedia.org/
wiki/File:Achilles_Agamemnon_Pom-
pei_mosaic_NAMNaples_10006.jpg
License: Public Domain

Fig. 60: Mosaic of Nestor
Location: Getty Villa
Date: 2nd century AD
Attribution: Dave and Margie Hill
URL: https://commons.wikimedia.org/
wiki/File:Getty_Villa_-_Collection_
(3151231788).jpg
Changes: Background removed
License: CC BY-SA 2.0

Fig. 61: Fresco of Thetis and Achilles
Location: Villa Valmarana ai Nani
Date: 1757
Artist/Attribution: Giovanni Batista
Tiepolo
URL: https://commons.wikimedia.
org/wiki/File:Giovanni_Battista_Tie-
polo_-_Thetis_Consoling_Achilles_-_
WGA22339.jpg
License: Public Domain

Fig. 62: Parthenon sculpture with cattle for sacrifice
Location: British Museum
Date: 5th century BC
Attribution: Marie Lan-Nguyen
URL: https://commons.wikimedia.org/
wiki/File:South_frieze_132-136_Parthe-
non_BM.jpg
Changes: Background removed
License: CC BY 2.5

Fig. 63: Thetis asking Zeus for help
Location: Granet Museum
Date: 1811
Atrist and Attribution: Jean Auguste
Dominique Ingres
URL: https://commons.wikimedia.
org/wiki/File:J%C3%BApiter_y_Te-
tis,_por_Dominique_Ingres.jpg
License: Public Domain

Fig. 64: Sculptural relief of Hephaestus thrown from Olympus
Location: Museum of Ostia
Date: 2nd century AD
Attribution: Sailko
URL: https://commons.wikimedia.org/
wiki/File:Fregio_con_storie_di_atena_
ed_efesto,_II_secolo,_dalle_terme_del_
foro_e_le_terme_bizantine_06.JPG
Changes: Background removed
License: CC BY 3.0

Fig. 65: Achilles triumphs over Hector
Location: Achilleion
Date: 1892
Artist and Attribution: Franz von
Matsch
URL: https://commons.wikimedia.org/
wiki/File:Triumph_of_Achilles_by_
Franz_von_Matsch.jpg
License: Public Domain

Fig. 66: Map of Odysseus' journey
Attribution: Giulia Zoccarato, Densi-
tyDesign Research Lab
URL: https://commons.wikimedia.org/
wiki/File:Odysseus%27_Journey.svg
Changes: Cropped
License: CC BY-SA 4.0

Fig. 67: Head of Odysseus

Location: National Archaeological Museum, Sperlonga

Date: 1st century AD

Attribution: Jastrow

URL: https://commons.wikimedia.org/wiki/File:Head_Odysseus_MAR_Sperlonga.jpg

Changes: Background removed

License: Public Domain

Fig. 68: Circe and Odysseus

Location: Academy of Fine Arts of Vienna

Date: 1785

Artist/Attribution: Hubert Maurer

URL: https://commons.wikimedia.org/wiki/File:Hubert_Maurer_-_Circe_und_Odysseus_2.jpg

License: Public Domain

Fig. 69: Engraving of Odysseus and the Lotus-Eaters

Location: Rijksmuseum

Date: 1633

Artist/Attribution: Theodoor van Thulden

URL: https://commons.wikimedia.org/wiki/File:Lotus-eaters.png

License: Public Domain

Fig. 70: Polyphemus mosaic

Location: Piazza Armerina, Italy

Date: early 4th century AD

Attribution: psub

URL: https://commons.wikimedia.org/wiki/File:Villa_del_casale_12.jpg

Changes: Background removed

License: CC BY-SA 2.0

Fig. 71: Krater depicting Odysseus stabbing Polyphemus

Location: Archaeological Museum of Argos

Date: ca. 670 BC

Attribution: Mary Harrsch

URL: https://commons.wikimedia.org/wiki/File:Archaic_or_late_geometric_period_krater_depicting_Odysseus_and_a_friend_stabbing_the_giant_Polyphemus_in_his_only_eye,_clay,_670_BCE,_Archaeological_Museum_of_Argos.jpg

Changes: Background removed

License: CC BY-SA 4.0

Fig. 72: Amphora of Odysseus stabbing Polyphemus

Location: Archaeological Museum of Eleusis

Date: ca. 660 BC

Attribution: Napoleon Vier

URL: https://commons.wikimedia.org/wiki/File:Polyphemus_Eleusis_2630.jpg

Changes: Background removed

License: CC BY-SA 3.0

Fig. 73: Bronze statuette of Odysseus underneath ram

Location: Archaeological Museum of Delphi

Date: ca. 550-500 BC

Attribution: Zde

URL: https://commons.wikimedia.org/wiki/File:Odysseus_under_the_belly_of_a_ram,_small_archaic_bronze,_AM_Delphi,_201355.jpg

Changes: Background removed

License: CC BY-SA 4.0

Fig. 74: Odysseus in the cave of Polyphemus

Location: Pushkin Museum of Fine Arts

Date: 1630-35

Artist/Attribution: Jacob Jordaens

URL: https://commons.wikimedia.org/wiki/File:Jakob_Jordaens_009.jpg

License: Public Domain

Fig. 84: Parthenon frieze showing equestrian riders
Location: British Museum
Date: 5th century BC
Attribution: Marie Lan-Nguyen
URL: https://en.wikipedia.org/wiki/File:Cavalcade_west_frieze_Parthenon_BM.jpg
Changes: Background removed
License: Public Domain

Fig. 85: Bust of Socrates
Location: Louvre Museum
Date: Roman copy of a Greek original from the 4th century BC
Attribution: Eric Gaba
URL: https://commons.wikimedia.org/wiki/File:Socrate_du_Louvre.jpg
Changes: Background removed
License: CC BY-SA 2.5

Fig. 86: Bust of Plato
Location: Vatican Museums
Date: Roman copy of a Greek original from the 4th century BC
Attribution: Marie-Lan Nguyen
URL: https://commons.wikimedia.org/wiki/File:Plato_Pio-Clemetino_Inv305.jpg
Changes: Background removed
License: Public Domain

Fig. 87: Theater of Epidaurus
Location: Epidaurus, Greece
Date: 4th century BC
Attribution: Robert Stephan
License: CC BY-SA 4.0

Fig. 88: Black-figure vase with Greek hoplites fighting
Location: National Archaeological Museum of Athens
Date: 6th century BC
Attribution: Grant Mitchell
URL: https://commons.wikimedia.org/wiki/File:Hoplite_fight_from_Athens_Museum.jpg
License: CC BY 2.0

Fig. 89: Bust of Alexander the Great
Location: Capitoline Museums
Date: 3rd to 2nd century BC
Attribution: Jean-Pol Grandmont
URL: https://commons.wikimedia.org/wiki/File:0_Alexander-Helios_Capitolini_(1).JPG
Changes: Background removed
License: CC BY-SA 3.0

Fig. 90: Silver coin of Alexander the Great
Date: 333-327 BC
Attribution: CNG Coins
URL: https://commons.wikimedia.org/wiki/File:KINGS_of_MACEDON_Alexander_III_the_Great_336-323_BC.jpg
Changes: Background removed
License: CC BY-SA 3.0

Fig. 91: The Alexander Mosaic:
Location: National Archaeological Museum of Naples
Date: ca. 100 BC
Attribution: Berthold Werner
URL: https://commons.wikimedia.org/wiki/File:Battle_of_Issus_mosaic_-_Museo_Archeologico_Nazionale_-_Naples_2013-05-16_16-25-06_BW.jpg
License: Public Domain

Fig. 92: The so-called Alexander Sarcophagus
Location: Istanbul Archaeological Museum
Date: late 4th century BC
Attribution: Ronald Slabke
URL: https://commons.wikimedia.org/wiki/File:Alexander_Sarcophagus_Battle_of_Issus.jpg
License: CC BY-SA 3.0

Fig. 93: Ptolemy I as Greek
Location: Louvre Museum
Date: 305-282 BC
Attribution: Marie-Lan Nguyen
URL: https://commons.wikimedia.org/wiki/File:Alexander_Sarcophagus_Battle_of_Issus.jpg
Changes: Background removed
License: Public Domain

Fig. 103: Tomb of Xerxes I

Location: Naqsh-e Rostam
Date: ca. 465 BC
Attribution: Dynamosquito
URL: https://commons.wikimedia.org/
wiki/File:Tomb_of_Xerxes_I_Soldiers_
of_all_ethnicities_supporting_the_
throne_of_Xerxes_with_names.jpg
License: CC BY-SA 2.0

Fig. 104: Leonidas at Thermopylae

Location: Louvre Museum
Date: 1814
Artist/Attribution: Jacques-Louis David
URL: https://en.wikipedia.org/wiki/
File:Le%C3%B3nidas_en_las_Ter-
m%C3%B3pilas,_por_Jacques-Lou-
is_David.jpg
License: Public Domain

Fig. 105: Map of Italy from ca. 750 to ca. 500 BC

Attribution: Javierfv1212
URL: https://commons.wikimedia.org/
wiki/File:Roman_conquest_of_Italy.
PNG
License: Public Domain

Fig. 106: The Seven Hills of Rome

Attribution: Renata3
URL: https://commons.wikimedia.org/
wiki/File:Seven_Hills_of_Rome.svg
License: CC BY-SA 4.0

Fig. 107: The so-called Hut of Romulus

Location: Rome, Italy
Date: 8th century BC
Attribution: Sailko
URL: https://commons.wikimedia.org/
wiki/File:Veduta_degli_scavi_coi_fori_
neolitici_di_capanne_sul_palatino,_02.
jpg
License: CC BY 3.0

Fig. 108: House-shaped funerary urn

Location: Walters Art Museum
Date: 8th century BC
Attribution: Walters Art Museum
URL: https://commons.wikimedia.org/
wiki/File:Villanovan_-_Urn_in_the_
Shape_of_a_Hut_and_a_Door_-_Wal-
ters_482312.jpg
Changes: Background removed
License: Public Domain

Fig. 109: Diagram of the cursus honorum

Attribution: C. K. Ruppelt
URL: https://commons.wikimedia.org/
wiki/File:Cursus_Honorum.png
License: CC BY-SA 4.0

Fig. 110: The Roman Senate (Cicero denounces Catiline)

Location: Palazzo Madama
Date: 1899
Artist/Attribution: Cesare Maccari
URL: https://commons.wikimedia.org/
wiki/File:Maccari-Cicero.jpg
License: Public Domain

Fig. 111: Map of Hannibal's Route of Invasion

Attribution: Courtesy of the United
States Military Academy Department
of History
URL: https://commons.wikimedia.org/
wiki/File:Hannibal_route_of_inva-
sion_-_en.svg
License: CC BY-SA 3.0

Fig. 112: Map of Roman territory in the 2nd century BC

Attribution: Courtesy of the United
States Military Academy Department
of History
URL: http://www.emersonkent.com/
map_archive/roman_republic_2nd_cen-
tury_bc.htm

License: Public Domain

Fig. 113: The Aqua Claudia
Location: Rome, Italy
Date: 1st century AD
Attribution: Roundtheworld
URL: https://commons.wikimedia.org/
wiki/File:Aqueduct_Rome.jpg
Changes: Background removed,
cropped
License: CC BY-SA 4.0

Fig. 114: Statue of Mithras
Location: Louvre Museum
Date: 2nd century AD
Attribution: Serge Ottaviani
URL: https://commons.wikimedia.org/
wiki/File:Mithra_sacrifiant_le_Tau-
reau-005.JPG
Changes: Background removed
License: CC BY-SA 3.0

Fig. 115: Bust of Livy
Location: National Museum of
Warsaw
Date: 15th century
Artist: Andrea Riccio
Attribution: Artinpl
URL: https://commons.wikimedia.org/
wiki/File:Briosco_Titus_Livius_01.jpg
Changes: Background removed
License: Public Domain

Fig. 116: Manuscript of Livy's
History of Rome
Location: Vatican Library
Date: 5th century AD
Attribution: Pylaimenes
URL: https://commons.wikimedia.org/
wiki/File:Livius,_Fragments.jpg
License: Public Domain

Fig. 117: Statue of Mars Ultor
Location: Capitoline Museums
Date: 2nd century AD
Attribution: Rabax63
URL: https://commons.wikimedia.org/
wiki/File:Mars_Ultor_(Avenger).jpg
Changes: Background removed
License: CC BY-SA 4.0

Fig. 118: Statue of Aeneas fleeing
Troy
Location: Galleria Borghese
Date: 1618
Artist: Gian Lorenzo Bernini
Attribution: Daderot
URL: https://commons.wikimedia.org/
wiki/File:Aeneas,_Anchises,_and_As-
canius_by_Bernini,_1618-1620,_mar-
ble,_view_1_-_Galleria_Borghese_-_
Rome,_Italy_-_DSC04797.jpg
Changes: Background removed
License: Public Domain

Fig. 119: Map of Etruria
Attribution: NormanEinstein
URL: https://commons.wikimedia.org/
wiki/File:Etruscan_civilization_map.
png
License: CC BY-SA 3.0

Fig. 120: Statue of Rhea Silvia
Location: Santa Maria della Scala,
Siena
Date: 1414-19
Artist: Jacopo della Quercia
Attribution: José Luiz Bernardes
Ribeiro
URL: https://commons.wikimedia.org/
wiki/File:Rhea_Silvia_by_Jacopo_del-
la_Quercia_-_Santa_Maria_della_Scal-
la_(from_Fonte_Gaia)_-_Siena_2016.
jpg
Changes: Background removed
License: CC BY-SA 4.0

Fig. 121: The Capitoline Wolf
Location: Capitoline Museums
Date: 13th-15th centuries
Attribution: Jastrow
URL: https://commons.wikimedia.org/
wiki/File:Capitoline_she-wolf_Mu-
sei_Capitolini_MC1181.jpg
Changes: Background removed
License: Public Domain

Fig. 122: Etching of Romulus killing Remus

Location: British Museum
Date: 1575
Artist: Giovanni Battista Fontana
Attribution: Venzz
URL: https://commons.wikimedia.org/wiki/File:Augurs,_Resort_to_Arms_and_Remus_is_Killed,_pl.8_from_the_series_The_Story_of_Romulus_and_Remus.jpg
License: Public Domain

Fig. 123: Hercules and Cacus

Location: Frans Hals Museum
Date: 1613
Artist/Attribution: Henrik Goltzius
URL: https://commons.wikimedia.org/wiki/File:Hendrick_Goltzius_-_Hercules_and_Cacus_-_43_-_Mauritshuis.jpg
License: Public Domain

Fig. 124: The Rape of the Sabines

Location: National Trust, Antwerp
Date: 17th century
Artist/Attribution: Peter Paul Rubens
URL: https://commons.wikimedia.org/wiki/File:Peter_Paul_Rubens_-_The_Rape_of_the_Sabine_Women_-_WGA20310.jpg
License: Public Domain

Fig. 125: Sculpture of Tarpeia killed by the Sabines

Location: National Museum, Rome
Date: 1st century BC to 1st century AD
Attribution: Marie-Lan Nguyen
URL: https://commons.wikimedia.org/wiki/File:Frieze_Basilica_Aemilia_Massimo_n3.jpg
Changes: Background removed
License: Public Domain

Fig. 126: Etching of the apotheosis of Romulus

Location: Rijksmuseum
Date: 1573
Artist: Giovanni Battista Fontana
Attribution: Mr.Nostalgic
URL: https://commons.wikimedia.org/wiki/File:Hemelvaart_van_Romulus_Exercitum_lustrans_Romulus_a_suis_colitur_(titel_op_object)_Leven_van_Romulus_en_Remus_(serietitel),_BI-1937-0095-27.jpg
License: Public Domain

Fig. 127: Statue of the Gracchi

Location: Musée d'Orsay
Date: 1848-53
Attribution: Sailko
URL: https://commons.wikimedia.org/wiki/File:Eug%C3%A9ne_guillaume,_i_gracchi,_1853.JPG
Changes: Background removed
License: CC BY 3.0

Fig. 128: Bust of Marius

Location: Glyptothek
Date: ca. AD 10
Attribution: Bibi Saint-Pol
URL: https://commons.wikimedia.org/wiki/File:Marius_Glyptothek_Munich_319.jpg
Changes: Background removed
License: Public Domain

Fig. 129: Bust of Sulla

Location: Glyptothek
Date: ca. AD 10
Attribution: Bibi Saint-Pol
URL: https://commons.wikimedia.org/wiki/File:Sulla_Glyptothek_Munich_309.jpg
Changes: Background removed
License: Public Domain

Fig. 130: Map of the Roman Republic at time of Caesar

Attribution: Historicair, Ifly6
URL: https://commons.wikimedia.org/wiki/File:Map_of_the_Ancient_Rome_at_Caesar_time_(with_conquests)-en.svg
License: CC BY-SA 3.0

Fig. 141: Diagram of Caesar's defenses at Alesia
Attribution: Courtesy of the Department of History, United States Military Academy
URL: http://www.emersonkent.com/map_archive/siege_of_alesia.htm
License: Public Domain

Fig. 142: Recreation of Caesar's defenses at Alesia
Attribution: Prosopee
URL: https://commons.wikimedia.org/wiki/File:Mus%C3%A9op-arc_d%27Al%C3%A9sia_fortifications.JPG
License: CC BY-SA 3.0

Fig. 143: Map of the Siege of Alesia
Attribution: Courtesy of the Department of History, United States Military Academy
URL: http://www.emersonkent.com/images/siege_of_alesia.jpg
License: Public Domain

Fig. 144: The Dying Gaul
Location: Capitoline Museums
Date: Roman copy of a Hellenistic original form the 3rd century BC
Attribution: BeBo86
URL: https://commons.wikimedia.org/wiki/File:Dying_Gaul.jpg
Changes: Background removed
License: CC BY-SA 3.0

Fig. 145: The Surrender of Vercingetorix
Location: Musée Crozatier
Date: 1899
Artist/Attribution: Lionel Royer
URL: https://commons.wikimedia.org/wiki/File:Siege-alesia-vercingetorix-jules-cesar.jpg
License: Public Domain

Fig. 146: Engraving of Plutarch
Location: National Gallery of Art, Washington, D.C.
Date: 1561-1641
Artist: Leonard Gaultier
Attribution: National Gallery of Art
URL: https://www.nga.gov/collection/art-object-page.78575.html
License: Public Domain

Fig. 147: Title page of Plutarch's Parallel Lives
Date: 1727
Attribution: Jacob Tonson
URL: https://commons.wikimedia.org/wiki/File:Plutarchs_Lives_Vol_the_Third_1727.jpg
License: Public domain

Fig. 148: Bust of Pompey:
Location: National Archaeological Museum of Venice
Date: 1st century BC
Attribution: Sailko
URL: https://commons.wikimedia.org/wiki/File:Ritratto_di_pompeo_magno,_20_a.C._circa.jpg
Changes: Background removed
License: CC BY-SA 4.0

Fig. 149: Bust of Caesar
Location: Vatican Museums
Date: 1st century BC
Attribution: FDRMRZUSA
URL: https://commons.wikimedia.org/wiki/File:Gaius_Iulius_Caesar_(Vatican_Museum).jpg
Changes: Background removed
License: Public Domain

Fig. 150: Bust of Crassus
Location: Louvre Museum
Date: 1st century BC
Attribution: Voism
URL: https://commons.wikimedia.org/wiki/File:Head_of_Marcus_Licinius_Crassus,_middle_of_1st_century_BC,_from_Italy,_Moi,_Auguste,_Empereur_de_Rome_exhibition,_Grand_Palais,_Paris_-_14649017884.jpg
Changes: Background removed
License: CC BY-SA 2.0

LIST OF FIGURES

Fig. 159: Statue of Commodus dressed as Hercules
Location: Capitoline Museums
Date: AD 180-92
Attribution: Marie-Lan Nguyen
URL: https://commons.wikimedia.org/wiki/File:Commodus_Musei_Capitolini_MC1120.jpg
Changes: Background removed
License: Public Domain

Fig. 160: Map of the "barbarian" invasions
Attribution: MapMaster
URL: https://commons.wikimedia.org/wiki/File:Invasions_of_the_Roman_Empire_1.png
License: CC BY-SA 2.5

Fig. 161: Colossal statue of Constantine
Location: Capitoline Museums
Date: early 4th century AD
Attribution: Vicenç Valcárcel Pérez
URL: https://commons.wikimedia.org/wiki/File:Fragments_de_l%27estatua_colossal_de_Constant%C3%AD_(313-324),_Museu_Capitol%C3%AD_(Roma).jpg
License: CC BY-SA 4.0

Fig. 162: Gold bust of Charlemagne
Location: Aachen Cathedral Treasury
Date: 14th century
Attribution: Beckstet
URL: https://commons.wikimedia.org/wiki/File:Aachen_Domschatz_Bueste1.jpg
Changes: Background removed
License: CC BY-SA 3.0

Fig. 163: Marble bust of Marcus Aurelius
Location: Louvre Museum
Date: AD 161-69
Attribution: Marie-Lan Nguyen
URL: https://commons.wikimedia.org/wiki/File:Marcus_Aurelius_Louvre_MR561_n02.jpg
Changes: Background removed
License: Public Domain

Fig. 164: Denarius of Maximinus Thrax
Date: AD 235-36
Attribution: Nicolas Perrault III
URL: https://commons.wikimedia.org/wiki/File:Aureus_of_Maximinus_I.jpg
Changes: Background removed
License: Public Domain

Fig. 165: Bust of Pupienus
Location: Capitoline Museums
Date: AD 238
Attribution: Jastrow
URL: https://commons.wikimedia.org/wiki/File:Pupienus_Musei_Capitolini_MC477.jpg
Changes: Background removed
License: Public Domain

Fig. 166: Bust of Balbinus
Location: Hermitage Museum
Date: AD 238
Attribution: George Shuklin
URL: https://commons.wikimedia.org/wiki/File:Balbinus_Hermitage.jpg
Changes: Background removed
License: CC BY-SA 3.0

Fig. 167: Map of Italy showing Aquileia
Attribution: TUBS
URL: https://en.wikipedia.org/wiki/File:Italy_provincial_location_map_2016.svg
Changes: Text added
License: CC BY-SA 3.0 DE

Fig. 168: Roman seigecraft and defensive works
Attribution: The Air War College
URL: https://commons.wikimedia.org/wiki/File:Roman_siege_machines.gif
License: Public Domain

Fig. 169: Roman coin depicting Pupienus
Date: AD 238
Attribution: CNG Coins
URL: https://commons.wikimedia.org/wiki/File:PUPIENUS-RIC_IV_11a-155504.jpg
License: CC BY-SA 2.5

Fig. 170: Roman coin of Gordian III
Date: ca. AD 240
Attribution: Rasiel Suarez
URL: https://commons.wikimedia.org/wiki/File:Gordian_III_Antoninianus.jpg
Changes: Background removed
License: CC BY-SA 3.0

Fig. 171: Diocletian's palace at Split
Location: Split, Croatia
Date: ca. AD 305
Attribution: Dennis Jarvis
URL: https://commons.wikimedia.org/wiki/File:Croatia-01239_-_The_Peristil_(9551533404).jpg
Changes: Background removed, cropped
License: CC BY-SA 2.0

Fig. 172: Statue of Diocletian and the Tetrarchy
Location: San Marco Cathedral, Venice
Date: ca. AD 300
Attribution: Nino Barbieri
URL: https://commons.wikimedia.org/wiki/File:Venice_%E2%80%93_The_Tetrarchs_03.jpg
Changes: Background removed
License: Public Domain

Fig. 173: The Colosseum
Location: Rome, Italy
Date: completed in AD 80
Attribution: FeaturedPics
URL: https://commons.wikimedia.org/wiki/File:Colosseo_2020.jpg
Changes: Background removed
License: CC BY-SA 4.0

Fig. 174: Yankee Stadium
Location: New York, NY
Date: completed in 1923
Attribution: BuickCenturyDriver
URL: https://commons.wikimedia.org/wiki/File:New_Yankee_Stadium.JPG
Changes: Background removed
License: Public Domain

Fig. 175: The Birth of Venus
Location: Uffizi Gallery
Date: 1485
Artist/Attribution: Sandro Botticelli
URL: https://commons.wikimedia.org/wiki/File:Sandro_Botticelli_-_La_nascita_di_Venere_-_Google_Art_Project_-_edited.jpg
License: Public Domain

Fig. 176: The Pantheon
Location: Rome, Italy
Date: completed in AD 126
Attribution: NikonZ7II
URL: https://commons.wikimedia.org/wiki/File:Pantheon_(Rome)_-_Right_side_and_front.jpg
Changes: Background removed
License: CC BY-SA 4.0

Fig. 177: The Jefferson Memorial
Location: Washington, D.C.
Date: completed in 1943
Attribution: King of Hearts
URL: https://commons.wikimedia.org/wiki/File:Jefferson_Memorial_Washington_April_2017_002.jpg
Changes: Background removed, cropped
License: CC BY-SA 4.0

Fig. 178: St. Peter's Basilica
Location: Rome, Italy
Date: completed in 1626
Attribution: Alvesgaspar
URL: https://en.wikipedia.org/wiki/File:Basilica_di_San_Pietro_in_Vaticano_September_2015-1a.jpg
Changes: Background removed
License: CC BY-SA 4.0

Fig. 179: Plan of St. Peter's Basilica and the Circus of Nero
Attriubtion: Joris
URL: https://commons.wikimedia.org/wiki/File:Plan_of_Circus_Neronis_and_St._Peters.gif
License: Public Domain

Fig. 180: Roman wine amphorae

Creative Commons Links

CC BY 2.0
https://creativecommons.org/licenses/by/2.0/

CC BY-SA 2.0
https://creativecommons.org/licenses/by-sa/2.0/

CC BY-SA 2.0 FR
https://creativecommons.org/licenses/by-sa/2.0/fr/deed.en

CC BY 2.5
https://creativecommons.org/licenses/by-sa/2.5/deed.en

CC BY 2.5
https://creativecommons.org/licenses/by-sa/2.5/

CC BY 3.0
https://creativecommons.org/licenses/by-sa/3.0/deed.en

CC BY-SA 3.0
https://creativecommons.org/licenses/by-sa/3.0/

CC BY-SA 3.0 DE
https://creativecommons.org/licenses/by-sa/3.0/de/deed.en

CC BY-SA 4.0
https://creativecommons.org/licenses/by-sa/4.0/

We hope you've enjoyed getting to learn about classical antiquity through the words of the ancients themselves. If you enjoyed your journey into the Greco-Roman past, make sure to check out some of the Argos Publishing's other offerings. We release original translations of ancient works for modern students.

ARGOS PUBLISHING, LLC

Made in the USA
Monee, IL
14 March 2023

29838237R00215